*Gospels before the Book*

# GOSPELS BEFORE THE BOOK

MATTHEW D. C. LARSEN

OXFORD
UNIVERSITY PRESS

UNIVERSITY PRESS

Oxford University Press is a department of the University of Oxford. It furthers
the University's objective of excellence in research, scholarship, and education
by publishing worldwide. Oxford is a registered trade mark of Oxford University
Press in the UK and certain other countries.

Published in the United States of America by Oxford University Press
198 Madison Avenue, New York, NY 10016, United States of America.

© Oxford University Press 2018

All rights reserved. No part of this publication may be reproduced, stored in
a retrieval system, or transmitted, in any form or by any means, without the
prior permission in writing of Oxford University Press, or as expressly permitted
by law, by license, or under terms agreed with the appropriate reproduction
rights organization. Inquiries concerning reproduction outside the scope of the
above should be sent to the Rights Department, Oxford University Press, at the
address above.

You must not circulate this work in any other form
and you must impose this same condition on any acquirer.

Library of Congress Cataloging-in-Publication Data
Names: Larsen, Matthew D. C., 1982– author.
Title: Gospels before the book / by Matthew D. C. Larsen.
Description: New York, NY : Oxford University Press, 2018. |
Includes bibliographical references and index.
Identifiers: LCCN 2018001337 | ISBN 9780190848583 (hardcover) |
ISBN 9780190848606 (epub) | ISBN 9780190848613 (online resource)
Subjects: LCSH: Bible. Mark—Criticism, interpretation, etc.
Classification: LCC BS2585.52 .L37 2018 | DDC 226.3/06—dc23
LC record available at https://lccn.loc.gov/2018001337

*For Lauren*

"Nothing conclusive has yet taken place in the world, the ultimate word of the world and about the world has not yet been spoken, the world is open and free, everything is still in the future and will always be in the future."
—M. M. Bakhtin, *Problems of Dostoevsky's Poetics,* 166

"Nothing is absolutely dead: every meaning will have its homecoming festival."
—M. M. Bakhtin, "Methodology for the Human Sciences,"
in *Speech Genre and Other Late Essays,* 170.

# Contents

*Images and Illustrations*   xi

*Preface*   xiii

1. Reading Gospels "before the Book"   1
2. Unfinished and Less Authored Texts   11
   Cicero, Caesar, and Hirtius   12
   Pliny the Younger and the Curious Case of the Exorbitantly Expensive *Commentarii*   17
   Plato and *Hypomnēmata* as Memory Aids and Working Texts   19
   Philo on *Hypomnēmata* and Their Potential Problems   23
   Plutarch's Creation and Use of *Hypomnēmata*   26
   Galen's Unfinished Texts   29
   Damis's *Hypomnēmata* as a Scrapbook of Textual Raw Material   34
   Conclusion   36
3. Accidental Publication and Postpublication Revision   37
   Cicero's Wound, Textual Healing, and Pseudepigraphical Pseudepigraphy   38
   Diodorus Siculus on How to Handle Accidental Publication   41
   Horace and Examples of Accidental Publication in the Ancient Roman Imagination   43
   The Idea of Accidental Publication as Asset: *4 Ezra*   45
   Arrian as Writer but Not Author   47
   Cicero and the Inability to Control One's Own Manuscript Tradition   50
   Josephus on Pre-Writing, Rewriting, and Postpublication Revision   52

4. Multiple Authorized Versions of the Same Work — 59
    Versions of the Community Rule as Memory
        Aids for Instructors   59
    The Herculaneum Library and the "Working Desk" of
        Philodemus   69
    Comparing the Scrolls in Qumran and Herculaneum   72
    Conclusion   75

5. The Earliest Readers of the Gospel according to Mark — 79
    The Gospel according to Luke on the Gospel
        according to Mark   83
    Papias on the Gospel according to Mark   87
    Irenaeus on the Gospel according to Mark   93
    Clement of Alexandria and Eusebius on the Gospel according to
        Mark   96

6. The Earliest Users of the Gospel according to Mark — 99
    The Gospel according to Matthew as Continuing the Gospel
        according to Mark   100
    The Many Endings of the Incomplete Gospel according to Mark   114
    Conclusion   120

7. Reading Mark as Unfinished — 121
    Understanding the Order and Logic of Unfinished Notes   123
    Ancient Organization of Notes   125
    The Logic and Structure of the Gospel according to Mark as
        Unfinished Collection of Notes   127
    Unfinished Notes and Voices in Tension   135

Epilogue — 147
    The Gospel according to Mark, the Interpreter, and the
        Unfinalizable Future   147
    Paths for Future Work on Gospel Writing   149

*Appendixes*

A. *A Side-by-Side Comparison of Selections of Philodemus's
    On Rhetoric Book III as Found in P.Herc. 1506 and P.Herc. 1426*   155

B. Codex Bobiensis of Mark 16 with "Shorter Ending" in Parallel
   Columns with the NA28 Greek Edition and the Latin Vulgate    157

Notes    159

Bibliography    193

Index of Modern Authors    207

Subject Index    211

Index of Ancient Sources    221

# Images and Illustrations

| | | |
|---|---|---|
| 4.1 | Image of the Corrected Punishment from 1QS Column 7, line 8 | 65 |
| 4.2 | Image from Col. LVII of *PHerc.* 1506 | 72 |
| 4.3 | Image from Col. XV of *PHerc.* 1426 | 73 |
| 4.4 | Theory of Ancient Writing and Textuality | 76 |
| 6.1 | Two-Source Hypothesis | 102 |
| 6.2 | Farrer Hypothesis | 102 |
| 6.3 | Neo-Griesbach Hypothesis | 103 |
| 6.4 | Proportional Venn Diagram of Overlap Between the Gospels of Mark and Matthew | 105 |

# *Preface*

THIS IS A book about unfinishedness and unfinalizability. It is also a book about writing practices, reading practices, and the intersection of the two. I cannot tell you how many times over the past six years, after a colleague read a draft of some portion or prior paper and offered feedback, that I heard the joke, "your own work, like the claims it makes for early textual traditions of the gospel, is itself unfinished, rough, and in need of polishing." They were not wrong, both in terms of style and argumentation. The manuscript and the ideas it attempts to convey were consistently being reworked and altered over many years, in many contexts, and received feedback from many colleagues, both formally and informally (too many to cite here). The work remains in my mind (to use the language of Eva Mroczek) more of a process, rather than a product. It exists in a more polished form today than it did previously. Yet I cannot avoid the sense—even now, as I take the "final" step of writing the preface before sending the manuscript to the printer—that my book is still unfinished. It has been said that authors never truly finish books; they just release them. Given the topic of my book, I welcome, acknowledge, and accept this humbling reality. My book makes its aim to point out the problems that have beset scholars on early gospel writing for some time and to gesture toward new paths for future research. Such a book, if successful, can never be a final or definitive word on a matter. The goal, to use Bakhtin's terms, is to produce centrifugal rather than centripetal discourse.

In terms of influence and thanks, there are many to mention. Eva Mroczek's and Sean Gurd's scholarship have been constant conversation partners throughout my project. I have cited them often throughout the book, though I also want to cite them here as important contributors to my overall thinking throughout the argument. Both have offered helpful insight and encouragement over conversations and emails through the years. Professors during my time at Yale provided the ideal intellectual environment for my research. I thank especially my doctoral advisor Dale Martin and my dissertation readers, Steve Davis, Ann Hanson, and Harry Attridge. Many others deserve hearty thanks for their guidance, support, and mentorship, especially Hindy Najman, Adela Yarbro Collins, Irene Peirano Garrison, Katie Lofton, Michel Beth Dinkler, Andrew McGowan, Felicity Harley McGowan, Greg Sterling, JanJan Lin, Kirk Freudenburg, Steven Fraade, Chris Hayes, John Collins, Bentley Layton, and Maria Doerfler. Several scholars outside of the Yale community generously offered guidance, helpful critique, and inspiration over the years. Especially worthy of mention are Jennifer Knust, AnneMarie Luijendijk, Brent Nongbri, Eldon Epp, René Falkenberg, Liv Ingeborg Lied, and Abraham Smith. Many days and evenings were spent discussing ideas related to this book with my graduate cohort: Olivia Stewart Lester, Zachary Smith, Sonja Anderson, Tyler Smith, Christina Harker, James Nati, Laura Carlson, Matt Croasmun, Mary Farag, Simcha Gross, Pratima Gopalakrishnan, Dan Schriever, Mark Lester, Dan Bohac, Dexter Brown, Tim Gannett, Tom Schmidt, Stephanie Machabee, Danny Eastman, Austin Rivera, Shlomo Zuckier, and Justin White. To all of you, the next pizza at Wall Street is on me. I must offer thanks to Greg Given and Mark Letteney both for their joyous friendship and their tremendously insightful feedback on previous drafts of the manuscript. Each of these colleagues has enriched and improved this work in their own way.

I thank Steve Wiggins, my editor, and his colleagues at Oxford University Press, as well as Anitha Jasmine Stanley at Newgen, for their work and guidance through the process of review and publication. I also want to thank Acacia Chan for her hard work on the project and especially for her help in indexing the book. My family deserves more space here than I fear I am allowed in this preface or than many readers would endure. It is not hyperbole when I say: I cannot thank them enough. My wife, Lauren Carter Larsen, is the perfect partner in life, dearest friend, ideal co-adventurer, co-parent, artist, creative inspiration, and inimitable running partner. I can only thank you unequivocally and with a full heart for believing in my work on this project and the sacrifices you've made to allow me to write this book. I dedicate it to you, because you believed in it the most, even (especially) at the times when I felt most weary. I apologize for how often I pestered you with the question, "hey, does the sentence sound better like this or this?" But I reluctantly admit I don't really regret it because the book is so much better as a result of your input. If the reader finds the prose herein not too burdensome, thank Lauren. My children, Lucy, August, and Eleanor, grew up with this book in a very real sense. This book was produced in the midst of your births, upbringing, schooling, joys, tears, laughter, excitements, and frustrations. It came into being despite broken bones (both yours and mine), illness (both yours and mine), sleepless nights (both yours and mine), travel, life transitions, and various other obstacles. Your joy and excitement in life inspire me. I am thankful every day to be your father. I hope, when you read this book one day in the future, it makes you proud and you remember its creation fondly. I also thank my parents, David and Vicky Larsen. Your lives are an example of faithfulness and generosity. I am sure, had it not been for your influence both as a child and as an adult, I would not have written this book.

The image on the cover of the book is of Titian's *Agony in the Garden*. I came across the image in 2016 at the New York Metropolitan Museum of Art's exhibit *Unfinished*. It is an unfinished work from Titian of Jesus in the garden before his arrest and execution. Its unfinishedness can be discerned in the lack of detail in much of painting, including important places such as Jesus's face. Other places in the painting, however, possess a remarkable level of detail. Most noticeable (to me, at least) is the clothing on the left shoulder of the person in the foreground. Titian's *Agony in the Garden* exists in multiple versions of the same work. Some of the versions are believed to be produced with the help of collaborators, all of which raises important questions of unfinishedness, multiplicity, originality, and reception.[1] As the reader will see, this painting has several points of comparison to my own argument about the process of textualizing early gospel tradition.

*Gospels before the Book*

# *I*

# *Reading Gospels "before the Book"*

PICK UP ALMOST any commentary or article on the Gospel according to Mark (or, for that matter, the Gospel according to Matthew, Thomas, and so forth), and you will find such concepts as book, author, and perhaps even publication at work within the scholarly discourse. A standard set of historical questions are brought to bear on the text: Who wrote it? When did the person write it? From where did the person write? Who is the intended audience? In seeking answers to the above questions, scholars try to locate a specific time and place of origin where an author worked on and finished a book. From such an origin, then, historians try to configure a scenario in which the meaning of the text can be attained in its proper first-century context.

For the Gospel according to Mark, the author is usually thought to be anonymous, although the name "Mark" is preserved for the sake of convenience.[1] The text is usually dated to either immediately before or after 70 CE.[2] The location and intended audience is also debated. The Gospel according to Mark has traditionally been associated with Rome, and some modern scholars find a Roman provenance likely.[3] Other scholars have suggested somewhere in Syria, Palestine, or in the Decapolis as the Gospel according to Mark's provenance.[4]

All these inquiries have a priori assumptions that are rather modern and "bookish." They presuppose an author producing some sort of finished book at a particular time and for a specific situation. It is not uncommon to see scholars use the word *publication*, often in scare quotes, to talk about a moment when the Gospel according to Mark was first put into circulation.

There is a subtle yet serious problem here. There is no evidence of someone regarding the gospel as a discrete, stable, finished book with an attributed author until the end of the second century CE, and a gospel *qua* discrete authored book does not really become a dominant discourse for talking about "the gospel(s)" until the third century CE. That is, though gospel became textualized in the first and second centuries, there is no evidence of the idea of gospel as a gospel book with an author until much later.

The earliest evidence comes from the Christian apologist Irenaeus of Lyon around 180–190 CE.[5] In his *Against Heresies* 3.1.1, Irenaeus defends his "orthodox gospels" as published books, created in specific times and places by known authors.[6] While his approach may seem intuitive to modern readers, his comments stand in stark contrast to prior discourses of gospel textualization and authorship. For others in the second century, like Celsus, Justin Martyr, and Theophilus of Antioch, and in texts like the *Didache* and 2 Clement, the gospel is a textualized tradition, but the configurations of the textual tradition are far too unbounded and messy to conflate with concepts like book, author, and publication.[7] In the first century and throughout most of the second century, the gospel, though textualized, nevertheless remains contingent, malleable, and subject to change—more rhizomatic than arborescent.[8] Textualized gospel constituted a diverse, living, mushrooming textual constellation (or constellations) that has been altered and remodeled time and time again.

Yet many modern historical-critical inquiries about first-century gospel texts participate, unwittingly perhaps, in later Christian discourses about the textuality and authorship of the gospels, presupposing and prioritizing a definitive moment when a stable book and a unique author simultaneously came into existence. The final version of the text and the author's intention are conjoined, locked in time for later readers to decode. The earliest discourses about gospel textuality and authorship, however, do not share such assumptions. Ignoring, or at least unaware of, the disjointed discourses about gospel textuality and authorship in the first centuries of the Common Era, modern historians of first-century texts speak about the first-century gospel texts in ways unknown in the first- and second-century discourses about the gospel. At the foundation of the historical-critical questions mentioned here lies a misleading anachronism regarding books, authors, and publication.

Ironically, then, while modern critical gospel scholars deny the historical reliability of Christian apologists' constructions about the historical origins of the gospels, many have been blind to the same apologists' more significant ideological invention: the very idea that there are four separate, finished, and fully authored books called the Gospels according to Matthew, Mark, Luke, and John, as opposed to a more fluid constellation of written residue. What if we take Celsus, Justin Martyr, and others seriously, not equating the process of textualization with the creation of "books" nor the producers of texts with "authors"? What if gospel texts are not stable, finished, discrete books?[9] How would our constructed knowledge about "the gospels" shift? What would it look like to construct a narrative of gospel production that does not use ideas about stable books, author figures, or publication? What would it mean to think about the text we now call the Gospel according to Mark before the book, before authors, and before publication?

An insightful point of comparison is Eva Mroczek's book, *The Literary Imagination in Jewish Antiquity*.[10] Mroczek demonstrates how the concepts of books and bible have anachronistically been applied to texts in Jewish antiquity. The "book," however, is more than an anachronistic concept; it is also a metaphor that shapes our thinking.[11] While Mroczek focuses her research on ancient Jewish writers, she points toward more historically nuanced ways of discussing textual growth and textual traditions that can be applied to a wide range of texts in antiquity. There was no "Book of the Psalms" in the Second Temple period of Judaism, she argues. Rather there was an unbounded textual tradition of liturgies. David is not an "author" but, rather, a figure in search of more and more liturgical texts to "colonize." While the Wisdom of Ben Sira is attached to a named author and does refer to itself as a book (though the Hebrew word for book [*sefer*] is missing from the Hebrew manuscripts), the metaphors the Wisdom of Ben Sira uses to describe itself, its manuscript tradition, and the reception of Ben Sira as a figure and text suggest an incompatibility with modern notions of book and author. Mroczek writes, "Despite the use of his name, Ben Sira is continuous with the anonymous and pseudepigraphic textual culture of early Judaism, and the text associated with him is *not* the originary intellectual product of an individual author—and was not understood to be either original or complete, either by Ben Sira or by his heirs."[12] Ben Sira is not a "finished product" but a nomadic text with "no origin an no endpoint."[13] She concludes about Ben Sira—its textual metaphors, manuscripts, and reception:

> In other words, what Ben Sira says about the role of the scribe and wise man as a transmitter of traditions, and what imagery he chooses to reflect on the work of writing—all this already points to the possibility of a complex bibliographical history. The imagery of movement and progression—channels and rivers, growing trees, and gleaners after grape harvesters—places Ben Sira's textual activity in a longer history that is both ancient and ongoing. It is as if the text itself was highlighting, or even enabling, its own openness, as a moment in a long process of writing, reading, and collection.[14]

Not just in relation to Ben Sira but also to a wide variety of ancient Jewish texts, Mroczek has shown how rereading texts without the framework of authors and books—without using "book" as a metaphor for organizing questions and information—creates new and innovative understandings of texts and the communities that produced and reproduced them.

The modern historical approach to investigating gospels is built on assumptions of concepts like book, author, and publication. Yet a historical understanding of such concepts, I argue, calls for nothing less than the need for a new model for thinking about the process of gospel textualization in the first few centuries. The evidence, I will argue, suggests a first- or second-century reader of the texts we now call the Gospel according to Matthew and the Gospel according to Mark would not have thought of them as two separate books by two different authors. Rather, they would have regarded them as the same open-ended, unfinished, and living work: the gospel—textualized. Thus are called into question the validity and utility of source, redaction, and textual criticism as traditionally practiced.[15] For example, what does it mean to talk about the "Synoptic Problem" without recourse to ideas like books, authors, and textual finality?

I point out problems with the current way of thinking about the gospels and begin the process of coming up with a way of describing gospel textualization. In order to point out such problems, at times I use tools that I myself ultimately find problematic. For instance, when I discuss the relationship between the textual traditions we now call the Gospel according to Matthew and the Gospel according to Mark, I use the standard critical edition of the Greek New Testament: Nestle-Aland, 28th edition (NA28). Yet, while some may take the NA28 to reflect the original version of the Gospel according to Mark, or at least as close as we can get to it, I will ultimately conclude there was no conception of something called "the Gospel according to Mark" in the first century. It was also not the type of text that would have had "an original."[16] Furthermore, we cannot be certain that the earliest manuscripts of the Gospel according to Mark reflect exactly what a reader in the first or second century would have encountered. This is especially so, since I argue that, in the first two centuries, the text we now call the Gospel according to Mark was fluid and unfinished; and thus the possibility that it existed in a different version—in fact, perhaps many different versions simultaneously—in the first two centuries seems realistic.[17] Even so, for the purpose of rethinking the relationship between the textual traditions we now call the Gospel according to Matthew and the Gospel according to Mark, using the NA28 remains my best option. I trust my reader will understand that, in doing so, I do not believe I am referring to *the* first-century text of the Gospel according to Mark.

It is customary to capitalize *Gospel* when referring to a written document and not to capitalize *gospel* when it refers to the spoken proclamation of good news. Such a custom works against the ways I am trying to complicate a clean distinction between written and oral, as well as between text and book, or writer and author. Thus, throughout this book I do not capitalize the word *gospel* unless (following the *SBL Handbook of Style*) I refer specifically to the texts we now call the Gospel according to Mark, or Matthew, Luke, and so forth, even though the use of these names and titles presents its own problems.[18] As an analogy, autobiography is a genre of literature, and consequently *autobiography* does not get capitalized. *The Autobiography of Malcolm X*, however, is the title of a book, and thus in the title, the word *autobiography* gets capitalized.[19] Further work remains to be done around the work of naming and terminology in order to describe gospel textualization in the first two centuries CE.[20]

In order to reimagine the narrative of gospel textualization and proliferation in ways native to the first- and second-century discourses on textual fluidity and growth, we must understand ancient writing practices and conceptions of authorship throughout the ancient Mediterranean world. What is needed is an investigation of a complex constellation of ideas: textual unfinishedness, unauthored texts, "publication," textual revision, and a variety of diverse uses and functions of different kinds of texts. Each idea is fluid and unique to its own context. While I look for some common elements, I do not mean to imply that all the examples I discuss, which come from a wide variety of times and places throughout the Mediterranean basin, are the same. They are not. Nevertheless, a survey of certain concepts and examples will allow us to dislodge our own assumptions about textuality and authorship, and begin to place our feet on the soil of the ancient world. While no example is a perfect parallel to the production of gospel texts in the first couple of centuries, each one provides a useful point of comparison. The goal in chapters 2 through 4 is (1) to gain a better understanding of some less frequently discussed aspects of ancient writing practices and modes of authorship in antiquity, and in so doing, (2) to become more aware of our own modern "bookish" assumptions, which are the result of printing-press technologies.

There is no one right path into the constellation of ideas about textuality and authorship, but a brief look at modern scholarship on ancient publication illuminates how the concepts of publication, textual finalization, and authorship hang together in the historical constructions of modern scholars.

Recent scholarship on book making and publication, or making a book public, hypothesizes, prioritizes, and perhaps even fetishizes the moment when the book is "finished."

Bernard A. van Groningen, in his 1963 article "ΕΚΔΟΣΙΣ," distinguishes among three terms: publication, distribution, and transmission (*ekdosis, diadosis,* and *paradosis*).[21] Whereas distribution (*diadosis*) is the more social activity of the text's being passed around among persons, tranmission (*paradosis*) is the mechanical act of transmitting the text from one manuscript to another. *Ekdosis,* however, is the publication of the book, and it is "the act of the author and no one else. It was he who, at one point, noting that his work is finished, makes the text available to others, abandons it to those who want to read it, exposes it to all the adventures that circumstances and men can make it incur."[22] In terms of publication, it is, for van Groningen, the controlled moment when the author and no other consciously decides to make public his or her finished text. Distribution and transmission follow after the moment of publication. The finished and final version of the text is the goal, and the finished text is the work of the author, whose active choice it is to make the book public.

Raymond Starr's 1987 article, "The Circulation of Literary Texts in the Roman World," adds nuance to the issue by speaking about concentric circles of publication.[23] Starr shows an awareness of complicating issues, yet chooses to prioritize the definitive moment of publication, discounting postpublication revision (the continued revision or reworking of an already "published" work) as a mere concession.[24] Starr knows it exists, but for the sake of his argument, he acts as though it does not. Like van Groningen, Starr focuses his attention on the definitive moment of publication, emphasizes ideas of textual finality, and prioritizes the control of authors alone to intend the publication of their books. Whereas van Groningen distinguishes between the moment of publication, in which the text becomes finalized, and the various postpublication activities of distribution and transmission, Starr adds complexities leading up to the moment of publication, theorizing concentric circles of wider and wider availability.[25] Neither acknowledges the possibility of accidental publication having an important place in their constructions.

Like van Groningen and Starr, Tiziano Dorandi, as well as scholars of early Christianity such as Harry Gamble, think of publication, or making a book public, as the act of no one but the author, who, maintaining entire control over the text, at one point notes that the work is finished and in a definitive version and makes the conscious decision to place the work in the public domain. Dorandi acknowledges that he limits his own research on publication, or making public (*ekdosis*), to the moment when the author, "having arrived at the definitive version of his manuscript, makes the decision (spontaneous or solicited, it does not matter) to make his work available to the public."[26] Gamble understands publication similarly and operates with a comparable focus.[27] He writes, "Only after the author had tentatively proffered a composition and then revised it would he or she make it available to a larger audience."[28] Both Dorandi and Gamble fix their attention on the revised, polished, and definitive version of a book, while they minimize or brush aside other potentially complicating issues.[29] Issues like unfinished texts, accidental publication, postpublication revision, author variants, and multiple authorized versions of the same work are placed on the Procrustean bed—and then lopped off. The author is the sole agent. The final, finished, definitive text is the object. Of course, simplification has both pros and cons. As we will see, such a focus is reductive to the point of being misleading.

In attempting to define publication, the proverbial wheat—the finished, definitive version of the authored text—has been separated from the chaff. While these definitions show an awareness of complicating issues, they focus on the final, definitive, published version of the book. Yet in order to understand how to think about texts before the book, before authors, before publication, we need to understand the chaff: unfinished texts, textual raw material, accidental publication, postpublication revision, multiple versions of the same work, and so on.[30] Especially (though not exclusively) for the pre–printing press world, I argue that we cannot simply assume that all texts, not even all texts that make their way down to the modern era, were finished, polished, revised, authored, published, or singular in form. Moreover, we cannot conflate the original text with the authorial version of a text, one that enjoys the full support of an author figure and has been formally brought out into the public by the author and no other. Nor can we assume there was only one authorial version of a text. By beginning to give an account of such issues, I hope to offer a more textured picture of how (the other side of) writing worked in the ancient Mediterranean world. How can we think about textual production—before the book? The answer moves us into a world of messy texts and textual production and continual alteration. To our modern sensibilities, it is a world full of new possibilities.

Before I turn to look at examples from antiquity, it is important to familiarize the concept of the fluid or open text. John Bryant, in his book *The Fluid Text*, argues that the fluid text is a fact, not a theory.[31] Bryant defines "a fluid text [as] any literary work that exists in more than one version."[32] While his claim about fluidity of texts extends even into the post–printing press technological milieu, it is more obviously true for the ancient world, which lacked the ability to mass-produce identical versions of a text. His claim about the ubiquity of fluid texts applies to practically every copied text in the ancient world. On the one hand, even texts that were not meant to be fluid underwent changes every time they were reproduced, since every text was copied by hand. On the other hand, some ancient writers produced texts they described as purposefully fluid and unambiguously presented as open, unfinalized, and unauthored texts with the purpose of being revised, finished, and authored, whether by the same writer or someone else.

It is also important to foreground a discussion of authors and writers before turning to examples from antiquity. John Bryant notes the difference well:

> *Author* is a title conferred, late or soon, upon an individual whose writings have circulated to such an extent that the culture concedes and confers upon it a reputation, and while many have achieved this status in greater or lesser degree, the title itself is an acknowledgement of status and "authority." But whereas an "author" appears only at the moment of cultural recognition, a "writer" is simply the *one who writes* and is born at the moment of his or her act of writing, not through the conferring of status of social recognition. An author is a social construct; a writer is one who performs a human process.[33]

Bryant's definition of the author vis-à-vis the writer helpfully distinguishes between the materiality of writing and the cultural capital or recognition of status conferred upon the producer or source. We may, however, add further nuance to this quote: if "authorship" is culturally recognized and negotiated, then we also need not think in a binary of "authored" and "nonauthored" texts. Rather, there are different types and degrees of "authoriality"; the level to which a work is "authored" may be mapped in a variety of ways. Foucault appears to fall into the authored and nonauthored binary, in his famous "What Is an Author?" essay:

> As a result, we could say that in a civilization like our own there are a certain number of discourses that are endowed with the "author function," while others are deprived of it. A private letter may well have a signer—it does not have an author; a contract may well have a guarantor—it does not have an author. An anonymous text posted on a wall probably has a writer—but not an author. The author function

is therefore characteristic of the mode of existence, circulation, and functioning of certain discourses within a society.[34]

Here Foucault seems to function with two alternatives: authored texts and texts without an author.

When we recognize, however, that authorship is culturally recognized and conferred, we must also recognize that there is in fact a wide range of degrees, variations, and types of "authorship." The status and "authority" attached to the source of an academic monograph is not necessarily greater or lesser but, perhaps, altogether different from the one who writes a famous novel or who ghost-writes an autobiography or pens a love letter to his beloved. Someone who writes a commentary on a classical text is not an "author" in quite the same sense as someone who wrote or otherwise produced the classic itself. Aristarchus, when he writes a commentary on Homer's *Iliad*, is qualitatively a different type of author from Homer. Alternatively, a text like the Dead Sea Scroll's *Rule of the Community* has neither an ascribed author nor a formal title, yet it nevertheless possesses an authority of yet a different type (as I will discuss more in chapter 4). Moreover, the signer of the private letter may not initially be experienced as an "author," but in certain scenarios he or she may come to be understood as the "author" in due course.

# 2
# *Unfinished and Less Authored Texts*

IN ORDER TO understand unfinished and less authored texts in antiquity, we must introduce the Greek term *hypomnēmata* and the Latin term *commentarii*.[1] The lexical range of both words is wide. Both words can refer to things as disparate as rough drafts, public records, commentaries, birth announcements, lists, and more. One of the most unifying features in their lexical constellations, perhaps, is that *hypomnēmata* and *commentarii* represent more fluid, less authored, and less "bookish" texts—things put down in writing not so much to become literature as to be memoranda. They are more practical than formal. *Hypomnēmata* and *commentarii* are not literature per se, at least not yet. They are inchoate, provisional, and often exist specifically for the creation of other texts. As the root of both words indicates, although they are often textual objects, they relate to memory more than writing. They are skeletons that need the breath of human memory to bring them to life. They are a concession to the absence of a source of knowledge, designed to protect against memory loss.

Christina Shuttleworth Kraus offers the following definition of a *commentarius*: "It is thus billed as unfinished in a very particular way: unpolished, unmade-up, unadorned, un-(or para-) literary."[2] Its production was not restricted to the normal "run of the mill literary producers," but included such writers as doctors, builders, soldiers, and other "lower status specialists."[3] That is, it would have been less odd for literate slaves or freed people to write *hypomnēmata* than for them to write history, poetry, or tragedy.[4] It was not uncommon for *hypomnēmata* or *commentarii* to have no ascribed authors and no affixed titles. They could also involve collective authorship, and both words also refer to lecture notes and informal treatises.[5] As will be clear, in what follows I refer to unfinished rough drafts or textual raw material, not to lists of raw data, private letters, or commentaries.

## Cicero, Caesar, and Hirtius

I think we can all agree: Cicero was a megalomaniac. Many have shared Augustine of Hippo's assessment that Cicero's tongue was easy to love, but his heart was not.[6] Cicero spent much time wringing his hands over how his illustrious career, and specifically his consulship, would be celebrated for generations to come. He didn't want people to miss out. What he needed was someone to write a book praising him and his time as consul. Preferably the book should be written in his own lifetime so he could bask a bit in his glory.[7] Writing his own panegyric, however, would break social mores. Many would perceive it simply as tooting his own horn, which would have the opposite of the desired effect.[8] Cicero knew it would take another Cicero to accomplish such a task. How would he ensure it was properly written? Answer: if you want something done right, do it yourself. Cicero engaged in the recognized task of scripting notes that someone else could revise, rework, correct, finish, author, and publish. In short, he wrote something for someone else to author.

An ongoing minor subplot in the first two books of Cicero's letters to Atticus is Cicero's struggle to find someone to write about his consulship.

> I have sent you [Atticus] a memoir [*commentarium*] about my consulship that I composed in Greek. If there is anything in it that to an Attic person seems inferior Greek or insufficiently learned, I will not say what Lucullus said to you—I think—at Panhormus about his histories, that he, in order that his histories might be easily recognized as the work of a Roman, peppered it with barbarisms and solecisms; if there is anything like that in my writing, it remains there without my knowledge and against my will. If I happen to finish the Latin version, I will send it to you. Thirdly, you can expect a poem, lest any form of my praise be neglected by me. Make sure you do not say, "Who will praise his father?" If, however, there should be any topic more able to be praised by writers, let it be praised. I would blame myself for not praising the worthier topic. But it is not panegyrics I write, but histories.[9]

Cicero uses the word *commentarius*, but since he says he wrote in Greek, we could say he wrote a *hypomnēma*, which is the Greek translation and carries a similar sense.[10] *Hypomnēmata*, in this context, were textual raw materials: not yet pieces of literature themselves, but preliminary to the creation of formal literature. Lucian, for example, in his *How to Write History*, refers to a *hypomnēma* as a rough draft to be used in the creation of a history, adding order (*taxis*) and polish to create the final draft.¹¹ Cicero, at the time of writing, was working on another rough draft of his consulship—a Latin counterpart to go with the Greek. Lucullus's reported comment allows insight into the nature of *commentarii* or *hypomnēmata*. Cicero says Lucullus intentionally interspersed his text with barbarisms and blunders, so that he might be recognized as a Roman and not come off as too Greek. *Commentarii* or *hypomnēmata* were the kinds of texts that were more tolerant of, and perhaps even demanded, rough style and imperfections in grammar, because they remained in an emergent, pre-polished, and undeveloped stage. Apparently both Cicero's and Lucullus's goal was to script unfinished pre-literary raw material so that someone else—in these cases, a Greek author—could turn their texts into proper pieces of literature, ostensibly about themselves and for their praise. While authoring one's own biography would look like off-putting self-praise, writing one's own material so that someone else can author the history seems to be a recognized literary activity. Cicero's request is effectively the inverse of ghostwriting an autobiography in modern culture: whereas in ghostwriting, an author asks another person to write the author's story in the author's name, in Cicero's case he wrote material about himself for someone else to author the finished story.

In the first letter in book 2, we find out that Cicero was not the only one who wrote raw material about his consulship. Atticus also wrote a notebook of Cicero's consulship in Greek and sent it to Cicero (*commentarium consulatus mei Graece scriptum*).¹² Atticus followed the expectation of *commentarii* or *hypomnēmata* and wrote notebooks that were rough and lacking in literary adornment (*horridula . . . atque incompta*). The idea was that someone else would clean them up and finish them. Otherwise an author would be competing with the writer in quality of writing style, which would demotivate a potential author from finishing the writer's textual material. Cicero, however, in a sly move of self-congratulation, laments that his notebook is simply too polished and ornamented with rhetorical flair. Poor Cicero can't write inadequately even when he tries. Even then it comes out with rhetorical flair and fireworks.¹³

Cicero wrote a notebook (in fact he wrote two, one in Greek [*hypomnēma*] and one in Latin [*commentarius*]) about his consulship, and shared both with Atticus, who had himself written a notebook in Greek about Cicero's consulship. Atticus, however, was not the only person who received Cicero's notebook; Cicero also delivered his notebook through Lucius Cossinius, who was expected to pass the same notebook along to Atticus (*Att.* 1.9; 2.1). Cicero similarly circulated the notebook to Posidonius in Rhodes, explicitly asking him to create from it something more polished (*ornatius*), finishing his unfinished textual material into a real piece of literature for public consumption (*Att.* 2.1). This time Cicero uses the Greek *hypomnēma*, not *commentarius*.[14]

Moreover, Cicero sheepishly begged Lucius Lucceius to incorporate some notes about his consulship into his history (*Fam.* 5.12), which would save Cicero the embarrassment of having to write his own panegyric. There was also the prospect that somehow an unspecified mass of "others" might come across Cicero's notebook and want to write about it (*Att.* 1.20). In Cicero's mind, practically every literary Greek must have coveted some unfinished raw material from Cicero to finish up and author. Although, strangely to Cicero, no one seemed to be pestering him for the material.[15]

Eva Mroczek offers a parallel example of textual unfinishedness in Ben Sira. She shows how "the idea of a definitive text does not match Ben Sira's own understanding of his text as an overflow or ingathering of older traditions, and a compendium of wisdom that is necessarily unfinished: 'the first man did not know wisdom fully, not will the last one fathom her' (24:28)."[16] She argues Ben Sira is an "open book," and "some authors' 'intent' was precisely *not* final."[17]

In sum, according to Cicero's admission, lots of texts about Cicero's consulship existed. Cicero himself had written several, although he was careful not to "author" them. He wanted to leave them unfinished, so that others could polish them up. Although they were in circulation, Cicero did not want them to be thought of as public. Just the opposite, in fact. Cicero wrote his own *hypomnēmata* in Greek, as well as *commentarii* in Latin, and shopped them around Rome, looking for someone to author a book about his consulship by using the literary raw materials he himself had written, which would allow him the glory of praise without the shame of self-praise. Atticus had also written separate notes about Cicero's consulship with similar goals. Yet for all his shopping of his memoirs around Rome, much to his chagrin, Cicero apparently found no takers.[18]

Cicero was not the only person in Rome at the time to write his own *hypomnēmata* or *commentarii*. Cicero's political rival Julius Caesar also wrote *commentarii* of his war in Gaul.[19] Four different ancient writers reflect on the purpose and nature of Caesar's notes on his wars: Cicero, Asinius Pollio, Hirtius, and Suetonius. Each provides us with an important insight into the expectations and experiences of those who read Caesar's *Gallic Wars*. They tell us that the genre of Caesar's work (*commentarii*) was more to provide others with material for writing history than for writing his own autobiography per se.[20] Thus, it was not so much a book itself, but a "pre-book."

Cicero wrote in his book of rhetoric entitled *Brutus* about the nature and quality of Caesar's *Commentarii*:

> Then Brutus said: "Caesar's speeches seem very excellent to me. I have read a lot of them as well as the *Notes* [*commentarii*] he wrote about his own deeds."
> "Yes, very excellent." [Cicero] said, "They are nude, erect, sexy,[21] having been stripped of all ornament of speech as if stripped of their clothing. But while he intended to prepare material for others who wanted to write history, perhaps he did something pleasing for those who are senseless, who want to burn it with their curling irons. Rational people, however, he frightened from writing. For nothing is sweeter in historical writing than pure and bright brevity."[22]

Cicero counters Brutus's praise by offering a backhanded compliment. When Cicero compares Caesar's *commentarii* to beautiful nude figures, standing erect, stripped of all their clothes, he effeminizes them—a regular accusation against men who overperformed their masculinity.[23] While they ostensibly had the purpose of being pre-documentary materials for other historians, they were so ornate and so perfect in their syntax and style that they overperformed their pre-documentary purpose. Those foolhardy few, who would try to finish Caesar's *commentarii* by improving upon them, are characterized as hairstylists excessively concerned to primp Caesar's coiffure. As if while using a hot curling iron, their zeal to primp up Caesar leads them to burn the hair. As the saying goes, "if it ain't broke, don't fix it," otherwise one's efforts to improve it may backfire. Such behavior calls the hairdressers' masculinity into question along with the status of Caesar's stripped naked, erect, beautiful *commentarii*. Thus, while advertised as unfinished and unadorned, rough drafts for someone else to author, Caesar's *commentarii* were actually so finely crafted, so overwrought that only a numbskull would dare try to improve them. Sober-minded people are too frightened to attempt to finish them. They are already perfect. Too perfect, in fact.[24] That they are the *commentarii* "of Caesar" marks them as already "authored" in some sense. Caesar was able to write his own history without authoring it per se. Cicero felt that was a tricky way of having your cake and eating it, too, since surely no one would add to Caesar's *commentarii*.

Aulus Hirtius, however, was the person Cicero said there would not be. Caesar had left off at the end of book 7, so Hirtius continues the story with his preface to book 8. Aulus Hirtius knew that he risked being labeled a literary nincompoop when he undertook the task of finishing Caesar's *Gallic War*, so he had to walk a fine line between praise of Caesar's *commentarii* and justification for his own effort as Caesar's continuator. Aulus Hirtius writes to Lucius Cornelius Balbus,

> Compelled by your incessant requests, Balbus, which seem to view my daily refusals not as an excuse due to difficulty but as an apology due to laziness, I have undertaken a difficult thing. I have made a continuation of the *commentarii* of our Caesar's actions in Gaul, since his previous and subsequent writings were not set in order, and I have finished his last work, which was left unfinished from his actions in Alexandria, all the way to the end—not, mind you, the end of civil rivalry, of which there is no end in sight, but the end of Caesar's life. I would assume that everybody who would read it would understand how reluctantly I wrote, so that I, who would introduce myself in the middle of Caesar's writings, might quite easily free myself from the charge of stupidity and arrogance. For everyone agrees that nothing was ever so perfectly finished by others that it is not surpassed by the refinement of these *commentarii*, which were published so that historians would have knowledge of such things. And everyone approves of them so much that it seems he has not provided but robbed historians of such an opportunity.[25]

Hirtius agrees with Cicero's assessment that by their title Caesar's *commentarii* cry out for someone to finish them, yet at the same time, it would be potentially foolish to try to improve them since they are already perfect. He straddles both issues in his preface. Caesar's *commentarii* are more polished than other similar documents and yet they are also incomplete. They leave out what happened in 50 BCE.[26] Part of his defense is to suggest that he is privy to special knowledge about the textual origins of Caesar's notes: although Caesar had first-rate literary skills, he wrote his notes very rapidly.[27] Perhaps he was so rushed in his writing that even he needed a little finishing.[28]

The best way to make sense of Cicero's *hypomnēmata*, Caesar's *commentarii*, Cicero's remarks on Caesar's *commentarii*, and Hirtius's continuation of Caesar's *commentarii* is to allow for the category of intentionally unfinished and unauthored texts. By calling them *commentarii*, Caesar claimed simply to write down some notes, but Cicero complains he transgressively presents already authored material as "just notes." The writer is not the author per se, and cannot be. The writer is the one who puts stylus to wax tablet, ink to parchment, pen to paper, and so forth. The writer comes into being at the very act of writing, while the author is a social construction of the one who authorizes a text.[29] Cicero and Caesar could not authorize their own self-praise, so they wrote textual raw material, which gave them "plausible deniability" against the accusation of immodestly singing their own praises.[30] No one finished Cicero's notes as a history of his consulship. Neither did another finish Caesar's, but for different reasons. Hirtius understood that, while the quality of Caesar's writings was quite good, *commentarii* were specifically designed to provide others with material to author, and so Hirtius continued the task of writing the story. While Bryant's theory of the fluid text purports to apply to all copied texts, it especially applies to *hypomnēmata* and *commentarii* of this sort.[31] They are self-consciously fluid and unfinished because they are written for the purpose of being later authored by someone else.

## *Pliny the Younger and the Curious Case of the Exorbitantly Expensive* Commentarii

Pliny the Elder had a voracious appetite for literature. He liked to read it; he liked to write it. Pliny the Younger reports that one important aspect of his uncle's writing was reading and taking copious notes of things he liked, which he would do at nearly every free moment. In *Ep.* 3.5.17, Pliny the Younger's famous letter to Baebius Macer, we find a curious financial detail that has received surprisingly little attention.[32] Having detailed the rigorous reading and writing schedule of his uncle, Pliny the Younger notes

> So it was with this intention that he [Pliny the Elder] worked up those volumes and left for me 160 *commentarii* of excerpts, written on both sides and in extremely small script, for which reason the number is actually quite a bit higher. He himself always used to say that, when he was procurator in Spain, he could have sold these *commentarii* to Larcius Licinus for the price of 400,000 sesterces—and that was when they were fewer [in number than 160].

How much did a book cost in the ancient Roman Empire? It is impossible to say with any kind of precision owing to variations in book quality, currency, time, and geographical dispersion.[33] Suffice it to say, though, that Licinus's offer was remarkably high; 400,000 sesterces was also the amount of money needed to become a Roman knight, and thus equivalent to the entire fortune of a moderately well-off Roman. One could either join the class of Roman knights or buy Pliny's *commentarii*.

Pliny's contemporary, Martial, tells us in *Ep.* 1.66 that one could buy a little book for 6 or 10 sesterces. Of course, this would seem a rather cheap book by ancient standards. One could expect to pay a good deal more for an expensive book made from the highest quality materials and with a good scribal hand. But what Martial goes on to say may prove helpful in our attempt to understand Licinus's extravagant offer.

> *You are wrong, o greedy thief of my writings,*
> *Who thinks a poet is made*
> *For the cost of a cheap book and copying.*
> *"Bravo!" does not come at the cost of six or ten sesterces.*
> *Look for unpublished poems and raw pieces of writing,*
> *which only one person knows, and which sealed up in a book-box*
> *the father himself of the virgin sheet guards,*
> *[raw unpublished poems] which have not bristled when rubbed by*
> *    scratchy chins.*
> *A famous book cannot change its master.*
> *But if there is one with an outer end not yet polished by the pumice stone*
> *And not yet decorated with roll and parchment*
> *Buy it: I have one just like this, and no one will ever know.*
> *For whoever recites other people's poems and seeks fame*
> *Must buy not the book, but the silence [of the one who produced it].*

Martial cites the cost of producing a cheap volume and copying at 6 or 10 sesterces. Indeed, 6 or 10 sesterces represents an unrealistically low cost of producing an average book, one more representative of a satirical epigram than normal economic realities of the ancient Roman world. Nevertheless, Martial indicates what might make a piece of writing more valuable. If it remains still in an unfinished, unpublished state and either does not have an author or at least is not perceived by the public at large to have an author, its value could skyrocket. To Martial, unfinished, unauthored, unpublished texts possess greater value because one can take such textual raw material, attach one's name, and become its author. In fact, he admits (jokingly?) that he already has rough drafts of someone else's poem, and he plans to capitalize on that person's efforts by finishing them and authoring them himself. So, sort of like an unfinished manuscript of a novel by a deceased famous author, unfinished and unpublished literary raw materials were worth more because you could author the literary raw material someone else wrote.[34]

Understanding the potential and value of authorless rough drafts may help us make sense of Licinus's seemingly overpriced offer for the elder Pliny's *commentarii*. According to the younger Pliny, his uncle was a literary giant who spent enormous amounts of time reading and excerpting the most valuable tidbits. His *commentarii*, then, represented a product that could rarely be matched by others in terms of time commitment or talent. Yet they also remained what Martial might have called *rudes curas*—rough or raw textual material, not yet a recognized piece of literature. They therefore offered the opportunity of valorization by polishing, arranging, authoring, and publishing. Licinus could author the text by working with the rough textual material and excerpts, which had been industriously and tastefully compiled by one of the great authors of the day. The value of Pliny's *commentarii* came not from the fact that Pliny was the author but from the fact that Pliny was not yet the author per se. Thus, it seems Licinus's wild offer depends on the unfinished state of the texts and their ability to be authored by Licinus himself. They are a means to an end, not an end in and of themselves.

## *Plato and* Hypomnēmata *as Memory Aids and Working Texts*

Any discussion of *hypomnēmata* must mention Plato. In the *Phaedrus*, Socrates famously discusses the nature and purpose of writing. Writing is like painting insofar as it looks like a living being, but when one poses a question to it, it remains reverently and hauntingly silent.[35] One can ask the text the same question again and again and always get the same answer: a silent text does not speak back. Without the presence of the author, the written word is like an orphan without a father to defend it.[36] Its purpose is not so much to communicate new information clearly to uninformed readers as it is to remind a specific readership of what they already know.[37] *Hypomnēmata* play an important role in Plato's theory of writing: they are memory aids, physical extensions of human memory. Someone writes *hypomnēmata* to treasure up reminders as a safeguard against forgetfulness.[38] Thus, *hypomnēmata* are inherently personal. They cannot defend themselves among an anonymous or public audience of readers who are not already familiar with the content. They leave too much ambiguous, and in the ambiguity lies potential danger.

In *Pol.* 295, the Stranger and the younger Socrates (who is a different character in *Statesman* from Socrates) discuss the nature of laws, both written and unwritten. The issue of the permanence and mutability of laws comes into question. In order to build his case that laws can be updated, altered, and improved, the Stranger offers a hypothetical scenario about physicians and physical trainers: "Let us suppose a doctor or a physical trainer is about to go on a journey and be away from his patients for a long time. If he thinks his trainees or his patients will not remember his instruction, he will want to write notes (*hypomnēmata*) for them, don't you think?"[39] The notes in question are by no means literature; rather, they are meant to jog the memory of a specific reader, not to inform an anonymous readership about new information. They are practical and technical texts, not formal literature.

The younger Socrates agrees that the Stranger's scenario is entirely reasonable, and then the Stranger continues:

> What if he should come back again after a briefer absence than he expected? Would he not venture to substitute other rules for those written instructions if others happened to be better for his patients, because the winds or something else had, by act of God, changed unexpectedly from their usual course? Would he persist in the opinion that no one must transgress the old laws, neither he himself by enacting new ones nor his patient by venturing to do anything contrary to the written rules, under the conviction that these laws were medicinal and healthful and anything else was unhealthful and unscientific? If anything of that sort occurred in the realm of science and true art, would not any such regulations on any subject assuredly arouse the greatest ridicule?[40]

As he did before, the younger Socrates consents to the likelihood of the Stranger's hypothetical scenario: a doctor or a physical trainer who had written *hypomnēmata* would surely feel free to revise his written instructions for his patients or trainees, if it so happened that he came across a better plan of treatment or training. In fact, such alteration and improvement would be incumbent upon the one who wrote the *hypomnēmata*. While the larger argument relates to the art of ruling and the updating of laws, the Stranger relies on a point of uncontested mutual agreement to score a larger point: both the Stranger and the younger Socrates (and, it is assumed, the reader) agree on how a doctor or a physical trainer would act in relation to his notes and how *hypomnēmata* work. The notes are functional texts, designed to help remind people of something they already know. They assume a close relational proximity between the writer and the reader, one in which things can be left presumed that might appear too ambiguous to an anonymous reader but nevertheless jog the memory of the intended reader. The texts are fluid, just like the current opinion of the doctor or physical trainer. Fluid, of course, because the possibility for improvement in the future remains always open for this kind of text.

The logic of the stranger's argument, with which (at least in this portion) the younger Socrates agrees, is contingent upon understanding that *hypomnēmata* are impermanent, fluid, improvable, parochial texts rather than frozen, timeless, definitive, bounded pieces of literature.[41] Doctors or physical trainers are among the kind of people who write *hypomnēmata*. It would not be surprising if such texts lacked a title or an ascribed author, since paratextual features serve to control the reading of an anonymous reader, and in the scenario of the Stranger, such information would be redundant. Geographical distance and the absence of the teacher create the need for *hypomnēmata*.[42]

In Plato's *Theaetetus*, we find similar uses of the term *hypomnēmata*. Before getting to the main act—the dialogue between Socrates and Theodorus—Plato gives us a brief prelude in which Eucleides and Terpsion talk about a certain Theaetetus. Their conversation provides the framing for the main dialogue. Eucleides knows of an interesting conversation with Socrates, and Terpsion asks him if he can tell him about it. In *Theaet.* 142d–143a, Eucleides, perhaps surprisingly, responds,

> Of course not, at least not off the cuff (*apo stomatos*), but I did jot down notes (*hypomnēmata*) as soon as I got home. Later I wrote what I could remember in moments of leisure (*kata scholēn*), and every time I visited Athens I asked Socrates about what I could not recall, and then I came here and made corrections, with the result that I have just about the whole conversation written down.[43]

After the narrative framing of the conversation between Eucleides and Terpsion, Plato then presents the main body of the Socratic dialogue as none other than Eucleides's *hypomnēmata*. In so doing, Plato stages a literary representation of how he himself wrote Socratic dialogues. Eucleides warns Terpsion that he has made two changes. First, although Socrates was speaking with Eucleides about Theaetetus and Theodorus, Eucleides presents the dialogue as between Socrates and the two geometrists. Second, Eucleides removes the small bits of narration between the conversations, such as "and I said," "and he agreed," and the like, since they would be annoying in the written account. A slave boy then reads aloud this modified version of the dialogue between Eucleides and Terpsion.

Thus, while the Socratic dialogue offers the reader an implicit yet practical entrée into the nature of Plato's *hypomnēmata*, Eucleides's comments in

*Theaet.* 143a provide an account of the compositional process, unfinishedness, and revisability of *hypomnēmata*, as well as a vignette of the complications in talking about authorship of unfinished notes.

While in Athens, Socrates told Eucleides about a conversation he had had with Theaetetus. Eucleides subsequently turned their conversation about a conversation into a textual object, and he did so in three stages. First, he wrote *hypomnēmata* as soon as he arrived back home in Megara. Second, he later more carefully wrote down everything he could remember in the style of the conversation itself. The third stage entails an indefinite number of revisions: he often went to Athens and asked Socrates to clarify what remained fuzzy in his mind. After Socrates had explained the unclear or forgotten to him, he would go back to Megara and correct his notes.[44] We are to imagine them having conversation after conversation about the textualized version of a prior conversation about a conversation. Plato here externalizes his thinking and writing style into a literary description.

What can we say about the nature of the *hypomnēmata*? As in *Pol.* 295, the notes are more functional than formal, designed to preserve the memory of a conversation. Textual fluidity is an indispensable part of understanding their function. How could it not be, since they are a textualized extension of human memory? In Plato's presentation, it is not possible to count the number of revisions; the Greek word *hosakis* points to an indefinite number. So, while they are preserved in a written form, they are not stable but change regularly. Eucleides's *hypomnēmata* are not public or widely read texts (at least not before plugged into Plato's *Theaetetus*). Terpsion expresses an awareness of the existence of Eucleides's notes, but has never seen them or heard them read. The text apparently had a limited circulation, if any.

What's more, *hypomnēmata* complicate the relationship between the one who did the material act of writing and the one who authorizes the discourse or from whom the discourse originates—the "author." While Plato presents Eucleides as the one who wrote the *hypomnēmata*, Eucleides hardly authored or even authorized the conversation. Socrates does. Further complication comes from the fact that throughout the third stage of textual revision, Socrates himself collaborates with Eucleides in the textualization of the conversation. So, in a sense Socrates is both the (co-)writer and the author, but Eucleides too can be seen in another sense as both writer and author. The notions of writer and author are certainly not identical, but they interpenetrate. Of course, we may also step back and consider how Plato is also both the writer and the author, but simultaneously neither the writer or authorizer, but such would only muddle things further.

## *Philo on* Hypomnēmata *and Their Potential Problems*

In her book *Literary Imagination in Jewish Antiquity,* Eva Mroczek reimagines how various Jewish writers in antiquity thought about texts, writing, and literature. She applies the image of the Miltonian author and the vial to describe modern conceptions of authors and books. In the modern imagination, books and authors are clean, unified, discrete, and self-contained things. Such ideas, of course, are modern social constructs. Consequently, they often function to import subtle modern anachronisms into the discussion of antiquity. Mroczek then shows how a variety of Jewish writers and communities described their texts, paying careful attention to the metaphors the writers themselves use, as well as to material philology and manuscripts. Ideas like fluidity, openness, and unbounded textual traditions play important roles in her book. She directs her attention predominantly to the Psalms, Ben Sira, the Dead Sea Scrolls, Jubilees, *4 Ezra*, and Josephus.[45]

While the word *hypomnēmata* does not appear in her book, many of the ideas discussed here about how writing worked and how readers conceived of texts bear striking similarities to the texts Mroczek investigates. This does not mean, however, that ancient Jewish writers did not use such words or deploy such concepts. Two first-century Hellenistic Jewish writers discuss *hypomnēmata*. In addition to the historian Josephus, whom I will look at in the next chapter, Philo of Alexandria, the first-century Jewish philosopher, uses the concept of *hypomnēmata* frequently in his writing, which is unsurprising for a thinker so heavily influenced by Plato. Philo, however, offers an understanding of how this particular type of text worked and functioned, illuminating an important aspect of our picture of social elements connected with ancient writing practices, textual perceptions, and readerly *habitus*. Philo reflects on the dangers and potential downfalls of *hypomnēmata*. He recognizes that their style and mutability present unique complications and potential snares. For him, to label something as *hypomnēmata* can function as a form of disparagement.

In the Philonic corpus, *hypomnēmata* can be used in reference to things as dissimilar as clothing, festivals, or excrement.[46] Basically *hypomnēmata* can refer to anything that serves to remind people of something, an idea which follows nicely the Platonic notion of writing discussed above. Not surprisingly, *hypomnēmata* can also refer to texts and writing. In some texts, Philo uses the word in connection with scripture.[47] Most frequently, however, it denotes non-scriptural and more "everyday" kinds of writing. Like other examples discussed in this chapter, Philo knows that *hypomnēmata* are the kinds of texts that, in contrast to polished style, reflect everyday language.[48] They are more colloquial. They are the kinds of texts an historian might produce for the use of later readers and writers.[49] One's own *hypomnēmata* are easier to understand (as one rereads them) than reading someone else's. That is, they are for more private or limited use than intended for public consumption, so the producer of the *hypomnēmata* knew what information could be left assumed and what information needed to be communicated more explicitly.[50]

Philo gives two examples of particular interest for the purposes of the present chapter. Both examples portray in negative terms the run-of-the-mill nature of *hypomnēmata*, as well as their textual fluidity. In both cases, Philo deploys the textual nature of *hypomnēmata* to denigrate an opponent. Philo is not the only person in antiquity to speak of *hypomnēmata* in negative terms. Lucian of Samasota, writing in the middle of the second century CE, wrote the following in his treatise *How to Write History*:

> Then someone else produces a *hypomnēma*, collecting together in writing events that have happened—just as bare, prosaic, and down to earth as some soldier would put it together when writing in a daily journal, or a manual laborer, or some merchant traveling along with an army. But at least this everyday kind of writer does something quite fitting. He is quite upfront about what he is doing: he has worked up materials ahead of time for some accomplished person who is competent to handle the writing of history. But here is precisely where I find fault. He [Kallimorphos] presents his writings in a rather highfalutin manner or in the position of proper books (*kata tēn tōn suggrammatōn tuchēn*): "*History of the Parthians*, by Kallimorphos, doctor of the sixth pikemen." Then he goes on to inscribe a number to each volume. And, what's more, he wrote the very regrettable preface that concludes: "It is fitting for a doctor to write history, since Asklepius was the son of Apollo, and since Apollo was the leader of the Muses and the head of all learning." Also, he starts writing in Ionic but then, for no apparent reason, completely out of the blue switches over to everyday Greek. While he sometimes sprinkles in some Ionic words here and there, most of the time he uses the language of a commoner—in fact, so common that it is actually vulgar.[51]

Lucian's comment here comes in a string of faux pas in history writing. The particular problem addressed in *How to Write History* stems from two interrelated points, both about elite culture and social status. First, the history was written by a doctor, and for Lucian, doctors are not literarily sophisticated enough to write history. Doctors write everyday texts like *hypomnēmata*, not histories. Second, the style and language of Kallimorphos's texts are far too ordinary for a book that claimed to be a work of history.

From a paratextual point of view, readers expect *hypomnēmata* not to have titles, volume numbers, prefaces, and other such literary accoutrements. Such paratextual features were associated with more finished, polished books. Furthermore, common people like doctors, soldiers, and tavern-keepers write *hypomnēmata*; they do not write histories. Lucian, then, effectively labels the doctor's *History of the Parthians* as an *hypomnēma* in order to insult the literary quality of his history.

In *Flacc.* 125–34, Philo similarly utilizes the concept of *hypomnēmata* as a part of his negative portrayal of Lampo. Lampo had once worked for the prefect Flaccus in the courts in Alexandria. Philo portrays Lampo as a bad person who used his place in the legal system to get rich at the expense of others, even at the expense of their lives. Lampo was the note taker at the court. The nature of *hypomnēmata* afforded Lampo an avenue to game the legal system to his financial advantage.

> For [Lampo] stood alongside the rulers as they issued judgments and he took down notes (*hypemnēmatizeto*) on the cases and introduced an organization [to the notes] (*eisagōn hōs echōn taxin*). Then, in some cases, he erased certain parts or purposefully omitted other things. Some times he interpolated some things that were not said. And other times he changed, remodeled, altered the notes, turning the words completely upside down, aiming to get rich with every letter—with every stroke of the pen—like someone who pores over records.[52]

Lampo writes *hypomnēmata* on the cases and then catalogues his notes into an organized structure in order to revisit them later. For Philo, the goal is to make Lampo look crooked and to call into question his character. The inherent fluidity of *hypomnēmata* provide Lampo the ability to fiddle with the records—to his benefit and others' peril. Moreover, not everyone would have had access to his notes, as they are not public documents. They are revisable texts to which only a few people ever had access. Thus, he could alter the records to state something financially beneficial to Lampo and his associates, without other people being privy to his nefarious actions. Philo clearly has a strong sense of the problems of Lampo tampering with the records. Yet Philo's ire does not stem from the mutability of *hypomnēmata*, strictly speaking. It is not the sheer fact that *hypomnēmata* are easily revisable that bothers Philo. Rather, for Philo, the assumed mutability of *hypomnēmata* is the means, not the cause, of Lampo's wicked actions. They create the space in which an already wicked person can act wickedly.

In *Legat.* 162–65, Philo again writes about *hypomnēmata* in less than positive terms. Philo portrays the emperor, Gaius Julius Caesar Augustus Germanicus—better known as Caligula, which may be translated "Little Boots" or even "Bootikins"—as hubristic and foolish.[53] He believed that the Alexandrians actually thought he was a god. Consequently, Caligula credulously assumed the innovations made in the synagogues in Alexandria were done with a heartfelt respect for him.

> Next, he supposed the innovations of their prayers were all done with clear conscience and out of pure honor for him. He was persuaded, on the one hand, by note-like journals (*tais hypomnēmatikais ephēmerisin*) that some people had sent along from Alexandria, because he loved to read these so much that he thought the writings of other authors and poets were distasteful compared to the joy of reading these journals. On the other hand, he was persuaded by some of his slaves who were always mocking things and being sarcastic with him.[54]

Caligula's problem, according to Philo, is that he liked too much reading journal entries sent from Alexandria—more than reading proper literature.[55] In this passage, Philo compares the style of speech in *hypomnēmata* with the everyday speech of Caligula's slaves, as opposed to the proper speech of more educated elite people. Their speech is mocking and sarcastic, less serious and proper, and therefore less trustworthy. Caligula's affinity for such note-like journal entries is part of what led him to make such stupid decisions as allowing the changes made in the Alexandrian synagogues. While people like Cicero and Pliny can use the openness of *hypomnēmata* (or *commentarii*) to imagine positive outcomes for themselves, Philo and Lucian offer a glimpse in the potential problems caused by the fact that *hypomnēmata* are relatively fluid and known to only a few people. For some people and in some social contexts, to call a piece of writing *hypomnēmata* could have been a snub.

## *Plutarch's Creation and Use of* Hypomnēmata

The provisional and intermediary nature of *hypomnēmata* comes through in the writing practices of Plutarch, who was born sometime around the middle of the first century CE and died sometime shortly before 120 CE.[56] Plutarch both consumed and produced *hypomnēmata* as subliterary textual objects. In a passage at the beginning of his *De tranquillitate animi*, Plutarch apologizes to Paccius for the quality of his treatise by offering a glimpse into his writing process.

> I just received your letter urging me to write you something on the topic of contentment and on some passages in the *Timaeus* that require more careful explanation. At just that same moment our friend Eros needed to sail to Rome right away, because he had received a letter from the most excellent Fundanus, who, in his usual custom, asked him to come quickly. Since I neither had time to produce the book you requested, as I would have preferred, nor could I have born the thought of him arriving from me at your house completely empty-handed, I picked out *Contentment* from the notes that I just happened to have made for myself (*peri euthumias ek tōn hypomnēmatōn*), since I considered that you also wanted this discourse not for the purpose of hearing some writing striving to be elegant but for practical living purposes.[57]

Plutarch's apology to Paccius works only if we understand what *hypomnēmata* are, as well as what they are not. Plutarch, like many others, would read actively and takes notes, or more likely dictate notes to slaves. The purpose of the notes was to remind Plutarch of the useful tidbits and stories he had read. So, while Paccius asked for a piece of literature from Plutarch on the topic of contentment, presumably of a literary quality like some of Plutarch's other *Moralia*, due to the short time frame between the receipt of Paccius's request and Eros's departure for Rome Plutarch had no time to craft a piece of literature.[58] In keeping with the Platonic understanding, the *hypomnēmata* functioned to remind what was already known more than inform what was not yet known. Though written, they were not (yet) literature, as literature is designed for elegance and enjoyment, whereas *hypomnēmata* are more like working texts, written for more practical purposes. One is elegant, like a luxury vehicle; the other useful, like a pickup truck.

Since he didn't want to refuse the request, he simply picked out the section from his notes (*hypomnēmata*) on the topic of contentment and sent it with Eros to Rome. Plutarch could have made his *hypomnēmata* on the topic of contentment with a number of goals: memory aids, literary raw material, or both. In any case, they remained in a rough, open, incomplete state, and for this Plutarch creates the need to make prefatory remarks apologizing for their lack of elegance by pointing to their usefulness. We may theorize a Plutarchan axis of textuality: a vertical axis going from elegant to inelegant, a horizontal axis going from useless to useful. *De tranquillitate animi* falls on the inelegant but useful quadrant, as is customary for *hypomnēmata*.

Scholars have investigated the nature of Plutarch's *hypomnēmata*, and the use of the term in *Tranq. an.* 464e–f has been widely discussed.[59] Luc van der Stockt and others have tried to rescue Plutarch from the source critics, who took him to be a slavish reproducer of sources and not a creative author.[60] Redeploying the tools of source criticism, they sought to find Plutarch's own *hypomnēmata* as a source for Plutarch, with the idea of "establishing the noncoincidental repetition of a cluster of data and identifying that cluster as a *hypomnēma*."[61] While I remain skeptical about the possibility of successfully reconstructing a lost *hypomnēma* source, careful analysis does suggest that Plutarch produced and made use of *hypomnēmata* that contained clusters of stories or patterns, or perhaps both.[62]

Plutarch not only wrote *hypomnēmata*; he also used others' *hypomnēmata* in the authoring of his *Lives*. Cicero's and Caesar's notes were not the only pieces of literary raw material circulating in the ancient Roman world. Many others also wrote *hypomnēmata* or *commentarii* on many topics, ranging from military stratagems to ethical topics to their own lives. Sulla was among those who wrote his own *hypomnēmata*, which he reportedly finished immediately before his death in 78 BCE. Plutarch claims to have used Sulla's notebooks (*hypomnēmata*). He makes explicit reference to them several times in his *Life of Sulla*.[63] According to Plutarch, Sulla wrote twenty-two *hypomnēmata*, which covered the entirety of his life up to his own death.[64] The purpose of attaching the name Sulla to the *hypomnēmata* Plutarch uses is to add credibility to his own *Life of Sulla*. His *hypomnēmata* were dedicated to a specific person, Lucullus, and in the dedication Sulla offers an exhortation.[65] Plutarch sometimes says that Sulla "wrote" something in his notebooks.[66] Often, however, Plutarch says that he "exhorts," "says," or "speaks in his defense."[67]

Plutarch also uses the word *hypomnēmata* in connection with rites done to commemorate something, which may provide a clue to the perception of their textuality.[68] Thus, Sulla's notes do not fit neatly into a simple oral/written binary, but seem rather to be an extension of Sulla's memory in the physical form of writing. They also complicate a private/public or unpublished/published binary. On the one hand, what he wrote were presented as mere notes or memoranda, but on the other hand, they were dedicated to a specific person and were also collected into a set of twenty-two *hypomnēmata*, which Plutarch takes as a sign of their completion. Even though they were "finished," they were nonetheless designed to be changed and rewritten into a proper historical biography. They seem to function as a kind of historical subgenre. Regardless of how finished or public they were, Plutarch felt that they were the kind of writing he could rework in the creation of his *Life of Sulla*.

## *Galen's Unfinished Texts*

Galen reflected lucidly and self-consciously on himself as a producer of texts and literature. He differentiated among a variety of types of texts, modes of authorship, and avenues of "publication." At the beginning of his *On My Own Books*, Galen tells Bassus about a certain kind of text he had produced that was especially prone to textual fluidity, alteration, and being co-opted and redeployed by others: notes or *hypomnēmata* not intended for publication (*ou pros ekdosis*) but, rather, were for those of his circle or his students who would be separated from their oral source, Galen. He informs us that many people in other places presented his writings as if they were their own. They wrongly claim to be the owner of the content. They present themselves as the origin and authority behind it, when they in fact are not. They mutilated his texts in a variety of ways: taking parts out, or adding parts, or altering them in some other manner.[69] The reason why some of his works are especially fluid, prone to alteration, and able to be revised and presented as another person's work is that they were nothing more than notes (*hypomnēmata*), given to friends or students, without a title, and in no way intended for a public readership. Associates who had heard Galen speak wanted a memory aid of what he said, so they asked him to write some notes. Such writings did not require a title or an ascribed author. We can infer, then, that had Galen's writings been intended for a public audience, they would have had a title and an ascribed author. Galen's *hypomnēmata* were para- (or pre-) literary and especially open to being revised, finished, and reauthored by someone else.

Why bother to explain the writing practices and textual origins of Galen's notes? Galen hopes that readers, once they are aware of the fact that these are notes given to those in his circle, will be able to account properly for the roughness and unfinished nature of some of his texts. Probably some of these *hypomnēmata* will have been augmented while others will have been condensed, with each varying in its completion in terms of both style and content.[70] As Galen puts it, "It is perfectly clear that the writings I just mentioned are neither finished in terms of their content nor examined with precision, since they [the readers] would have had neither the need nor the ability to learn everything accurately (*akribōs*) before having had some training in the basics."[71] Galen thought his *hypomnēmata* lacked a completeness and accuracy that one would find in books aimed at a general and anonymous readership. Writers of *hypomnēmata* address specific students and therefore know precisely what information can be assumed, what information must be directly addressed, and what information can be omitted. It matters to Galen that the prospective reader know not only that Galen wrote something but also when he wrote it (for example, as a young man, or in a moment of anger, or during a demonstration) and to whom he wrote it (beginners, associates, advanced students), so that he can try to control the way his writings are read.[72] Try as he may, Galen's efforts were futile since his writings were already out of his hands, and—as every writer knows—one's readers cannot be controlled.

Galen had produced lots of notes and operates with a refined theory of their uses. In the recently discovered *Avoiding Distress* (*Peri alupias*), Galen talks about the loss of his notes (*hypomnēmata*) in the context of the loss of many other books in his library. He says, "None of these losses grieved me, even though they were substantial, valuable and hard to replace, any more than the loss of my own writings, which were of two kinds: some were so well fashioned as to be of use to others as well, while others were similarly produced for myself alone as an *aide-mémoire*."[73] While Galen claims he was not grieved by the loss of his books, he wants his reader to know the loss even of his notes had not caused him grief, presumably because the impossibility of reproducing such private and limited texts, which had not yet developed into disseminated literature, would have caused grief upon grief. Their real value comes from their usefulness, their inaccessibility to the public, and therefore the difficulty to reproduce them.[74] He details two different purposes and functions of his notes: some are written to be useful for others and some were written to be useful for himself. In both cases, their usefulness derives from their aiding memory of an oral tradition or teaching. In this way, Galen participates in the Platonic tradition of *hypomnēmata* as extension of human memory in the physical form of human writing.

For Galen, notes were necessary for those who wanted to remember his teachings while away from him. Think of the doctor and the physical trainer, and the creation of their notes in Plato's *Statesman* previously discussed. But unfinished notes also presented certain challenges. In the beginning of his *On Anatomical Procedures*, Galen details his reason for writing the present version of his work.

> Anatomical procedure was the subject of a previous work written on my coming to Rome [162 CE] not long since.... I have now resolved to write again on the subject, for two reasons. Firstly because Flavius

> Boëthus, the Roman Consul, as keen an anatomist as ever lived, on leaving Rome for his native Ptolemais [165 CE], urged me to record these "procedures." I gave him, among other works, my *De anatomicis administrationibus libri duo*. These were of notes [only] for, while he was with us [162–65], he had made many observations in a short time and had asked me for some such records as memoranda. But since he is now dead and I have no copies (for those I had in Rome were destroyed by fire), at the urging of friends I decided to write others to give them. I was the more inclined thereto because the work would be much better composed, for meanwhile I have made many new observations. For clarity it is enlarged into a more detailed and accurate account.... *De thoracis et pulmonis motu libri tres* I wrote long ago, as a youth. It was for a fellow-student, returning to his own country after a long absence. He wished to display his talents in public, but lacked lecturing ability. He, too, died and thus this book became public property, so that many got hold of it, though it was not for publication.... But the treatise that I wrote for Boëthus falls far short in lucidity and accuracy of what I propose now.[75]

While the present version is much more polished and refined, the previous version had been personally addressed memoranda (*hypomnēmata*), and thus less polished and less complete in its scope. He cites two reasons for undertaking the newer version. First, the previous version was circumstantial, as is common for notes. They were given to a certain Flavius Boëthus before his departure from Rome and consequently from Galen, the source of the information. Boëthus had since died and a fire in Rome had destroyed all of Galen's copies, with the result that the people who wanted a copy urged Galen to write another version. Second, the rising demand created the need for Galen to supply another version, but this time he would not write in the same fragmentary, provisional style. Galen took the opportunity to write a more complete version of his *On Anatomical Procedures* that would be more detailed and more accurate.

One of the questions Galen had to address was why ancient doctors (ancient from his perspective) did not write *hypomnēmata* on anatomical procedures. At the beginning of book 2 of *On Anatomical Procedures* he takes on the question.

> I commend Marinus, who has written on anatomical procedures, without criticizing my other predecessors who have not. For them

it was superfluous to compose memoranda for themselves or others since they practiced dissection from childhood under parental instruction, as they did reading and writing. . . . One so instructed from his earliest years would no more forget what he had learned from experience than would others the alphabet. In time, however, the art came to be customarily imparted not only to kinsmen but to those outside the family. Thus the habit of dissection from early years came to be discontinued. For when the Art was communicated to [any] favoured adult it followed that the instruction became poorer. . . . Formerly, then, there was no need for accounts of anatomical procedures, nor for the sorts of handbooks that were first written, so far as I know, by Diocles [ca. 360 BCE]. . . . In addition to their deficiencies such treatises have not made clear the usefulness of their matter, but fling together indiscriminately things that can be of the greatest service to the Art with others that contribute little or nothing thereto. . . . But, since there is danger that such studies may perish, because of the little regard that my contemporaries have for the arts and science, and further since they themselves no longer have practice from the earliest years, I feel justified in writing these memoranda (*eikotōs hypomnēmata graphomen*). Yet had it been possible to preserve oral tradition, such writing would have been superfluous. . . . Wherefore I have nothing but praise for Marinus for recording his anatomical experience, though I was myself compelled to write another work on the same theme, since I have found his both incomplete and obscure.[76]

Standing firmly in the Platonic tradition, Galen describes the purpose of *hypomnēmata* as a memory aid in the absence of the source of the teaching.

Not all *hypomnēmata* were equally rough, unfinished, or obscure. Like Galen's previous version of writing on anatomical procedures, Marinus's texts are incomplete and vague. Galen's present version, while still identified by Galen as notes, is more polished and accurate. When describing the literary nature of the constellation of *hypomnēmata*, unfinishedness and roughness are not a sine qua non. Neither is addressing the specific needs of one reader or one group of readers. Both are common but not ubiquitous. Perhaps a more common family resemblance of *hypomnēmata*, at least to Galen, is usefulness as an aid for remembering what was taught while absent from the source of the teaching.[77]

Galen claims to know the writings of Hippocrates so well that he is able to determine when a writing of Hippocrates is not finished or intended for publication.⁷⁸ In *In Hippocratis librum VI epidemiarum commentarii* 17b.13K, Galen comments on Hippocrates, *Epidemics* 6.3.1, which reads, "Watch for the sign of purification at the same time of day." Galen elaborates as follows:

> It is not unclear that this sentence goes with what was written before, where he was teaching how one should effect the purification. And so that we can know if we have got the right amount for it, he now writes the sign. But the text is unclear to us because, as I have already said several times, this book was not written for publication but as an outline sketch and draft for himself. If he were writing for publication he would have said everything he needed to say, specifically what time of day we should watch for the sign of the purification.⁷⁹

Galen feels he can safely assume Hippocrates's writings were not finished, but were mere sketches and outlines created for his own use. He can operate with such an assumption because the text is ambiguous. The gaps and ambiguities would not have thrown Hippocrates off, nor would they have confused those in his circle of students. On the contrary, his texts assume a proximity between readers and writer that allow quick movement through a topic. Yet Galen goes even further. As Sean Gurd points out, Galen claims to so understand Hippocratic theory of medicine and Hippocrates's style that he rewrites Hippocrates's aphorism into a more finished form. Commenting on Hippocrates, *Epidemics* 6.2.25, "because in a warmer place, more solid, on the right-hand side and dark because of this and the veins are rather on the outside [and with more bile]," Galen writes

> It is not surprising that the whole explanation is lacking, for this book was not written for publication, but contains sketches and outlines, as we are ourself accustomed to make. If it were a text for publication, beginning this way (as he wrote in the *Aphorisms*) he would have added the rest, making the whole text read as follows: Male foetuses are usually found to be constituted on the right side of the mother, while female foetuses are normally found in the other sinus [*scil.* of the womb], the left one. For it is probable that the warmer [sex] should be constituted on the warmer side of the mother. And the male is the warmer, as can be gather from the magnitude of the veins and the skin. For men are darker than women. If Hippocrates had written a text for publication [*suggramma*] he would have expressed himself thus, as he

did in the *On Fractures and Joints* and in the *Prognosticon* and in other such.[80]

Here Galen provides for us a rare opportunity to compare how an unfinished text might differ from a finished one. Not only that, Galen also illustrates a concrete example of what it might look like for someone to finish an unfinished text. His rewriting lengthens Hippocrates's aphorism by eliminating potential ambiguities. What is left as potentially unclear to an anonymous readership Galen demystifies, so that Hippocrates will not be misunderstood or misused by quacks or charlatans. Or, to put it in Galen's own terms, he finishes Hippocrates's drafts by making them more accurate and less ambiguous for an anonymous, more public readership.

## *Damis's* Hypomnēmata *as a Scrapbook of Textual Raw Material*

According to Philostratus's *Life of Apollonius*, a contemporary of Apollonius in the first century CE (perhaps early second) named Damis of Old Ninos wrote up a collection of notes (*hypomnēmata*) about his teacher, Apollonius of Tyana.[81] His notebooks included written memorials of Apollonius's journeys, sayings, speeches, and predictions. Philostratus recounts the following story about the notebooks' afterlives and how he came across them.

> The notebooks containing the memoirs of Damis were unknown until a member of his family brought them to the attention of the empress Julia. Since I was a member of her salon (for she admired and encouraged all rhetorical discourse), she set me to alter these discourses of Damis and to take care over their style, since the style of the man from Ninos was clear but rather unskillful.[82]

Several scholars have challenged the historicity of Damis's notebooks and by extension Philostratus's claim to historical reliability of his own sources. Some scholars argue that Damis's memoirs are a literary fiction, perhaps even one that ancient readers would have been expected to recognize as such.[83] Since I am not interested in historicity but the cultural understandings of textual unfinishedness and texts prone to reworking, the historical status of Damis's memoirs is of little relevance. Whether the memoirs of Damis come from the first century or are a literary fiction of Philostratus in the third century (more likely), they represent an interesting ancient instantiation of textuality and authoriality. Real or imagined, they reflect how some ancient readers understood *hypomnēmata* to function.

Philostratus describes Damis's memoirs in a specific and, as we have come to see in this chapter, well-known way. They were the collection of notes (*hypomnēmata*) of a student based on the teachings of a teacher, made as an extension to the memory for the student, so that nothing said or done might be forgotten. Such a situation, however, should not lead one to believe that they actually reflect the actions or word-for-word teachings, as the fluidity of the genre allowed ongoing revision, and human memory is active and flexible. In the case of Philostratus's work, we are dealing (ostensibly) with a couple hundred years of textual fluidity. Philostratus claims that memoirs were written and preserved on writing tablets (*deltous*), the kinds of writing material in which one might make initial drafts, write notes for later revision, or even perform school exercises.[84] For more than a century, at least in Philostratus's account, the writing tablets with the memoirs inscribed on them were not public but, instead, were possessed by Damis's family, the only ones to whom they were known.[85] Then, according to Philostratus, around the beginning of the third century CE (or perhaps late second), a member of Damis's family brought them to the attention of the empress Julia Domna, the wife of the emperor, Septimus Severus. Julia regarded Damis's collection of notes as the kind of writing that possesses a textual unfinishedness, lacks literary polish, and consequently leaves space for someone else to alter them and author them. Yet they were also the kind of text that merits being polished into a proper piece of literature.

In Philostratus's presentation, Damis's notebooks provide a surfeit of textual raw material. In *Vit. Apoll.* 1.19, Philostratus gives us another name for Damis's memoirs, which Christopher Jones translates as *Scrap Book*(*hē . . . deltos hē tōn ekphatnismatōn*).[86] One might more literally translate it as "the writing tablet containing the things that are cleaned out (or brought out) of the animal trough."[87] Certainly a less than complimentary image. Philostratus goes on to explain that a foolish and slanderous person accused Damis of recording not only the important events and sayings but also silly and unnecessary ones. In *Vit. Apoll.* 1.19, Philostratus defends the zealousness of Damis, but in 7.28 he himself acknowledges that Damis's memoirs contain stories and memories that are unimportant and unhelpful, which supports their identification as a notebook of manger remnants. So, whether his collection of notes come from the first century or is a third-century literary fiction of an imagined first-century text (the latter seems more likely), Damis's writings are presented as unfinished in a rather specific way, lacking literary polish. They contain stories and anecdotes that are unimportant as well as important. Though direct, they lack literary skill and therefore require alteration and reworking. In fact, they are the kind of text that invites such alteration, leaving space for another person to come along and author them into a piece of proper literature.

## *Conclusion*

I have reviewed a specific type of textual object, one which is not literature per se (at least not yet). It is occasionally created with the goal of becoming literature in the hands of another. Sometimes not. Such texts are especially associated with rough drafts of historical writers, or technical manuals for teachers, doctors, and other professionals, or students. They are texts possessed by a certain person or circle of people and are often self-consciously not made public by their writers. Openness is left in the text for another to rework them and attach their name to them to "author."[88] None of the examples discussed in this chapter provides a perfectly exact analogue for what I will argue in relation to the first- and second-century texts we have come to call gospels, with special attention to the Gospel according to Mark. Yet each example serves to help map out how unfinished texts, specifically *hypomnēmata*, were produced by ancient writers and experienced by ancient readers. Understanding *hypomnēmata* allows us to rethink the process of the production and textualization of the gospel.

A modern reader does well to keep in mind that many texts in the ancient world, perhaps even most, were considered not "literature" but, rather, textual objects and unfinished. Yet this vast sea of unfinished textual objects has not survived to the present. Rather, they have been lost to time. After all, it took a tremendous effort and money to keep a work alive. Nonetheless, one must not presume that a text, just because it has survived to the modern day, was a finished text. One should also not assume that all texts were published, and it is to the topic of publication that we now turn.

# 3

# *Accidental Publication and Postpublication Revision*

PUBLICATION IS A dangerous word for an ancient historian. It is often set off with scare quotes. And rightfully so. All too often, scholars wrongly and unknowingly bring in a host of modern ideas connected with the printing press when they talk about publication in antiquity. The printing press can lead one to imagine a textual uniformity and finality that is foreign to the ancient world. A text that has survived to the present must have been published and therefore be in its final form as intended by the author, so the line of thinking goes.

Of course, every word an ancient historian uses is anachronistic. It is a question of the kind of anachronism and whether the anachronism is potentially helpful in the historian's construction of the ancient world. I argue the word *publication* is helpful for two reasons. First, it contains in it the idea of a public readership, which is important to the ancient ways of thinking about making a text public, bringing a text out to a broader readership. Second, since the modern idea of publication is reliant on printing technologies, once the printing-press anachronism is clearly pointed out, since it is so patently anachronistic, the use of the word *publication* serves to remind people to place their reading beyond the printing press.

In the ancient world, publication is a cultural *habitus* (a "structured" and "structuring [social] structure" not perceived as obedience to rules, to use the language of Pierre Bourdieu) produced by social perceptions, structures, and practices, and not by printing presses.[1] It was a matter of readers' expectations and authors' attempts to control those readers' expectation. As I have shown, scholarship on publication in the ancient Roman world has overfocused on the clean, idealized process of making a text public. The author's control, intention, and execution have held pride of place. Yet there is another story to be told: the story of ancient writing practices, readers' expectations, and all that could go "wrong" with publication. In order to understand writing before the emergence of the book, we must understand the ins and outs of how a text became "public" in a variety of contexts in the area around the ancient Mediterranean basin.

Connected with unfinished, unattributed, private texts in antiquity is that of accidental publication. Implied in the definitions of ancient publication among the modern scholars discussed in chapter 1 is the idea that, if a text comes down to us, it must have been consciously made public at some specific time by the author. This is not the case. In this chapter I explore examples of accidental publication, in which the author claims to have no knowledge of how a text became public and such that publication was against his will. Exploring the textured nature of publication in the ancient world provides a helpful means for thinking about how differently textuality and authorship worked in the ancient world.

## *Cicero's Wound, Textual Healing, and Pseudepigraphical Pseudepigraphy*

It is sometimes thought that Cicero delivered his speeches solely from memory. He would prepare a speech, memorize it, deliver it, and then go back and edit a textualized speech for public reception as a piece of literature. No doubt this reflects some of his speeches—but not all. While this may represent Cicero's notional ideal, the process by which a speech might become public could be complicated at several points. For example, someone could have written down the speech and passed it around against Cicero's will. Cicero might have decided not to add a speech to his literary résumé and yet someone might somehow have got hold of it anyway and passed it around, which could be undesirable and even humiliating. Quintilian tells us that Cicero often used a draft of notes (*commentarii*) while on the rostrum or delivering a speech.[2] In this context the *commentarii* would not be memory aids for students to use at a later time when they are separated from the source of the teaching but, rather, for the speaker himself to use, helping him stay on track during his speech. It was not unheard of for a speaker's notes to become public through circulation, either without the speaker's consent or in an edited form.[3] Quintilian even cites one of Cicero's speeches still in note form (*commentarii*) as being in circulation in his own day, which was over a century later.[4]

Cicero complains from time to time that one of his speeches had become public against his will.[5] In *Att.* 3.12, Cicero is wringing his hands and scheming with Atticus about the political goings-on in Rome. Elections are coming up and Cicero wants his public image to be in top shape. Something embarrassing, however, has transpired.

> You cut me deep when you told me about my speech being published. If you can, please heal that wound, as you have called it. I did in fact write something a long time ago when I was angry with [Curio] for something he wrote first against me, but I had so suppressed it that I thought it would never become known. How it has escaped I have no clue. But since it so happens that I never had a word of dispute with him and since the speech seems to me to be less carefully written than my other speeches, I think we might be able to claim that it was not written by me. Please take care of this, if you think you can cure me. But if I am already a goner, I don't really care.

We find out only at *Att.* 3.15 that the opponent Cicero has in mind is Curio.[6] Probably in 61 BCE, Cicero wrote a speech against Curio and Clodius in a moment of anger. The speech remains extant in fragmentary form even to this day, even though Cicero never intentionally published it.[7] In *Att.* 3.12, he claims that, fortunately for him, he never delivered it and he never even had a public moment of dispute with either one of his opponents. The speech existed in written form, but had never been made public through oral presentation. Somehow the speech had become public against Cicero's will and to his embarrassment, because such a speech would not help him during upcoming elections.

The availability of Cicero's embarrassing speech in public upset him. Part of the back and forth between Atticus and Cicero in *Att.* 3.12 and 3.15 involves Atticus giving Cicero a hard time for distressing himself over the accidentally published speech, which served no purpose to Cicero and in fact was unfounded, as the debate in the Senate went well. Grief was thought by some ancient medical theories to cause sickness and even death.[8] The accidental publication of Cicero's undelivered speech against Clodius and Curio was the cause of Cicero's grief, and this explains the metaphor used by Atticus and Cicero. They analogize the accidental publication as a grievous wound (*vulnus*) that Atticus must heal. Cicero urges Atticus to try to heal the wound of its accidental publication by removing all copies of it from circulation. Cicero invites Atticus to play literary doctor and do his best to cure him, if he thinks he can. If the wound has already killed Cicero, then there is no use grieving any longer, since dead people have no reason to grieve.

Atticus was responsible for the curation, circulation, and protection of Cicero's literature and, by extension, his literary persona. He was his Aristarchus (which, of course, puts Cicero in the enviable place of Homer), because he had the responsibility of correcting and revising Cicero's writings.[9] He also knew his rhetorical "color-box," his rhetorical style and the sound of his literary voice.[10] Atticus employed copyists who reproduced Cicero's writings for public consumption.[11] Perhaps, then, Cicero expects Atticus to fix his current problem because Atticus himself was its cause, whether directly or indirectly. We cannot know whether a foe stole it or Cicero (or Atticus) shared it with a friend who then passed it along to another (and so on), but in either case an embarrassing textualized yet undelivered speech fell into public circulation. Cicero, however, knows and can assume that Atticus realizes his accidentally published speech did not match the style of his other speeches. It was "more ignored" (*neglectius*) than his other writings, which indicated its roughness when compared to the stuff Cicero and Atticus usually brought out to readers.

By way of solution, Cicero suggests a two-pronged approach. The best alternative would be to have the speech removed from public circulation. "Unpublishing" a piece of writing was another feature of publication in the ancient Mediterranean world that may seem strange to those accustomed to modern printing technologies. Undoing publication, however, while possible, would have been difficult, as it would involve locating and acquiring every copy of a text.[12] If unpublishing his speech was not possible, Cicero has another solution: he suggests they claim it was pseudepigraphically written in Cicero's name, but was not actually by Cicero. That is, the backup plan was to claim the authentic writing was a pseudepigraphon.[13] Claiming that some anonymous writer forged writings in Cicero's name was possible for two reasons. First, he claims to have never delivered the speech, so there was no cultural memory to prove the speech came from him. Second, because Cicero and Atticus (and others) never corrected, revised, polished, and finished the speech in preparation for public consumption, it had a more unkempt and rough style when compared to Cicero's other writings.[14] If neither unpublication nor (deceptively) labeling his authentic writing as pseudepigraphical were possible, then the "wound" had already killed Cicero, and he, like a dead man, need not concern himself with such things any longer.

## Diodorus Siculus on How to Handle Accidental Publication

We know nearly nothing about Diodorus Siculus apart from his enormous work called *Library of History* and the occasional tidbits of information we can mine about him from it.[15] He toiled away on his huge work for many decades, compiling information from a wide variety of sources. He boasts of having traveled throughout Asia and Europe hunting down information about the general history of the world, and that in a context in which travel was a risky, arduous, and expensive task.[16] In the preface, he writes that he has been working on his *magnum opus* for thirty years and the volumes are not yet published.[17] A picture emerges of him traveling, excerpting, writing, correcting, revising, and polishing his nascent piece of literature—all over a period of three decades. As we imagine the literary origins of *The Library of History*, we can envision him pining over, adding to, tinkering with, and rewriting his text for an extended period of time. The project was an open and ongoing one.

During these thirty years, some of his volumes made their way out onto the public stage before they were finished. He writes

> Some of the volumes were stolen and prematurely published before they were corrected and carefully completed (*tēn akribē sunteleian labein klapeisai proexedothēsan*). Therefore, I was not ready to give my stamp of approval to the writing. I disclaim these volumes. But in order that these prematurely published volumes might not ruin the entire history writing, I thought it necessary to write something defensive to set the matter straight. I treat my subject in forty volumes. In the first six volumes, I describe the actions and myths prior to the Trojan War.[18]

Thirty years is a long time to try to keep a piece of writing unpublished and out of the hands of untrustworthy readers, especially if, as seems likely, he would have asked others their opinions about his writing.[19] In fact, somewhere along the way the wrong readers had gotten their hands on some of Diodorus's volumes and spread them around prematurely. Diodorus laments that he had not had the opportunity to correct or revise the stolen volumes into a state of satisfactory completion. I say "satisfactory completion" because a finished work is little more than a work that a writer has decided no longer to change—a decision that, of course, itself could change, and, as we shall see, often did.[20] Some of Diodorus's writings were born before they had properly gestated and Diodorus takes the necessary action to address such writings for the sake of his whole project.

Diodorus, however, cannot be the one to identify and deal with such unfinished writings. He must rely upon and empower his anonymous readers to do so. His method to ensure that readers know to distinguish the legitimate books from the ones he disowns is to write an outline of the whole project. He enumerates the volumes and defines the topics of the volumes. By tabulating the contents, he allows an anonymous reader to ascertain what he stands behind and what he labels as illegitimate.

An accidentally published work is often perceived to be a more open and revisable work. Without titles, prefaces, and paratextual features geared toward controlling the text and the anonymous reader, ambitious readers could easily take an accidentally published text and use it as raw material for the creation of their own texts, or even just write their names on it, give it a title, and claim it as their own. Diodorus shows an awareness of the likelihood of such "mutilation" in his preface when he writes:

> So then, I have outlined [the subjects of my *Library of History*] beforehand, because, on the one hand, I want my readers to understand the whole project but, on the other hand, because I want to discourage those who are accustomed to revise their books for publication (*tous diaskeuszein eiōthotas tas biblious*) by abusing other peoples' works. May what I have written well throughout my whole history not incite envy among you, but may what I have written in ignorance meet with correction at the hands of those who are more competent.[21]

Diodorus's solution to the ever-present possibility of accidental publication is to create paratextual features such as section outlines, so that if readers read a copy that deviates from his authorized outline, they will know they read a pirated and unauthorized copy.[22] The preface with detailed outlines has two purposes. First, it attempts to guide readers by offering them a map of the whole work. Second, by defining his topics beforehand, Diodorus attempts to create a security system guarding against textual revisers, editors, correctors, and anyone else who might capitalize on the inherent fluidity of such texts in antiquity.

In the same breath, though, Diodorus also introduces a paradox regarding the revision of his *opus*. He acknowledges two types of textual revisers: those who are accustomed to revise or correct others' books in the creating and publishing of their own; and those more competent who might correct what is lacking or amiss in Diodorus's writings. The former he discourages by adding a preface with a detailed outline of subjects; the latter he explicitly invites. The difference between the two forms of textual alteration relates both to the cause and the outcome of the revision. To Diodorus, using his writings as a source in the creation of a new, separate work is bad. Reworking and improving his work is good.

## *Horace and Examples of Accidental Publication in the Ancient Roman Imagination*

How might accidental publication occur? Some writers employ the language of theft, which could refer to actually stealing a physical text, or to plagiarism, or simply to stealing one's ideas. Another commonplace was accidental publication as a result of the overzealous disciple's notes passing into the public sphere. Being so far removed, we are left to use a disciplined and careful historical imagination about how students might accidentally make their master's teachings public.[23] Luckily, Horace, a first century BCE author, and his satirical imagination help us think about how we may picture just such a moment.

Horace satirizes a moment of an eager lecture-listener named Catius rushing home to record what he had heard recently in a lecture. As he hurries home, Horace (or his satirical literary persona) stops him and then we hear the following exchange:

> Catius! Where are you off to? . . .
> . . . No time to stop, for I must jot down these new philosophical rules which are going to eclipse Pythagoras and the condemned Athenian and Plato's genius.
> I know I shouldn't delay you at such an awkward time; you will forgive me, won't you? But if anything slips your mind you'll soon recall it with that memory of yours, which is quite [amazing] whether it's a natural gift or something acquired by practice.
> Well, I *was* anxious to make sure of remembering the whole lecture, for it was all subtle material presented in a subtle style.
> Can you reveal the man's name? Was he a Roman or a stranger?
> I'll repeat the rules from memory; the source [Lat. *auctor*] must remain a secret. When serving eggs . . .[24]

He goes on to recount the lecture at some length and in detail. In his satire, Horace mocks ancient Roman "foodie" culture through the presentation of an Epicurean character named Catius.

In order for the joke to land, Horace's satire requires certain knowledge from the reader. It expects the reader to know that such philosophical lectures happen in Rome with some frequency. The lecture Catius attended is situated among and in competition with other established philosophical schools, such as the Pythagoreans and Platonists, who ostensibly would have been discussing matters of weighty philosophical significance. Since Catius himself sets up the philosophical teachings of famous philosophers as points of comparison, when the lecture begins with the words "When serving eggs, ... " we know we are firmly in the realm of satire.

Moreover, the satire also assumes the regularity of an enthusiastic student or lecture-auditor writing down entire lectures. If Horace thought his audience would never have seen or heard of students rushing home to record from memory whole lectures, the joke would not be effective. Yet in Horace's satire, the content that Catius rushes home to preserve in writing is not about the philosophical life but, rather, about the undignified (or at least less "elite") topic of food preparation, like how to serve eggs or prepare a sauce—tasks not suitable for a person of means but instead for slaves and people of lower classes. Thus, the satire strikes at certain people's garishness and overzealous concern for food. It is through the student's note-taking that the teacher's teaching receives its textualization. Even after it is textualized, though, it is not yet a piece of formal literature; it occupies a liminal space between oral teaching and written literature.

When Catius shares the whole lecture with Horace, Horace in turn shares the whole lecture with his readers, and the fictional "lecture" thereby becomes "public"—all without the permission of the anonymous teacher. While a satire and not the actual lecture of a real philosopher (or perhaps more accurately, a cook!), Horace's *Sat.* 2.4 enacts for us an imagined instantiation of how a spoken lecture might accidentally become published in a textualized form against someone's will and without her or his knowledge. Someone spoke, another wrote, who then shared with another, and thereby caused the piece of teaching to pass beyond the teacher's immediate circle of students. In such a scenario, the teachers would not have known that their teaching had become public.

As was often the case, when accidental publication occurred in this way the name of the source, or the author (*auctor*), was not attached to the document itself and was, even in Horace's satirical presentation, unknown. Paratextual features such as titles, ascribed authors, prefaces, and postscripts usually came along in the formal publication phase as a way of trying to inform and control, or at least negotiate, an anonymous reader's interpretation.

The teaching passes from the mouth of the teacher to the ears of the auditor, from the mouth of the auditor to the ears of Horace's literary persona, from the ears of Horace's literary persona to the text of *Sat.* 2.4, and from there to each new reader—and at every turn is refracted and altered through memory, rhetoric, rewriting, and interpretation.

### *The Idea of Accidental Publication as Asset:* 4 Ezra

The idea of once-private texts that have now, in one way or another, whether against the author's will or not, come to the attention of new and more public readerships was a problem to some in antiquity. To others, however, it could be an asset. Accidental publication is often associated with a text ascribed to an authoritative figure who did not write it.[25] Whether this is intentional pseudepigraphy or plagiarism, or whether it is imitation and emulation for the sake of continuing and animating a textual tradition, accidental publication creates the notional space to answer the question: if the text in question comes from X authoritative figure, why are we just now hearing about it, so many years/decades/centuries later?[26] This seems to be the logic behind one of the letters of Plato.

> Plato to Dionysius wishes well-doing.
> I hear from Archedemus that you think that not only I myself should keep quiet but my friends also from doing or saying anything bad about you; and that "you except Dion only." . . . For this reason I myself have never yet written anything on these subjects, and no treatise by Plato exists or will exist, but those which now bear his name belong to a Socrates become fair and young. Fare thee well, and give me credence; and now, to begin with, read this letter over repeatedly and then burn it up.[27]

Like a romance novel or a spy thriller, the reader is instructed to read the letter until its contents have been fully absorbed and then to burn it, so that the only evidence of its existence is in the reader's mind. The instructions lead the reader to imagine that, luckily, the original recipient was disobedient, with the result that the present reader gets to peek at information otherwise unavailable. A similar logic may be detected in the pseudo-Pauline epistles, some of which suggest the idea to the readers' imagination that other letters of Paul are circulating around out there, ones that they don't know about yet.[28]

While using different terms and language, the logic of once-secret texts that have now fortuitously become public plays an important role in some writings of early Judaism, especially in the Ezrean writings. Others have noted the importance of the passages in *4 Ezra*, where Ezra is made to create secret writings, but I would like to speak directly about the passages from the perspective of ancient writing practices.[29] The key passages in question read as follows:

> And [God] answered me and said, "Go gather the people and tell them not to seek you for forty days. Now you make for yourself many wooden writing tablets and take with you Sarea, Dabria, Selemia, Elkana, and Asiel. Take these five who have been trained how to write quickly. And you come here, and I will kindle in your heart a lamp of comprehension that will not be snuffed out until you have finished writing what you are about to write. And when you have finished, make some of them public, but entrust others secretly to the wise. And so, at this hour tomorrow, you will begin to write".[30]
>
> And so in forty days ninety-four books were written. And it so happened that when the forty days were up, the Most High said, "Publish the first books you wrote and let the worthy and the unworthy read them. But you must hold back the last seventy books so that you can entrust them to those who are wise from among your people".[31]

Ezra and his five men are to write on *buxos*, writing tablets made of boxwood. A writing tablet made of wood would often have been filled with wax. One pointy end of a stylus would scratch the wax to write, and the flat end would erase by smoothing the wax. Some ancient teachers recommended wax tablets because they made revision and rewriting easy.[32] They were frequently used by schoolchildren and by writers in the earlier stages of the composition process.[33]

Ezra is told to make many wooden writing tablets, apparently enough to hold ninety-four books. He is then told to make some public, but keep others back for the wise (*quaedam palam facies, quaedam sapientibus absconse trades*). *Palam facere* and *absonse tradere* are not the language typically used in Latin of the period to express the division between published and unpublished writings. One might expect *edo* or *effero*, or in Greek *ekdidōmi*, *ekpherō*, or the noun *ekdosis* (or its opposite *ou pros ekdosis*), which are all more technical terms to express publication.[34] Nevertheless, while not using the same technical language, the Latin translation of *4 Ezra* certainly participates in cultural expectations and *habitus* of publication. The phrase *Palam facere* is a common one used to refer to making something generally public knowledge.[35] Ezra and his scribes produce twenty-four books generally known to all the people. These published or public texts are compared with the seventy books that are handed down secretly to a limited group of insiders known as the wise (*sapientibus absconse trades*).

What's important for the present study is that the Torah revealed again through Ezra is imagined as a series of published books. Yet, in contrast to the published books, Ezra also produced a wealth of other unpublished, secret books. These are preserved for the eyes of the wise only. Until now. Now the secret books are being made known to a new set of privileged readers; they are invited to join the wise readers of the secret knowledge. Whereas the making public of previously unpublished, secret writings has often elsewhere been a problem to be solved and complained about by various ancient writers, here, in a growing Ezrean tradition, it presents a solution. The theme of formerly secret books now being brought to new readership runs throughout much of ancient Jewish prophecy and apocalyptic writings. A couple such examples would be Daniel 12:4 and 1 Enoch 68:1–2.[36] How is it that these new or newly found writings are so old, an ancient reader might ask. Answer: the texts were written long ago but previously kept for the wise. Now their apocalyptic teachings are being made available. Therefore, the *topos* of accidental publication provides the cover and the imagined space for creating more Ezrean writings.

## *Arrian as Writer but Not Author*

Exploring the possibility of accidental publication provides the opportunity to better understand some nuances of ancient writing practices and how they relate to different modes of authorship. Arrian's preface to Epictetus's *Discourses* offers a glimpse into how publication, writing, and authorship hang together. Sometime in the first quarter of the second century CE, Arrian heard the lectures of Epictetus. We have him to thank for Epictetus's spoken teachings becoming textual objects. But Arrian wants to be clear on how Epictetus's oral teaching came to be a published book.

> *Arrian to Lucius Gellius*
> Greetings. I neither authored (*sunegrapsa*) the *Discourses* of Epictetus in the same way as someone might author (*suggrapseie*) such things nor did I circulate it publicly among people—what's more, I don't even claim to have authored it (*oude suggrapsai phēmi*). But I tried to write

down everything I heard him saying in his own words as best I could in order to preserve memory aids (*hosa de ēkouon autou legontos, tauta auta epeirathēn autois onomasin hōs hoion et ēn grapsamenos hypomnēmata*) of his thinking and his candor for myself at a later time. The *Discourses* are the kind of thing someone might say to another on the spot when prompted, not the kind of thing someone might compose with the purpose of passing down to others to read at a later time. Being what they are, I don't know how they were brought out into public circulation without my consent and without my knowledge. But it really doesn't matter to me if I do not seem to be an adequate writer, and Epictetus doesn't care if someone disparages his words, because it was clear that when he said them his only goal was to move the minds of those hearing him toward the best things. If these *Discourses* produce the same effect, I think they would accomplish the very thing that philosopher's teachings are supposed to accomplish. But if not, let those who read them know this one thing: when Epictetus gave his lectures, they had the exact impact on those listening that he wanted them to have. But if these *Discourses* by themselves do not produce the same effect, maybe it's my fault, maybe it had just to be this way.[37]

Here Arrian comes off as a bit touchy. He defends Epictetus's *Discourses* and, by extension, his own literary abilities. It does not take an overactive imagination to hear echoes of what Arrian's critics might have been saying: his texts are not polished, they sound like pieces of oral presentation, they lack power and efficacy, and they are riddled with errors and mistakes. Such mudslinging sullied both Epictetus and Arrian. So Arrian, in a move of self-defense, makes a revision to the *Discourses* by (if not also other changes) adding a preface to explain the origins of his writings.[38] He asks the reader to understand that the *Discourses* were simply his lecture notes, written only for himself. Their purpose was to be a personal *aide-mémoire* of both the thoughts and the frank style of his teacher, so that later, when he was away from Epictetus, he could evoke his presence. But, being such, they were never intended to be circulated publicly and read by anonymous readers—they were defenseless orphans without their father to defend them.

In keeping with the Platonic idea, Arrian refers to his texts as *hypomnēmata*—notes of Epictetus's teaching to jog his memory, a precaution against the toll of time, a way of preserving Epictetus when he was no longer around. Though they are a textualization of oral teaching, it would be a mistake to think of them as pieces of literature. In a way, they are more like a speech genre that incidentally also happens to be written down—spoken words preserved in writing for the sake of memory, not for the sake of being literature.

Arrian protests he is not the "author" of the text he wrote, in the sense that he is not the source of the content and he wishes to situate the writing in a broader context of philosophical teaching and student note-taking.[39] While in modern usage, writer and author are often conflated, such was not the case in antiquity, where authorship was connected with authorization, among other things.[40] The author was the source or the one who gave authority to the content.[41] Arrian happened to be the one who textualized the *Discourses*, but he appears uncomfortable with the label of author, since the teaching does not originate with him nor does its authority stem from him. He is merely a conduit. Ambiguity or confusion between the writer and the author are especially muddled in the case of *hypomnēmata*, since they either derive from another source than the writer or in some sense are less authored.

Arrian is quite clear: he did not publish Epictetus's *Discourses*. Regardless, they had entered public readership in one way or another. How they became public baffles Arrian. While the definitions of publication at the beginning of the chapter make a firm connection between publication and the self-conscious decision of the author, accidental publication throws a wrench into such a configuration. While it may seem intuitive to concatenate authorship, intention, finality, and publication, all four concepts are complicated by the preface of *Discourses*. Arrian refuses to be identified as the author of the text he wrote, which was not in its definitive, polished form, and which was brought into the public domain against the will and without the knowledge of the writer (and presumably the author, Epictetus).

Several consequences flow from the *topos* of accidental publication, one of which is postpublication revision of a text. Van Groningen, Starr, Dorandi, and Gamble all focus their attention on the finished, definitive version of a piece of literature in their discussions of publication or making a book public in antiquity. Yet just because a work was published does not mean it was in its final or definitive state. The two should not be conflated. Authors could and often did go on and further revise their books, even after those texts came into the public space. Such revision, of course, was not confined to accidently published writings. Martial says he revised *Epigrams* Book 10 after it was made public, and the reader would find that over 50 percent of it was new.[42] Ovid, speaking in the voice of his books, says of his *Amores*: "We who were once five books / Are three, the author preferred it this way / That now, should you not be pleased to have read it / It will yet be a lighter punishment with two books having been removed."[43] Thus, even an intentionally published text could be quite substantially expanded or condensed after its publication. Only a subjective judgment on the part of the modern scholar determines which version—the earliest, the last, or one in between—deserves the stamp of being "the original text" or "the final text" or even "the best text." Furthermore, the relationship between works that have been revised by the author after the point of publication and the remaining manuscript evidence is not necessarily predictable.

## *Cicero and the Inability to Control One's Own Manuscript Tradition*

People make mistakes. But what happened when ancient authors wanted to correct a mistake in a work already brought out publically? Horace, speaking about the dangers of writing, famously warned: *Nescit vox missa reverti*, "A word, once spoken, does not know how to return."[44] Like toothpaste, once it is out, it is hard to get it back in. Nevertheless, when authors realized they had written in error, they sometimes tried to do the apparently impossible. And they sometimes even succeeded.

Cicero provides two interesting examples that help us understand the unpredictability of manuscript traditions and their relationship to authors' intentions. In *Att.* 12.6.3, Cicero writes to Atticus about an error in his *Orator*.

> If you love me, please send the book. It is certainly yours [to send] since it was dedicated to you. "Chremes, you have so little work to do"[45] that you are really reading my *Orator*? Go on! I am so grateful, and I will be even more grateful, if, not only in your scrolls but also in other peoples' scrolls, you have your copyists replace "Eupolis" with "Aristophanes."

Cicero writes to Atticus, who curates his literary *oeuvre*, to ask him to make a correction of an error in a published writing. In the section in question of his *Orator*, Cicero makes a point about Attic style and plain style. The quotation in question comes from Aristophanes, *Ach.* 530–31: "Pericles lightened, thundered, and threw all Greece into confusion" (*fulgere, tonare, permiscere Graeciam*).[46] A potentially insightful point about Attic style. The problem, however, is Cicero wrongly attributed the quotation to Eupolis, not

Aristophanes. Atticus and his team of copyists are tasked with making the correction in their own copies, as well as hunting down other copies with the "Eupolis" reading in it and changing it to "Aristophanes." In this case, Cicero got lucky—only corrected manuscripts come down to us today.[47] Had it not been for Cicero leaving indication of his blunder in a letter to Atticus, there would be no such evidence.

In another case, however, Cicero again admits to a gaffe in one of his published writings, but this time he would not be so fortunate. He returns to Atticus once more.

> Brutus told me what T. Ligarius said, that my mention of L. Corfidius in the speech in Ligarius's defense was an error. But, as they say, it was just *un trou de mémoire*. I had known that Corfidius was a dear friend of the Ligarii, but I understand that he died just before [the speech]. Do please ask Pharnaces, Antaeus, and Salvius to remove that name from all [copies of the speech].[48]

The context of the speech makes the mistake even more striking. He evokes the physical presence of Corfidius at the speech in order to drive his point home rhetorically. He had said,

> And do you mark the illustrious array before you—Brocchus and his household, Lucius Marcius, Gaius Gaesetius, Lucius Corfidius, all Roman knights who attend here in the garb of mourning—men who are not merely known to you, but known for good men and true, men who were on your side?[49]

Cicero's plea directs one's attention to the physical presence of a variety of respected people. An image comes to mind of Cicero pointing his finger at each of these men, who sit listening attentively to his speech. Without their presence, the power of his rhetoric wanes. And apparently Corfidius had worn his garb of mourning so profoundly that he himself had already died, and thus regretfully had to miss Cicero's speech. So, if Corfidius was not only absent from the speech but in fact already dead, Cicero's rhetoric does not quite work in his favor. It probably backfires. As he was wont to do, Cicero turned to his friend Atticus for help. In this case, however, Atticus was of less help to him. Whereas in the other case only corrected manuscripts remain to the present day, in *Lig.* 33 only uncorrected manuscripts remain.

The two examples from Cicero's speech just mentioned are particularly interesting to put side by side. In both cases, Cicero requested that a published speech be later altered to fix mistakes, yet these two examples suggest there is not necessarily a predictable relationship between what an ancient writer intended when and what remains to this day in the manuscript tradition. While the results are different in each case, in both cases had Cicero not given us information elsewhere, the manuscript tradition and the traditional tools of textual criticism would leave us unaware of the problem, all of which should prompt us to be a bit humbler in our claims to have reached any sort of authorial intention or definitive version through manuscripts and exegesis.

## *Josephus on Pre-Writing, Rewriting, and Postpublication Revision*

Josephus provides an especially helpful point of comparison for the larger purposes of rethinking gospel textualization in the first two centuries CE, since he was a knowledgeable Jew living under Roman rule and writing (at least ultimately) in Greek. While he lacks the sort of explicit theorization about ancient writing practices found in the writings of some of his contemporaries, certain clues in his writings suggest that he, like other writers of the period, produced textual raw materials during a preliminary stage of the creation of some of his works, which then remain works in progress for a long time. Some of his works received authorial revision even after their initial publication.

In *Ag. Ap.* 1.46–50, Josephus briefly touches on how he wrote the *Jewish War*. Aware of other attempts to write about the war, he describes how and why he had written as a way of justifying his own history. Others write and publish their histories without ever having been to the places they write about, which undercuts their claims to reliability.[50] By comparison, Josephus writes the true history of the war because he was there, acting as a general in the Jewish army, but later taken captive and held under guard by Vespasian and Titus in a Roman camp.[51] It was his dual role as general and then guarded captive that allowed him the opportunity to become the historian *par excellence* of the war. He claims,

> During that time, nothing happened that escaped my attention. For I saw everything that happened in the Roman camp and I was writing it all down carefully (*epimelōs*) and I alone understand all the news that the deserters reported. Later when I found some time for leisure

(*scholēs*) in Rome, after all my materials had been prepared, I used some literary collaborators for help with the Greek language. That's how I produced the tradition (*paradosin*) of what happened.[52]

Regardless of in what language Josephus wrote his preliminary notes, the relevant point here is that Josephus claims to have produced textual raw materials, as was customary for ancient historians.[53] He says that while captive, he wrote in a Roman camp all that he heard from other deserters, and many years later he reworked these notes into his *Jewish War*. Although he does not use the word here, Josephus was familiar with what *hypomnēmata* were and how they worked. He refers to Caesar's *commentarii* of his actions in Gaul (his *Gallic War*) as "Caesar's notes" (*ta Kaisaros . . . hypomnēmata*).[54] Shaye Cohen has argued that Josephus refers to writing a *hypomnēma* in *Ag. Ap.* 1.50, while other scholars have preferred other terms.[55] Whatever the case, his language is clear enough that he wrote textual materials that were not themselves finished texts but, rather, were raw material designed to be altered and rewritten into a piece of more formal literature—to become something else. Whether Josephus would have used the precise term *hypomnēmata* or not is unimportant. The function of the textual materials in the context of *Ag. Ap.* 1.50 fits with the idea of *hypomnēmata* as pre-literary memory aids.

To rewrite his preliminary notes, he worked together with some collaborators (*tisi . . . sunergois*). Their purpose was to help him turn his preliminary materials into a polished book in proper Greek. He may refer to translation assistance or, more likely, simply to a communal project of literary collaboration, as was common in Roman culture at the time.[56] Josephus uses the phrase *pros tēn Hellēnida phōnēn* (lit. "with respect to the Greek tongue"). The word *phōnē* may refer to the Greek language or proper Greek pronunciation or even just nuanced Greek phrasing.[57] Not surprisingly, the textual raw materials from which Josephus and his cohorts created his *Jewish War* have been lost, which is the destiny of most *hypomnēmata* or *commentarii* from antiquity. What he wrote as a captive in the Roman camp was not the *Jewish War*; it was provisional texts designed to give its life for the birth of another text.

Elsewhere Josephus offers another sideways glimpse into the literary genesis of his *Jewish War*. Steve Mason has made an observation about the expanding circles of publication of Josephus's *Jewish War*.[58] In the prologue to *Jewish War*, Josephus gestures toward others who have read preliminary versions of his work, disapprovingly.[59] In 1.1–3, he indicates he knows the works in progress of other writers in Rome, which would seem to imply that he either heard bits of their writing at prepublication recitals or through sharing of texts in some other similar situation. Mason thinks Josephus somehow came into contact with "advance copies or extracts" of others' writings.[60] Of Josephus's *Jewish War*, Mason, pointing to the digression in 1.13–16, writes:

> Of interest here is not only that Josephus again seems well aware of what his contemporaries are writing, but also that *they are fully apprised of his work*: they have "abused" him for it. What else are we to make of this lengthy and peculiar paragraph? These eloquent men "position themselves as judges" over great recent events (*sc.* the Judean war): "which expose the ancient wars as paltry by comparison, *while abusing those who rival them for honor*—in relation to whom, even if they prove superior in speech-craft, they are inferior in choice of subject." Oblique though this passage may be, for understandable reasons in a dignified prologue, it seems to show Josephus again in vigorous debate with other writers in the capital.[61]

Prior to Josephus's writing of his prologue, and therefore prior to the *Jewish War* being finished, it seems Josephus had shared some bits of his writing with others, as was customary in Roman literary culture, and they had shared their writing with him. Mason certainly reads the text closely, perhaps even a little too closely, possibly asking more of the text than it can deliver. Nonetheless, his proposal fits plausibly within the context of late first-century CE literary best practices in Roman writing culture. If Mason is right in his reading of 1.13–16, it allows us to note another moment in the literary origins of *Jewish War*: in addition to the preliminary notes Josephus claims to have written while Roman camps, provisional versions of *Jewish War* circulated to a limited circle in Rome while still a work in progress.[62]

Josephus's preliminary notes and possible pre-circulation of unfinished "advanced copies" of his *Jewish War* tells us about the prepublication life of one of his writings, but another of his writings, *Jewish Antiquities*, offers insights into his postpublication revision of his writings. Josephus has two endings to his *Jewish Antiquities*, one in 20.259 and another in 20.267. They read as follows:

> I will end my *Antiquities* here, after which I also began to write my *War*.[63]

> With this I will put an end to my *Antiquities*, which encompasses twenty books and sixty thousand lines.[64]

Richard Laqueur in 1920 noticed the two endings and concluded that Josephus originally published his *Antiquities* in 93/94 CE, but then revised them in response to a rival account from a certain Justus and republished them in 100 CE with an autobiographical appendix.[65] In Laqueur's theory, the first edition of *Jewish Antiquities* did not have 20.259–266, which contained both the first ending ("I will end my *Antiquities* here...") and his reference to an autobiography in 20.266. It did, however, have the second ending ("With this I will put an end to my *Antiquities*,...") and the time stamp of thirteenth year of the reign of Caesar Domitian, and "the fifty-sixth of my own life," which would place the writing to 93/94 CE. The second edition contained the first ending ("I will end my *Antiquities* here,...") but did not have the second one ("With this I will put an end to my *Antiquities*..."). Justus's history employed better Greek and even implicated Josephus and his role in the war. Such a situation left Josephus little choice: he had to revise his *Antiquities* and add an apologetic autobiography (Josephus's *Life*), and conceivably making other alterations, too.

While Laqueur's theory deals nicely with the oddity of two endings, which seem hardly able to stand together side by side, some critics have pointed out a potential problem. The manuscript tradition does not provide evidence of variation in the endings of Josephus's *Antiquities*.[66] Yet, as we have seen with the examples from Cicero, manuscript traditions are fickle, and it would be unwise to assume, much less demand, a connection between what an author did or intended and what manuscripts remains extant. Manuscript traditions may or may not show evidence of authorial postpublication revision.

Moreover, another piece of support for Laqueur's theory comes from Josephus's evidence of ongoing rewriting, even after the text was "finished" or "published." Josephus elsewhere expresses a desire to keep his writings up to date. Immediately after the second ending in 20.267 just mentioned, Josephus goes on to write,

> God willing, I will again make some notes cursorily (*kata peridromēn hypomnēso palin*) about both the war and the things that have happened among us all the way down to the present day (the thirteenth year of the reign of Caesar Domitian and the fifty-sixth of my own life).[67]

In addition to the various moments of the literary origins just discussed, Josephus here says he hopes to jot down some running notes about the war and then goes on to date his comments to 93/94 CE. Elsewhere, however, in *Vita* 363, he dates his *Jewish War* to the lifetime of Titus (ca. 75 CE).[68] What

Josephus meant and what he intended to do has been debated, but the words he wrote suggest that he continued to create *hypomnēmata* again about the Jewish war well over a decade after he claims Titus published Josephus's *Jewish War*. He continues to write and rewrite up through the present moment (*mechri tēs nun enestōsēs hēmeras*). He also focuses on writing up through the present day in *Life* 430. He draws his *Vita* to an end by saying,

> And these are the things that have happened throughout my whole life. Let others judge my character from them as they wish. But to you, Epaphroditus, most excellent of men, do I dedicate the whole composition of my *Antiquities*. Here I stop my writing *for the present* (*epi tou parontos*).

With the phrase "for the present" Josephus leaves a back door open for future alteration. He reflects on the provisional and impermanent nature of his own writings, which look a certain way today but might very well change tomorrow. Postpublication revision in antiquity should come as no surprise because publication not so much a material issue as it was as a social *habitus*. Nothing would have prevented someone from making future changes, even after the writing was made public, and many did just that. Josephus's propensity to textual revision, even after publication, and his desire to keep his writings up to date lends credence to Laqueur's two-edition theory of the *Jewish Antiquities*. The most likely explanation for the oddity of two endings is that Josephus wrote, published, and then continued to rewrite his *Jewish Antiquities*. Somehow over time the various manuscript traditions conflated into one another. But the text of his works remained fluid, even after having been brought out to a public readership. Furthermore, Josephus is not concerned with the finalized, definitive version of his works, frozen as a memorial for all time. Just the opposite. Josephus shows concern with keeping his writings up to date, a commitment that presupposes their fluidity and ongoing revision.[69]

Medieval Hebrew manuscripts offers an illuminating point of comparison. Eva Mroczek points to the work of Malachi Beit-Arié and Israel Ta-Shma, who identify certain medieval Hebrew manuscripts as "open books."[70] Ta-Shma writes, "quite often books were not meant by their authors to serve as final statements, but rather as presentations of an interim state of knowledge or opinion, somewhat like our computerized databases, which are constantly updated and which give the user a summary of the data known at the time of last updating. In a similar way, the medieval book was sometimes conceived of as no more than a solid basis for possible future alterations by the author himself."⁷¹ Mroczek argues that Ben Sira was analogously (though not identically) created as and treated by others as an open book.⁷²

Sean Gurd, speaking about texts in antiquity, has said that every new draft of a work functioned provisionally as a final draft—until someone, whether the author or someone else, decided to rework it again, in which case the newer text became the final draft.⁷³ Or, put differently, every new draft functions only provisionally and temporarily as a final draft, while the notion of a truly finished text in definitive version does not map neatly onto the material *realia* of the ancient world.

# 4
# *Multiple Authorized Versions of the Same Work*

ONE COROLLARY OF unfinished texts, accidental publication, and postpublication revision is that not all works are singular, that many exist in multiple versions.[1] John Bryant, in his theory about reading texts as fluid, distinguishes among different "versions of the version." Some versions are authorized; some are not. The original author creates some versions; sometimes another person creates the new version.[2] These are different types of authority and authorization. Here I look at a couple examples of a work existing in more than one version, with an eye to how texts change and why. Of special interest will be how ideas of authorship and authorization impact textual revision. I follow the impulses of material philology. Material (or new) philology attends to the materiality of texts.[3] Thus, it is interested in the manuscript not as a means to an end of establishing what text was written behind the manuscript but, rather, treats the material manuscript as an end in itself.

As we have seen, some texts remained for some time in an unfinished, provisional state—geared toward practical uses, not literary ones. Often this was intentionally so. Such unfinished and less authored texts could end up in the hands of others without the writers' awareness or permission, thereby effectively becoming published by accident. All of this makes it difficult to talk about a "final" version of a text. In such a context, it should not come as a surprise that works often existed in multiple versions—and the *Rule of the Community* is one such text.

## *Versions of the Community Rule as Memory Aids for Instructors*

The discovery of the Dead Sea Scrolls in caves near Qumran in the 1940s and 1950s was a watershed time for our understanding of ancient Judaism in particular and of antiquity more generally.[4] Subsequent discoveries occurred in 2017. Some have hailed the discoveries as one of the most, if not *the* most, important archeological discoveries in the twentieth century.[5] The Dead Sea Scrolls number just under a thousand manuscripts dating from the fourth century BCE to the first century CE. The relationship between covenant members of the *Yaḥad* and the broader cultures of Hellenistic and Roman culture has been debated. Yonder Gillihan has recently argued that the "Covenanters' civil ideology reflected their era," and that "certain features of the sect were very much like those of other associations—organization, initiation, rules for meetings, and so on."[6] Their discovery has had far-reaching implications for scholarly constructions of ancient Judaism, including how scholars think about textuality and writing practices, as we find different versions of the same work from the scrolls found at Qumran.[7]

The versions of the *Rule of the Community* (*Serekh ha-Yaḥad*) found in caves 1 and 4 differ in important ways. Paleographically, the version in Cave 1, which is the longer version, is written in older script; the copies of the *Rule* found in Cave 4, which is shorter and more fragmentary, is the more recent script. In a stemmatological approach to these textual variations, one wants to know whether the texts of Cave 1 or Cave 4 are earlier. Did Cave 1 texts use Cave 4, or vice versa? There are problems with either alternative. If one assumes Cave 1 is prior, as Philip Alexander does, then it is difficult to explain why Cave 4, the later text, shortened the earlier text as it did, omitting so much material. If one assumes Cave 4 is prior, as Sarianna Metso and Geza Vermes do, it is difficult to explain why the shorter text uses the paleographically later script. That is, if scholars want to imagine such a thing as *the* version of the *Rule of the Community*, why did some covenant members continue to copy a shorter and (if paleography is any guide) older version of the *Rule* when a lengthier and more recent version existed? So, if the shorter version is indeed the older version of the *Rule*, why did people continue to copy it when a longer and ostensibly more up-to-date version of the *Rule* was available? An even more fundamental question is: Why preserve multiple versions of the same work in the same general area of Qumran?

However one may want to think of the various versions of the *Rule of the Community*, the material evidence resists a simple, clean, and linear development.[8] Whether one opts for a traditional-source critical approach or whether one prefers a more nuanced account of textual growth that allows for rhizomatic multiplicity, it is clear that the text was fluid and in an ongoing state of development.[9] Even if one adopts the source-critical approach, as Sarianna Metso does, it is difficult to avoid the conclusion that "there never existed a single, legitimate and up-to-date version of the community rule. The community continued copying the older and shorter form of the text even when a more extensive version was already available."[10] But how can we account for such textual multiplicity? An honest assessment of the data will describe and appreciate the multiplicity without having to "solve" it or prioritize the earlier over the later, or vice versa.

Textual alteration raises issues of authority. Who has the right to change a text? Instinctively one might wish to answer: the author. Yet, it is difficult to talk about an author (or even a redactor, for that matter) of the versions of the *Rule of the Community*, because it has no author figure.[11] Unlike some other Jewish writings, the *Rule of the Community* does not claim divine inspiration.[12] But if it is difficult or even impossible to talk about an author, is it possible to talk about an authorizing figure? Who (or what) authorized the *Rule*?[13] The person (or thing, entity, etc.) who authorizes a text would—like an author figure—also have some claim to altering or updating it. Thus, even if one is not the "author" of a text, such persons may nonetheless have the authority to alter the text as a result of his or her role within a community. The question of authorization is a question of use. And the *Rule of the Community* does offer clues to the reader about who used it and how.[14]

The text of the *Rule* states clearly that it is a text "for the instructor" (*lemaskil*) of the community, which could mean that the book belongs to an instructor or that it is intended for his use as leader of the community, or (as seems likely to me) both.[15] Of course, it is possible that many members of the community could have read the *Rule*. Yet due to issues of literacy and the cost of producing a scroll, it is safe to imagine that not everyone in the community would have owned or even needed a personal copy, not even all literate members. It was primarily the instructor's book. He used it as a guide for carrying out leadership duties.

Furthermore, what is striking about the *Rule of the Community* is how much it demands of its reader or user. A good deal of prior knowledge is assumed, without which it is surprisingly unhelpful, and perhaps even frustrating. The *Rule* more reminded what must be done than explained how something ought to be done. If the goal is to use the texts to determine what was going on behind the texts, they can be frustrating. Yet the potentially frustrating lack of perspicuity about certain details in the *Rule*, as well as the other Dead Sea Scrolls, may in fact provide important clues to the users of the textual traditions.

Take, for example, the ritual washings described in 1QS 5.13. Apart from the *mikva'ot* found at Qumran, it would be hard—from the *Rule of the*

*Community* alone—to say much more about the ritual washings at Qumran than the mere fact that they did ritual washings and the ritual washing preceded participation in the pure food.[16] Someone who had no previous knowledge of how to do the ritual washing could scarcely perform the details of the liturgy itself simply by reading the *Serekh*, and that fact alone is telling. The community rules are for persons who were privy to the social and ritual processes of the community, who had the know-how and the experience of years in the life of the *Yaḥad*. The same goes for the annual renewal festival and induction described in 1.16–3.12. Despite all the rules and instructions recorded there, a reader from outside the community (such as modern scholars), having never seen or performed such a ceremony before, could in no way reproduce it.[17] We may wonder: exactly which just deeds are the priests to recite and what mercies to proclaim (1.21–22)? The same goes for the Levites: what are they to recite (1.22)? The text merely says that they should do a recitation, but does not give the content of the recitations and proclamations. The community rules serve more as reminding field guides than an instructional how-to manual for new or anonymous readers. Galen, had he read one of the *Rule of the Community* texts, might have thought the same thing about it as he did about some of Hippocrates's aphorisms in the *Epidemics*: the ambiguity in the text indicates something important about how it was designed to be used and by whom. Not just any reader could pick up the text and find it useful. Paradoxically, the texts found in Caves 1 and 4 present themselves as utilitarian, yet they are not useful to someone who does not already possess a good deal of knowledge about the ins and outs of community life.

Furthermore, 1QS 3.13–4.26 contain a lengthy section about two spirits, which the instructor is to teach to all the "sons of light." It details the ways of light and darkness and calls the community members to walk in light. It would be a mistake, however, to imagine somehow the actual members of the community individually reading this portion of the community rules.[18] Reading in the ancient world was a communal and performative act.[19] For the average members of the community, their experience of the text would have been not unlike those listening to Ezra read the Torah in Nehemiah 8— mainly aural, with the only visual component being the speaker's comportment and perhaps, if they are close enough, the reader's engagement with the physical text.[20] For them, what is heard is what is authoritative, not what they personally read off a manuscript with their own eyes. In this way, the reader, the user, and the authorizer are linked. Thus, the question of use of the text, as well as how one would have experienced it, is connected with authorization of the text, all of which relate to what textual content was experienced by the community with each reading.

Moreover, since the whole written content of 1QS 3.13–4.26 could be read aloud in a matter of six or nine minutes, and since certain portions—for example, the vice list—leave interpretive gaps that require explanation, the contents are more easily understood as script than as something the instructor would recite aloud verbatim.[21] As noted, it is a user's field guide or notes more than literature, as most would have encountered it orally from an instructor, and what they heard would likely have had a healthy dose of extemporization added to the script of 3.13–4.26. 1QS 9.12–26 indicates that the way the community will learn what they need to know is by the instructor's leading them in knowledge, not by their individually reading the *Rule*. The *Rule of the Community* thus looks like framing notes for the instructor—a skeleton or aide-mémoire intended for an instructor's use in teaching the community.[22]

In such a scenario, it is difficult to separate the written word and oral teaching in the reading of the *Rule of the Community* and the instructor's teaching of the rule. The two bleed into and interpenetrate one another. 1 QS 6.7–8 is a key text for understanding the reading practices of the *Yaḥad*. For the first third of the night, every night of the year, members of the community come together to read out loud from "the book" (*besefer*), examine what is right, and offer blessing together in the community. Their reading practices are collective and, for many, reading is experienced aurally, not visually. They move seamlessly between reading, interpreting, and blessing. This is not unlike the lecture event and reading practices of the president of the Therapeutae, as described by Philo in *On the Contemplative Life*.

> The President of the company, when a general silence is established—here it may be asked when is there no silence—well at this point there is silence even more than before so that no one ventures to make a sound or breathe with more force than usual—amid this silence, I say, he discusses some questions arising in the Holy Scriptures or solves one that has been propounded by someone else. In doing this [i.e., lecturing on the readings from Holy Scripture] he has no thought of making a display, for he has no ambition to get a reputation for clever oratory but desires to gain a closer insight into some particular matters and having gained it not to withhold it selfishly from those who if not so clear-sighted as he have at least a similar desire to learn. His instruction proceeds in a leisurely manner; he lingers over it and spins it out with repetitions, thus permanently imprinting the thoughts in the souls of

the hearers, since if the speaker goes on descanting with breathless rapidity the mind of the hearers is unable to follow his language, loses ground and fails to arrive at apprehension of what is said.[23]

Philo paints a picture here of the reading, lecturing, and listening of the Therapeutae. The president begins reading, but somewhere along the way slides out of reading and into oratory, and then back again. The text being read is a launch pad for his expositions and solving of exegetical riddles, with a seamless flow between reading and lecturing, with both speaking and listening being interactive and bodily experiences.[24] The function of the text of Holy Scriptures is to tie knots for the president to solve, with the reading of the text creating the problem that the president's oratory must resolve. The manual for the instructor, although not having the same status that scripture did for the president of the Therapeutae, seems to have functioned in a roughly analogous way: a reminder of his teaching to the community, a piece of writing from which he moved between reading and teaching.

Supporting the view that the text is a working text for the leader is the emendation of one of the legal stipulations in 1QS 7.8. At one point in the manuscript, the text offers two degrees of punishment for holding a grudge too long. In the main line of the text, it reads six months (ששה חודשים). It also supplies in smaller print above the punishment of six months another the punishment of one year (שנה אחת), which is usually taken to be an updating of the punishment meted out for nursing bad blood with other members of the community. James Nati points out the correction and thinks it points to a development of policy within the community.[25]

Apparently, the users and authorizers of 1QS presided over a community where some members had a hard time letting bygones be bygones. As a result, in order to motivate members not to hold a grudge, they upped the time of punishment by double. Moreover, the words "six months" (ששה חודשים) are not crossed out, leaving both punishments visible on the text (see figure 4.1). While the older reading of six months is placed in brackets, which seems to mean that the more recent punishment of one year has replaced the other, it is not unimportant that, from the perspective of the reader of the manuscript, both readings are legible.[26] The alteration of the punishment indicates 1QS (and other rule texts) are not eternal and unchangeable codes of crimes and punishments but, rather, more practical, impermanent, and revisable guides for the use of the leader(s) of local communities of the *Yaḥad*.

Moreover, the list of prohibitions and penalties hardly represents a systematic legal code. While it can be broadly lumped into prohibitions against verbal and/or social actions in 7.1–9 —like speaking maliciously for no reason

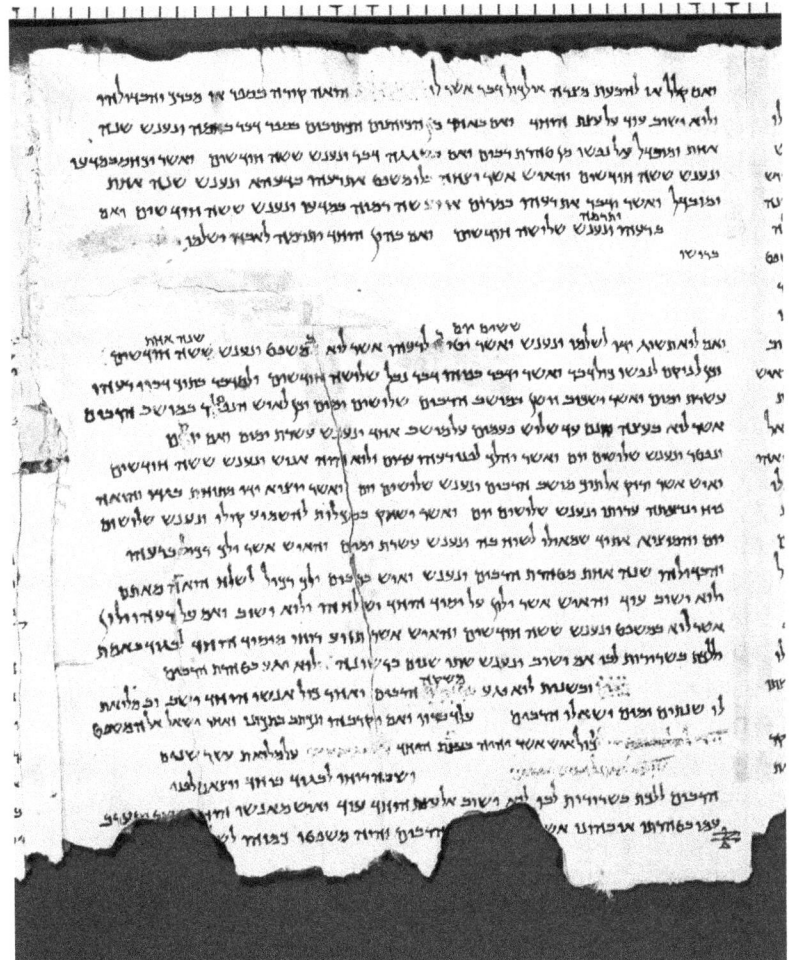

FIGURE 4.1 Image of the Corrected Punishment from 1QS Column 7, line 8

or interrupting someone, mismanaging community goods or money—and physical actions in 7.10–25, the exact actions described seem like a reactionary running list. The physical actions the text prohibits include spitting during the meeting, pulling out one's penis, falling asleep, giggling idiotically, walking around naked unnecessarily, gesturing with one's left hand while talking, and so forth. It reads like a situational codification of actions in reaction to their occurrence. About the relationship between use and textual multiplicity of the *Serekh* text in general, Sarianna Metso writes:

> Thus, we have textual phenomena, such as parallel editions, developing editorial stages, and evidence of cross-influence between different

documents, that pose challenges for those attempting direct historical reconstruction on the basis of rule texts found at Qumran. These textual phenomena become less puzzling if the function of these documents in the communal life of the Essenes is correctly understood. If we assume that the purpose of the document was not to serve as a prescriptive lawbook in the modern sense, but rather as a recording of different judicial decisions and a report of oral traditions, then the existence of contradictory regulations in compilations like the Community Rule is not so surprising.[27]

Textual use shows textual multiplicity to be an expected part of the life of the tradition. One gets the sense column 7 is more a working list of punishable actions and possible punishments, developed in a responsive manner, all of which could be updated by the authorized user, the instructor.

A central part of the life of the community seems to have been access to "the pure food."[28] Only after going through the purifying water was someone allowed to receive the pure food. Separation from the pure food was one of the possible punishments listed in 1QS column 7. The reality is, though, that we know almost nothing of the details of this pure food. What's more, in 1QS 6.4 the text says "when the table is prepared for eating and the new wine for drinking . . . ," yet it never offers any instructions for table preparation. It assumes the user already knows what the pure food is (Is it bread, wine, both, or something else altogether? Is it a meal?), as well as how to prepare and serve it. Consequently, there would be no need to explain; reminding is enough. Yet, if modern readers—and recently inducted members of the sectarian movement, for that matter—were asked to recreate the ritual of receiving the pure food from the *Rule of the Community*, they would be at an utter loss, since the text offers no clue. Rather, it assumes the user of the manual already knows and merely needs to be reminded about the moment of table preparation. Local leaders would need to know details of what the pure food is exactly, how to procure it for the group, and how the table is prepared.

Recently, though, scholars such as John J. Collins have argued for thinking about the Dead Sea Scrolls through a geographically dispersed model of the *Yaḥad*.[29] Collins mentions, among other things, 1 QS 6.1–8 and its reference to "in all their dwelling-places" in 6.2 and "in every place where there are ten men from the council of the Community" in 6.3. Such comments imply a multiplicity of geographical locations where the texts were in use. The *Yaḥad*, then, would be a larger movement with multiple local expressions of the community connected to a larger organization associated with Qumran, not unlike the way modern religious denominations conceive of their own identity: locally experienced and expressed, but connected to a larger entity.[30] In such a case, the *Rule of the Community* would not so much represent a single text as a moving, growing constellation of textualizations of a didactic tradition of the *Yaḥad*. Each different community rule was *the* rule text for each local instantiation of the community.

The different versions of the *Rule* display different approaches to community leadership. Charlotte Hempel identifies the *locus classicus* as 1QS 5 and 4Q258 (4QS$^d$) 1 and 4Q256 (4QS$^b$) 9.[31] In these texts, the community rules are variously identified as "the rule for the people of the community" (1QS) and "midrash for the instructor over the people of the law" (4Q258 [4QS$^d$] and 4Q256 [4QS$^b$]; translation by Hempel). Based on this variance alone, one might be tempted to say that 1QS reflects a more communal form of governance than the *Rule* texts in Cave 4, which reflect a more "top down" form of leadership. Yet, Hempel points out that whereas the Cave 4 texts say "they shall be accountable to the *many*," the Cave 1 text says "they shall be accountable to the sons of Zadok, the priests who keep the covenant and to the multitude of the people of the community who keep the covenant."[32] It is hard to paint a clear picture of how the instructor, the "many," the priests, and the Sons of Zadok relate to one another throughout the different iterations *Rule* texts, but if the community rules are in use at different locations and used by different people, it would be unwise to shoehorn the disparate data into an assumed identical form of leadership across the various local communities. Rather, we are dealing with varying forms of leadership across geographically dispersed communities.[33]

If there were many residences and locations of the sectarian movement, perhaps it would be correct to speak not of a single instructor but, instead, of multiple instructors or some other variety of local leadership.[34] Each instructor (or some other form of local community leadership) would have been the authorizer of the local *Rule*, which would have also derived authority both by its connection to the larger movement and by its connection to a base camp at Qumran and its leadership. Returning to the question of why they kept multiple different versions of the community rules at Qumran and its surrounding areas, we are in a position to think about the versions differently.

We should think, then, not of one location with a "final" version of the *Rule of the Community* (even if final was only final, until it was updated again), or of an "original" version from which others deviate or are contaminated, but, rather, of many locations each with its own modified and provisionally "final" instantiation of a community *Rule*, which would differ in big and small ways from the *Rules* of other local units of the organization. As James Nati has argued, we should think not of *the Rule of the Community*, but of rules for the communities.[35] It seems there never was an "original version" of the *Rule*, and perhaps it is misleading to use the word *version*. Rather, there were local iterations of the *Rule*, subject to alteration by the local authority, being authorized both by their connection to the larger community and by the local leadership of the community. Each local iteration of the *Rule* would likely have contained older material, which had been brought into a new and different spatial and geographical context, along with their own additions reflecting local traditions and experiences. No one version would have been more authentic than another. Likewise, it would be something of a fool's errand to try to trace the origin and its contaminations. Deleuze and Guatarri's theory of the rhizome, which lacks a stratified and linear beginning and end, may provide a better frame for thinking about texts like the various community rules.[36] Each version—and we cannot rule out the possibility that the ones preserved in Caves 1 and 4 were some of many more—is a unique instantiation and contribution to the work, which is better conceived as an energy or discourse than as a stable transcendent text or piece of literature.[37] All that remains are different, equally authorized versions or performances of the rules of various local communities. Likely some knew of other versions out there, but the one in their local community for all practical intents and purposes was *the Rule* for that community.[38]

In some ways, the caves of Qumran seem a long way from Greek and Roman theories of literature, yet there are important parallels to the textual functions of the various versions of the *Rule of the Community* and Greek *hypomnēmata* and Latin *commentarii*. All are primarily designed to be useful texts, not formal literature. They are not designed for general consumption. Ambiguities or inconsistencies remain in the texts. *Hypomnēmata* often referred to juridical or administrative records of a leader or ruler.[39] Josephus uses the term frequently to refer to records of a king or leader.[40] The Septuagint uses the term *hypomnēmata* similarly in 2 Samuel 8:16 and Ezra 6:2.

Like Greek *hypomnēmata* and Latin *commentarii*, the scrolls often lack an ascribed author figure, as well as a formal title or preface or other paratextual features. Lacking a high degree of textuality fixity, such texts remain (often intentionally) update-able and lithe, often existing therefore in a variety of forms. From place to place, textual difference is to be expected; in fact, a lack thereof would be surprising. The more they are used, the more they evolve and develop—and the only way to stop evolving is to fall out of use or be destroyed. The Platonic idea of *hypomnēmata* as a physical extension of memory in textualized form is not an unfit description for the texts contained in 1QS and 4QS. And if new and better information, or new ways of dealing with issues, comes to their attention, it is the local leaders' prerogative and perhaps even their bound duty to modify it. Unlike some *hypomnēmata* and *commentarii*, though, the community rules do not seem to have the aspiration of becoming a piece of formal literature after careful alteration. While *hypomnēmata* and *commentarii* could move in a trajectory from inception to completion, it is difficult to speak about an origin or even *telos* of the textual tradition of the *Rule of the Community*.

In summary, some similar ideas about useful texts and textual fluidity among Greek and Roman writers can also be seen in the various iterations of the *Rule of the Community* found at Qumran. This is not to suggest that members of the sectarian movement would have used the language of *hypomnēmata* to classify their community rules. It is to suggest, however, that a Hellenized Jew in the first century CE, such as Josephus or Philo, could reasonably have inspected the *Rule* and then classified it as *hypomnēmata*.[41]

## *The Herculaneum Library and the "Working Desk" of Philodemus*

In juxtaposition to the versions of the *Rule of the Community* of the Dead Sea scrolls stands Philodemus's library at Herculaneum. Tertullian's famous question, "What does Athens have to do with Jerusalem?" may be reworked for the purposes of this chapter to ask: What do the caves of Qumran have to do with the library at Herculaneum?[42] One is located in what was once a plush estate outside of Neopolis/Naples. The other is located in a dry and desolate location in the Judean desert. One is clothed in elite Greek and Roman culture, the other in Jewish sectarianism. The contrast comes out nicely in a comment from Greg Woolf:

> Philodemus had been brought up, however, in the city of Gadara in present day Jordan, just a hundred miles or so from where the Qumran community was, during exactly the same period, creating the collection which we now call the Dead Sea Scrolls. The Qumran library included portions of the Hebrew Bible, or of its Samaritan variant and also the Septuagint, the Greek translation mentioned by Isidore, along with idiosyncratic sacred texts and rules in Hebrew and Aramaic. Writing technologies, scripts, even one of the languages was shared between the library of Philodemus and that of the Qumran community, yet the vast

differences in genre, in notions of authority and in tradition give us no hesitation in assigning the two to such different literary traditions that the two libraries might have been assembled on different continents or planets!⁴³

Yet, despite the differences, both offer collections of writings serendipitously "frozen in time" and made available to modern readers in fragmentary form. The Dead Sea Scrolls were preserved from destruction by the elements in dry caves of the Judean desert. The Herculaneum library was simultaneously destroyed and preserved by the intense heat of the eruption of Vesuvius in 79 CE. In both, we find several versions of the same work preserved alongside one another. Comparing the different versions of the *Rule of the Community* with Philodemus's *Rhetoric* shows insightful similarities and differences.

Philodemus's writings make up almost half of the thus-far readable rolls in the Herculaneum library. Several of his writings are preserved in more than one copy, with each copy containing a different version.⁴⁴ For instance, Philodemus's *On the Stoics* can be found in two rolls. *PHerc.* 155, although quite fragmentary, seems to be a less "drafty," more polished edition of *On the Stoics* based on typological analysis. *PHerc.* 339 appears to be an earlier draft.⁴⁵ In the case of Philodemus's *History of the Academy*, Tiziano Dorandi makes the case that we get a sneak peek into Philodemus's writing procedure in *PHerc.* 1021 and *PHerc.* 164: 164 contains excerpts, possibly taken by a scribe; 1021 contains the excerpts and other content in a prose format, all of which suggests that Philodemus excerpted choice selections during his composition process and later worked them into a more ordered prose format.⁴⁶ Gigante thinks this provides the rare opportunity to see an "author's scribbling pad," a "provisional draft," and the "working desk" of an ancient writer.⁴⁷ Other texts contain subscriptions that mark their texts as *hypomnēmata* or as *hypomnēmatikon*, the adjectival form of the word *hypomnēma*.⁴⁸

> *PHerc. 89:* [ὑ]πόμνημα | [---].νδε[--- | Περ[ὶ ϑ]εῶν
> Note | ... On the gods
> *PHerc. 168:* Φ[ιλοδ]ήμου | .. [..] ατ .. ω .. κ .. | ὑπομνηματικὸν | Α
> Philodemus's | ..., hypomnematikon, Book 1
> *PHerc. 182:* Φιλοδ]ή[μου | ὑπό]μ[νημα πε]ρὶ ὀργῆς
> Philodemus's | note On Anger

Philodemus's *On Rhetoric* allows us to go a step further. *On Rhetoric* shows a textual tradition over a period of many years and even decades capturing in writing an evolving approach to teaching the topic in his school. Various rolls show the text in a draft, memory aid, or lecture note stage. Books 1–3 are preserved in five rolls:

Book 1: *PHerc.* 1427
Book 2: *PHerc.* 1672 and 1674
Book 3: *PHerc.* 1426 and 1506

The subscriptions in *PHerc.* 1427, 1674, and 1506 have the name of Philodemus, the title of the work, and its book number, but some of them also contain the word *hypomnēmatikon*.

*PHerc.* 1427: Philodemus's | *On Rhetoric* | *hypomnematic* | Book 1
*PHerc.* 1674: Philodemus's | *On Rhetoric* | *hypomnematic* | Book 2
*PHerc.* 1672: Philodemus's | *On Rhetoric* | Book 2
*PHerc.* 1506: Philodemus's | *On Rhetoric* | *hypomnematic* | Book 3
*PHerc.* 1426: Philodemus's | *On Rhetoric* | Book 3[49]

Book 1 is represented by only one roll and has no non-*hypomnematic* counterpart. Books 2 and 3, however, do. By attaching the adjective *hypomnēmatikon* here, the subscription is marking the copy as somehow less than definitive and still a work in progress or perhaps lecture notes and therefore intended only for limited circulation.[50] The fact that Books 2 and 3 exist in more than one form, with some rolls labeled as *hypomnematic*, not only shows us the multiplicities of textual forms preserved alongside each other in the same library but may also allow us to look at the evolution of these particular works over a period of time (see appendix A, this volume). The changes between the versions usually involve changing a word or phrase here or there.[51]

The differences between the *hypomnematic* versions and the non-*hypomnematic* versions of Book 3 are not wholescale rewritings but, instead, tweaking, rewording for emphasis, and occasionally rethinking sentences or paragraphs. It is interesting to note that the rewritten or revised version is usually the shorter one rather than the longer. In some ways, one may wish to argue that the visual and bibliographic changes are the more significant ones between *PHerc.* 1426 and 1506 (Book 3). The non-*hypomnematic* version contains different handwriting and fewer words on each column (see figures 4.2 and 4.3).

The non-*hypomnematic* version (*PHerc.* 1426) also contains the name of what seems to be the scribe, Poseidonactos of Biton (Ποσειδώνκτος τοῦ

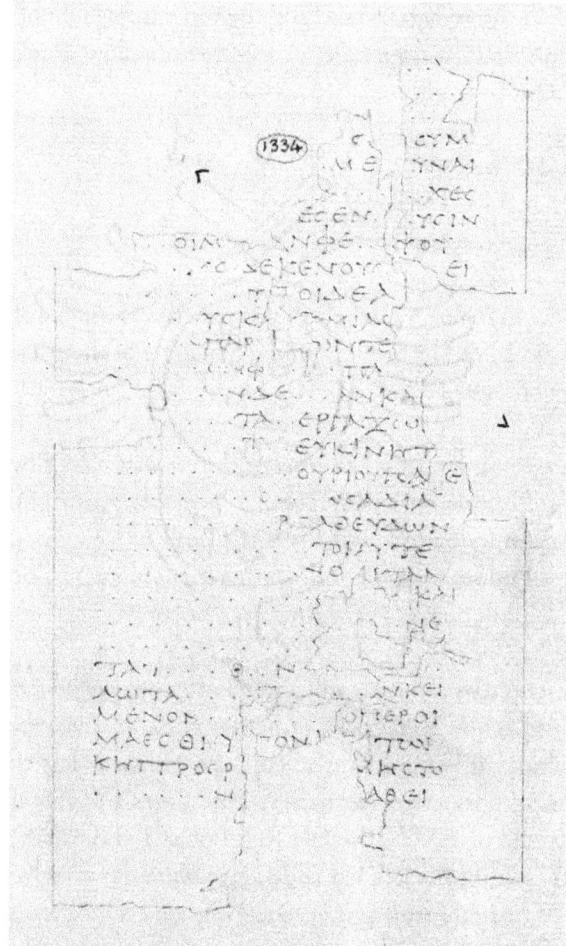

**FIGURE 4.2** Image from Col. LVII of *PHerc.* 1506

Βίτωνος), who notes the number of columns: 204 (σελιδ σδ). Such information is lacking in the *hypomnematic* version (*PHerc.* 1506).

## Comparing the Scrolls in Qumran and Herculaneum

Both in the scrolls found in the caves at Qumran and in the rolls found in the Herculaneum library, though very different cultural contexts, we find the prevalence of works existing and preserved in multiple versions. Each shows evidence of what John Bryant has called a work as concept and as energy.[52]

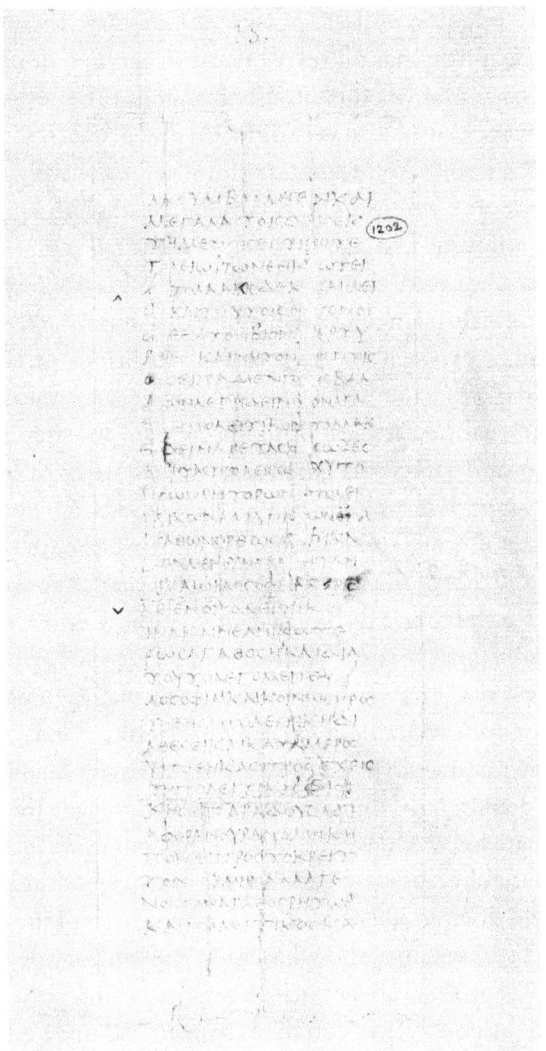

FIGURE 4.3  Image from Col. XV of *PHerc.* 1426

Texts remained open over a long period of time. Both show words and phrases changing, sometimes in ways that do not seem to make a real difference, and sometimes in ways that one might argue change the tone or even the meaning of a passage. In both cases, differing versions are preserved, which implies that the idea of *the* official text of *On Rhetoric* Book 2 or 3, or *the* definitive text of the *Rule of the Community* was not an idea native to the thinking of either of these two different ancient communities, or at least not one that the communities prioritized. Both appear open to further revision as a result of the respective ongoing projects of each community. These two examples do not, of course, prove that all texts existed in multiple forms, but it does suggest that in two "libraries fortuitously frozen in time" from the first century BCE and first century CE, in very different places and contexts around the ancient Mediterranean basin, textual multiplicity was hardly exceptional; it was a normal part of cultural *habitus* of making, reading, and preserving texts. The "best" text is not the first, the original, or the "final" but, rather, the most recent, the most improved, the most useful. Origin is not essence. Speaking about a final, original, or single version of a text is unproductive.

The differences between the two textual traditions of the *Rule of the Community* and Philodemus's *On Rhetoric* also gesture toward meaningful differences in textual trajectories. Both are forward moving, but one seems to be moving toward something whereas the other seems to be just moving. Even in the *hypomnematic* versions of Philodemus's *On Rhetoric* Books 2 and 3, the rolls contain a formal subscription. The subscriptions tell us the name of the author and the title of the book, as well as whether or not it is provisional or lecture notes or intended for limited circulation. Certain manuscripts at Herculaneum even give the name of a scribe or corrector.[53] *Hypomnēmata* did not always have a title or an author, so this particular example is insightful. Therefore, in the rolls containing *On Rhetoric* Books 2 and 3, a progression from lecture notes or memory aids toward definitive text can be seen. It is not clear that Philodemus or his disciple ever consciously made the effort to publish or disseminate his writings. The modern reader knows of his works only thanks to the fateful actions of Vesuvius in 79 CE, which may suggest that neither he nor his disciples ever circulated his texts beyond the confines of his school. The text still remains, though, within the category of technical texts designed not to impress someone with elegant prose but, rather, designed for useful, practical purposes. They could be changed and updated, and if an improvement could be made, it was the duty of the writer or scribe to make it. Nevertheless, the library contains descriptions of the literary genetics of certain texts, attaching an author's name to the subscription and a formal title, as well as a description about certain rolls as *hypomnemtic*.

By contrast, the different versions of the *Rule of the Community* do not contain formal titles. The "rule of the community" (*Serekh haYaḥad*) should not be understood as a formal title so much as a practical one (the same could perhaps be argued for the adjective *hypomnēmatikon* in the discussed title in the Herculaneum library). It is a community rulebook— a description of what it is and how it is used. It is not written by the instructor. Rather, it is *lemaskil*—for or belonging to the instructor. Thus, it is for the practical, real-life purposes of the instructors in the various camps where it is used. It has an authority, but not an author. It belongs to the instructors so they can use it to teach the holy ones in their various camps how to live in accordance with rules of the *Yaḥad*. Although the different versions demonstrate a textual fluidity and multiplicity, unlike the scrolls of Philodemus's *On Rhetoric* Books 2 and 3, the text contains no explicit self-reference about its literary genetics. By contrast, while Philodemus's *On Rhetoric* Books 2 and 3 point toward some sort of *telos*, though not necessarily publication. They circle in on or push toward a final or definitive version of the book, even though "final" and "definitive" are to be taken only in an provisional sense. Philodemus's *On Rhetoric* seems to have started as lectures to his students, which then became textualized by his students, and then became updated, improved, and shifted toward some sort of a *telos*. The different textual traditions of *Rule of Community*, however, resist a clear identification of origin or *telos*.

In summary, both "libraries," which differ in so many other ways, suggest that textual pluriformity was a normal part of textual culture. The communities seemed to have no qualms about preserving multiple, differing versions of the same work in the same place or general area. Yet in the Greco-Roman context of Philodemus's library, the scrolls tip off the reader to their own literary compositional processes, origins, and trajectories. They indicate an origin as memory aids from lectures, yet they also gesture toward a *telos* of a more polished or more finished version of a text. Connected with the trajectory is attachment of an author's name to the text, as well as occasionally the name of a scribe and the numbering of columns. In the versions of the *Rule of the Community*, however, no author appears. Rather we have an authorizer of the text who uses the text for practical purposes. The *Rule of the Community* contains no formal title comparable to the scroll subscriptions at Herculaneum. Moreover, while *PHerc.* 1674 and 1506 indicate more provisional or less literary versions of Books 2 and 3, and *PHerc.* 1672 and 1426 remove the label *hypomnematic*, the versions of the *Rule of the Community* resist such indications, the latter with its origin and its *telos* effaced.

## *Conclusion*

While modern scholarship on ancient publication has tended to prioritize the writing and publication of a work as a clean, controlled act of the author and no one else, there is ample evidence that such cleanness was not always the case, and perhaps not even usually the case. Things could go "wrong" at every turn, and often did, it seems. And the fact that things often went wrong could also be deployed to a writer's or a community's advantage. Texts could be altered, for a variety of reasons. Unfinished or unauthored texts were especially open to revision, by their very nature. They invited someone else to revise them by correcting and augmenting them or by adding to the ending. Technical texts like manuals, guides, notes, or rough drafts were often created intentionally with the purpose that someone, whether the original writer or someone else in the process, would improve upon them or make them more useful, polished, and well-ordered. Texts still in progress or otherwise not intended for a public readership could and often did slip out of the hands of their writers or readers and accidentally make their way into the public arena. Functionality often trumped formality. Geographical dispersion played a role. Once a text was away from its owner and in a new location, it acquired a new owner, as it were, and that new owner did with it what he or she willed. The more a text was used, the more it tended to be altered.

Within this configuration of textual alteration, a common trajectory can be traced. Writing, textuality, and authorship in the ancient world may be theorized and charted on the graphic shown in figure 4.4.

Depending upon the specific moment in time and upon the cultural location, a work may by placed at various spots on the chart. For instance, a classical text such as Livy's *Ab Urbe Condita* would be both public and literary; a published work of Galen or Vitruvius's *De Architectura* would be both public and practical; an as yet unpublished work of Pliny would be both private and literary; and Galen's unpublished lecture notes would be both private and practical. And a text's placement can change depending upon how a community uses, valorizes, alters, reads, and deploys the work. Within this theorization of ancient writing and authorship, certain trajectories may be seen. Texts tended to move from functional to formal, from unattributed to

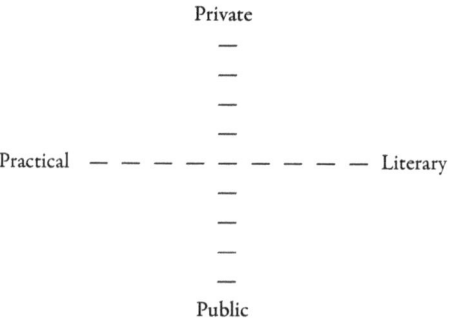

FIGURE 4.4 Theory of Ancient Writing and Textuality

attributed, from fluid to more stable.[54] It must be remembered, however, that an innumerable mass of textual objects from the ancient world would have never made a movement along this trajectory, and the great majority of them are now lost. The *Rule of the Community*, for example, shows little or no sign of moving toward being a stable, authored, formal piece of literature; nonetheless, the tendency holds true. If a text was altered, it tended to move from functional to formal, from unattributed to attributed, from fluid to more stable—and not vice versa.

# 5
# *The Earliest Readers of the Gospel according to Mark*

IN THE LAST three chapters, I did a close reading of a variety of texts across the ancient Mediterranean world. I explored such topics as unfinished texts, accidental publication, postpublication revision, and multiple authorized versions of the same text. In the remaining chapters, I look at how to think about the earliest gospels "before the book." While such an investigation is relevant to all early gospels in late antiquity, I take as an exemplar the text we now call the Gospel according to Mark, and more generally to its relationship to the texts we now call the Gospels according to Luke and Matthew.

I begin with three observations. First, what constitutes a book, an author, and publication is socially determined and contextually specific.[1] Second, no evidence exists of anyone using such concepts to discuss the gospel prior to the end of the second century CE. Yet, third, modern historical-critical scholars of first- and second-century gospel texts routinely use concepts like book, author, and even publication in their research and writings. This is a clear anachronism. By using a later discourse to talk about earlier textual traditions, modern readers and scholars shoehorn the textual objects of the earlier gospel tradition into later categories, making first- and second-century texts answer the questions of later readers.

A new way to talk about gospel as textual object in the first and second centuries must be developed, one that avoids the metaphor of the book and its concomitant author figure. Chapters 5 and 6 are my attempt to diagnose a problem and begin to redescribe the textualization and proliferation of "gospel" as textual object in the first couple centuries. My goal is to come up with a native theory of how to approach the textuality of the texts we now call the Gospels according to Matthew, Mark, and Luke that would be recognizable to the reading and writing practices and cultural *habitus* of ancient readers. I aim to reimagine how to talk about gospel texts before authors, before books, and before publication—a way that allows for the nuance and textured nature of gospel tradition to be taken seriously on its own terms. To begin such a redescription, I take the Gospel according to Mark in relation to the Gospels according to Matthew and Luke as my test case and starting point, though such an observation clearly has implications for many other gospel texts of the first few centuries.

To illustrate how our discourse shapes the state of our questions, consider the genre of the gospel. From the third century onward, the genre of the Gospel according to Mark, for instance, was not really debated. Gospel was a literary genre, and it was obvious that the Gospel according to Mark was a gospel. But with the dawn of the Enlightenment, scholars began to treat the Bible like any other text, the canon was shattered, and the question of the genre of the gospels was opened. The genre of the Gospel according to Mark (or of all other gospels) has thus been the subject of debate during the last couple centuries.

Scholars have tended to think of the Gospel according to Mark as one of three genres, broadly speaking.[2] Many have thought of gospel as the literary genre of "Mark," taking it as *sui generis*. In this view, "Mark" is the originator of a new and unique literary genre called gospel.[3] "Mark" took the early Christian preaching and made a new genre of literature out of it.[4] Another view is that the Gospel according to Mark is a *bios* or ancient biography. To different degrees and in different ways, some scholars have argued that the Gospel according to Mark (along with the other canonical gospels) conformed to the ancient Greek and Roman expectations of biographies (*bioi*), which were normally aimed at readers' emulation of the virtues of the main character.[5] More recently, there has been a trend toward viewing the Gospel according to Mark as a historical monograph or some other kind of historical writing. Noticing that the Gospel according to Mark lacks some important features characteristic of ancient biography, some have argued that the Gospel according to Mark is a history about a single person.[6] Many other theories exist, though they enjoy less widespread acceptance.

The main problem with all these theories is that they obscure the important issue of development, as well as the realities of disjointed discourses. That is, a more historically accurate answer to the question, "What is the Gospel according to Mark?" is the counterquestion, "When?" That the Gospel according to Mark becomes a gospel and that gospel, by around the third century, is a literary genre is clear. But gospel was originally a speech genre and only later became a literary genre. The development happened over a long period of time, and not necessarily in a simple or linear fashion. Throughout the late first and second centuries, there was a wide variety of ways to configure the authority and textuality of the gospel. As gospel became inscribed into textual objects, it did not automatically become a piece of literature, a possibility explored at length in chapters 2, 3, and 4. It remained fluid and open to revision. It was a text without being a book. It was written without being authored—at least in any strict sense of the term. It had a readership, but it was not formally "published," finished, or otherwise closed off.

What was the textual tradition we now call the Gospel according to Mark before it became the Gospel according to Mark—before it became a stable book attributed to a specific human author figure? There are serious problems with seeing it as a gospel, a *bios*, or some form of a history. First, when considering the Gospel according to Mark as literature, the idea that "Mark" wrote a gospel as *sui generis* is problematic. A genre consisting of only one example is contradiction, because to belong to a genre is to belong to an already existing, recognizable group. Genre is a socially constructed and learned category. That is, genre only happens in multiples. Genre is reader oriented. It is an issue of participating in a precedent. With no precedent, there can be no genre recognition.

Next, the Gospel according to Mark lacks many elements expected of ancient *bioi*. Most notably, it lacks stories about Jesus's family lineage, birth, childhood, ethical focus, and things after his death. Thus, if Mark were a biography, it would lack many of the features characteristic of ancient biography. Lucian's *Demonax* is often trotted out as an example of an ancient *bios* that also lacks some expected biographic features. In a Wittgensteinian approach, though, Lucian's *Demonax* does not broaden the "lines" or "circle" within which all ancient *bioi* are defined and therefore must operate. It is, rather, an "exception that proves the rule" of the constellation of family resemblances expected of ancient biography.[7] Even so, Lucian does in fact mention Demonax's family lineage, has a formal epilogue, and explicitly identifies itself a *bios*—unlike the Gospel according to Mark. It is perhaps feasible that ancient readers could have read Mark as a history, but it would be difficult to imagine someone reading it this way who did not already regard Jesus as an historically important person, since ancient histories were not often written about marginal people or events. Ancient histories usually dealt with more than one person, although there are exceptions to this rule. If the Gospel according to Mark was a history, it was a history that can be placed only at the fringes of ancient historiography.

Scholars have tried to imagine how ancient readers would have experienced the genre of the Gospel according to Mark. Yet to my knowledge a thorough treatment, which takes seriously ancient readers as data points of interpretation, has yet to be done. Detlev Dormeyer gives the longest treatment.[8] In the end, however, his treatment remains relatively brief.[9] I investigate how the Gospel according to Mark was read, experienced, and categorized by its earliest readers, as a means of trying to understand how to approach the textuality of the Gospel according to Mark from first- and second-century perspectives. The investigation will pay attention to how readers describe the Gospel according to Mark from the point of view of textual production, as well as how they categorize it. It will also look at the ways Mark's earliest users used it. While it is does not take their historical claims at face value, it does take their reading practices seriously. And, as we shall see, the earliest readers of Mark show us a way to connect the issues of textualization of gospel tradition, the speech genre of gospel, and the literary genre of gospel.

One major obstacle to speaking about the first and second-century textual tradition(s) behind the text we now call the Gospel according to Mark is the problem of naming. It is customary to offer a caveat that, while a historical person named Mark probably did not author the Gospel according to Mark, the name "Mark" will be retained for the sake of simplicity.[10] But simplicity can be seductive and ultimately unhelpful. By retaining the name Mark (or any other name, for that matter) to talk about the textual tradition later associated with its name, a whole host of ideas are implicitly introduced. Attaching the name of an author to a text leads the reader into thinking of a controlling authorial personality. The very act of retaining the name Mark (or any other name), therefore, makes it difficult to redescribe the textualization, production, and proliferation of gospel tradition because it already participates in later discourses by importing ideas about a human (albeit anonymous) author figure. For example, when scholars speak about Matthew's use of Mark, the names Matthew and Mark function to bring to mind two individuals, even if anonymous and faceless, and their interaction vis-à-vis two pieces of literature. Doing so introduces a later third-century discourse.

In this chapter, it is important to be careful about the language used in relation to the various textual traditions associated with the Synoptic Gospels. Since the first time the idea of a specific, stable book is connected to a gospel and is associated with a named author figure occurs is Irenaeus of Lyon toward the end of the second century (*Haer.* 3.1.1; discussed in detail later in this chapter), I attempt to avoid the ideas of book and author as much as possible in order to speak historically about first- and second-century texts on their own terms.[11] To that end, when referring to textual traditions extending back to the first and second centuries, I do not refer simply to the names of "Mark," "Matthew," "Luke," but to the Gospel according to Mark, the Gospel according to Matthew, and the Gospel according to Luke.[12]

Even as late as the third and fourth centuries CE, remnants of prior gospel discourses can be detected. Eusebius, for instance, who often thinks of the gospels as stable, published pieces of literature, nevertheless preserves the idea of the Gospels according to Matthew and John as recording *hypomnēmata*.[13] Origen likewise refers to the gospels as *hypomnēmata*.[14] Tertullian mentions something recorded "in the same *commentarius* of Luke" (*in eodem commentario Lucae*).[15] In an effort to preserve older traditions, late ancient Christian writers mine older sources and then reconfigure them into contemporary understandings of gospel textuality and authorship, usually for apologetic purposes.

The Gospel according to Mark, however, is the textual tradition most consistently regarded as less finished, less authored, and less bookish than other gospel constellations. The comments are often embedded in later writings as quotations or used by apologists in their own writings, so they must be read with care. I treat the examples as data points of the Gospel according to Mark's own readers in order to try to imagine a landscape of readers' expectations in relation to gospel textuality and authorship. What emerges is an understanding of gospel as a fluid, unfinished, and relatively open constellation of textual objects.

## *The Gospel according to Luke on the Gospel according to Mark*

The preface to the Gospel according to Luke (which I suspect itself represents a growth within the Gospel according to Luke's textual tradition) acknowledges an awareness of other attempts to textualize stories about Jesus.[16] I find it significant that the preface to the Gospel according to Luke does not call these stories "gospels" or even "the gospel," nor does it provide the names of authors. In other prefaces to biographies or histories, the author will frequently mention the names of previous works it rewrites. For example, the compiler's preface in 2 Maccabees 2:19–32 tips its hat to Jason of Cyrene's five-volume work and indicates that 2 Maccabees is an epitome of Jason's books (2 Macc. 2:23–32). In antiquity, such practices were common among writers throughout the Mediterranean basin. The Gospel according to Luke, however, does not mention any books or names of authors in the previous attempts to textualize the stories about Jesus. In fact, it does not even name its own author.

Loveday Alexander, in her analysis of the Gospel according to Luke's preface, notes significant similarities to prefaces in medical technical texts.[17] I find her analysis productive. Galen, as I discussed in chapters 2 and 3, routinely distinguished more finished works from less finished memoranda by noting that his more finished works were more careful or precise (*arkibēs*) than his less finished *hypomnēmata*. I return to one previously discussed example because it bears a meaningful resemblance to how the Gospel according to Luke characterizes the Gospel according to Mark. In his *On Anatomical Procedures*, Galen speaks about the nature of his text vis-à-vis a couple other texts.[18] Galen had written a second edition, which was clearer and more precise.[19] Similarly, one of Galen's predecessors named Marinus had written about anatomical experiments, and Galen commends him for this, even though his notes are incomplete and obscure. The present edition of *On Anatomical Procedures*, which Galen knows those outside his circle will read, is much more finished than his first edition. For the sake of clarity, it is enlarged, better composed, more detailed, and more careful (*akribēs*) than previous versions or editions of anatomical procedures. Galen says, "I have [here] communicated everything I have learned from the beginning to those who find they need it."[20]

Analogously, while others have made a beginning at arranging the story of Jesus's teachings and actions, the producer of the preface to the Gospel according to Luke had also resolved to produce a text about Jesus, but this one, in contrast to its predecessors, would (1) follow closely (2) everything learned (3) from the beginning.

> Since lots of other people have attempted to set in order the story about the things that have been fulfilled among us, just as the witnesses from the beginning and the servants of the story handed it down to us, it also seemed good for me, since I had followed closely (*parēkolouthēkoti*) carefully (*akribōs*) everything from the beginning (*anōthen*), to write [the story] for you, most excellent Theophilus, in order that you might know the convincing nature (*asphaleian*) of the things you were taught.[21]

The producer of the preface wants to give the impression that "Theophilus" could have been dissatisfied with previous accounts. Therefore, he also wants to textualize the gospel, as many others have attempted to do. What was it about the texts that could have produced such hesitations for a reader? The language in the preface of the Gospel according to Luke mirrors Galen's language about creating a more finished, authored, and publishable text from previous textual objects, which looked more like textual raw material. Its relationship to prior textual objects is similar to Plutarch's use of *hypomnēmata*, as discussed in chapter 2.

The one who wrote the preface to the Gospel according to Luke claims to have "followed closely" (*parēkolouthēkoti*) everything from the beginning (*anōthen*). What exactly does such a claim mean? It could mean, of course, that the Gospel according to Luke claims to follow a precise chronology of Jesus's life. But another meaning is also possible, one which takes into account the language of textual composition in antiquity. Theon's *Progymnasmata*, a school handbook of rhetoric and composition from around the end of the first century CE, delineates what elements it was customary to address about a character in a narrative: "Family, nature, education, bodily state, age, fortune, character, action, speech, death, and things after death follow closely with the character [of a narrative]."[22] Note the words Theon uses: these elements "follow closely" (*parakolouthei*) the character in a narrative. Here, to "follow closely" seems to be a technical term referring to a precise sense of adhering faithfully to the elements a reader might expect to find in a narrative. Nicolaus of Damascus marks similar elements as necessary for his story of Augustus: birth and breeding, parents, nurture and education from infancy, and means by which the character came to such an estate.[23] Theon uses *parakolouthein* to denote the expected elements and arrangement of a character in a *diēgēsis*.[24]

After the producer of Luke 1:1–4 labels previous attempts at telling the story of Jesus as narrative, he claims that he presents a precise and orderly (*kathexēs*) account that *follows closely* (*parēkolouthēkoti*) everything from the beginning (*anōthen*). Such a statement strongly implies that the one who produced the preface to the Gospel according to Luke does not take the Gospel according to Mark (or the saying source document called Q, or any other sources to which he may have had access) to be sufficiently careful (*akribēs*).[25] It was not a well-ordered narrative that *closely follows* from the beginning, thus necessitating the creation of the Gospel according to Luke. In order to meet ancient readers' expectations, the Gospel according to Luke reworks the Gospel according to Mark—perhaps most notably among other things—by adding stories from before Jesus's birth about his family (Luke 1:5–80), his birth (2.1–20), his childhood and education (2:41–52), his age (3:23), his speech (6:17–49), and events after his death (24:13–53), all of which are lacking in the Gospel according to Mark.[26] In this way, we may understand the preface to the Gospel according to Luke as reading the Gospel according to Mark as less ordered in the sense that it does not *follow closely* the arrangement and contents a narrative was expected to have according to reading habits in antiquity.[27] The person who wrote this preface is the earliest known reader of the textual tradition we now call the Gospel according to Mark.[28] He finds it to be poorly ordered. One need not wait until Papias to find a reader of the Gospel according to Mark. The writer of the preface to the Gospel according to Luke is just as much a reader as Papias, and perhaps more so. Both by the language in its preface and how its narrative differs, the Gospel according to Luke labels its sources, which includes the text we now call the Gospel according to Mark, as less finished, less accurate, and less structured like a narrative. It's more like *hypomnēmata* and less like a *suggramma* or *biblion*. For the writer of the preface, previous attempts to write the story of Jesus were failed attempts. They were failures because they, like *hypomnēmata*, were not careful enough (*akribēs*), did not follow things from the beginning in an orderly fashion, and did not discuss the topics customarily expected by ancient readers in stories about a person.

Eusebius's reading of the preface to the Gospel according to Luke confirms my analysis. Of course, Eusebius does not seem to be aware that he denigrates the Gospel according to Mark with the following comments, because for him there is no textual interdependence between the Gospel according to Mark and the Gospel according to Luke. Rather, he participates in a later discourse and thinks of named stable, discrete books that do not "use" each other:

> Luke himself at the beginning of his treatise prefixed an account of the cause for which he had made his compilation (*suntaxin*), explaining that while many others had somewhat rashly (*propetesteron*) attempted to make a narrative of the things of which he had himself full knowledge, he felt obliged to release (*apallattōn*) us from the doubtful propositions (*amphēristou hypolēpseōs*) of the others and related in his own Gospel the accurate account of the thing of which he had himself firmly learnt the truth from his profitable intercourse and life with Paul and his conversation with the other apostles.[29]

In Eusebius's reading of the Gospel according to Luke's preface, its sources, which (although he did not recognize this) were the textual traditions we now call the Gospel according to Mark, Q, and perhaps others, were hastily and sloppily put together. The Greek word translated as "somewhat rashly" is *propetesteron*, a comparative adjective functioning adverbally. Eusebius uses it metaphorically here, but its literal meaning has to do with falling forward—headlong and quite out of control.³⁰ Their unfinishedness and lack of polish or clarity, Eusebius says, had resulted in some readers not taking these prior gospel texts seriously, thinking of them as dubious and contested assumptions, not carefully and thoughtfully arranged and put together. Their rough and unfinished nature created a troublesome situation from which readers needed to be rescued. Luckily, "Luke," so Eusebius tells us, provides the necessary remedy. The Gospel according to Luke adds organization and structure (*suntaxis*) to the previous rough versions. *Suntaxis* is what Lucian says must be added to a rough draft (*hypomnēmata*) in order for it to be finished into a proper piece of history.³¹

Eusebius shows us how a late ancient reader might have read the Gospel according to Luke's characterization of prior attempts to textualize the story of Jesus. Thus, Eusebius corroborates my reading of the Gospel according to Luke. Eusebius sees the preface to the Gospel according to Luke as demonstrating the rough literary quality of the textual tradition we now call the Gospel according to Mark. Thinking of the gospel as textualized in the form of *hypomnēmata* does not suddenly disappear in late antiquity with the advent of later discourses of published books and authors. While Eusebius can describe gospels as books published by authors, he also calls the Gospel according to Mark and other gospels *hypomnēmata*.³² Thus, in late antique Christianity, we see multiple and divergent discourses on configuring gospel textuality, authorship, and authority existing side by side for multiple centuries.

## *Papias on the Gospel according to Mark*

Around 130 CE, Papias, the bishop of Hierapolis in Asia Minor, wrote five books called the *Narrative of the Dominical Logia*.³³ In his writings, Papias also remarks on a figure called "Mark." None of Papias's writings remain extant apart from their preservation in other peoples' writings.³⁴ Papias is always cited as a source and made to do work in someone else's argument. It is easy, then, to conflate Papias's fragments and his purposes of writing with the books and purposes of the person using him as a source.

In the comments related to the textual tradition we now call the Gospel according to Mark, Eusebius is the one who preserves Papias's relevant comments in his third book of *Ecclesiastical History*. Eusebius's book 2 ends with Peter and Paul in Rome under Nero and book 3 gives an account of the period after the apostles (although he included the apostle John here). Book 3 also uses the writing of Philo and Josephus to construct a history of the time period. Papias is the last of the generation after the apostles discussed in Eusebius's third book.[35] Eusebius's main interest in Papias comes from his writing called *Narrative of the Dominical Logia*.[36] Eusebius wants to draw a clear and trustworthy link between Papias's writings and the apostolic period.

It is important not to import later discourse of Gospel textuality and authorship into Papias's world of the early second century CE. Even a scholar as preeminent as François Bovon falls into the trap of anachronistically participating in Eusebius's later gospel discourse when he writes, "Papias (first half of the second century) uses the formula *euaggelion kata* ("Gospel according to . . .") for Matthew."[37] Papias, however, never uses the formula *euaggelion kata* to describe any gospel in his writings. In fact, Papias (in the fragments that remain extant) never refers to any piece of writing as a gospel or even uses the word *gospel* (*euaggelion*). Some later readers come to think of gospels as discrete books with authors, and the temptation to buy into later "bookish" discourse is strong. It must be resisted nonetheless.

Papias does not view his own project as writing about the histories of the gospel books and their authors so as to demonstrate their reliability; that is Eusebius's concern. It is Eusebius, not Papias, who writes a history of gospel writing. Rather, Papias seems to think of himself as continuing and expanding the project of textualizing gospel tradition about Jesus and refining the constellations of textual objects into a more literary format. Papias is more productively thought of as analogous to the producer of the Gospel according to Luke, expanding written gospel tradition and traditions, than as analogous to Eusebius the historian. Compare the comments from Papias's preface to his *Narrative of the Dominical Logia* with the preface to the Gospel according to Luke just discussed. Papias writes, "I also will not hesitate to draw up in arrangement (*sugkatataxai*) for you with my explanations everything I learned and remembered well from the elders; I confirm their truth."[38] He goes on, then, to add an element that the Gospel according to Luke lacks, but using a word we have already seen. He describes his method of combing through source material as follows:

> For unlike most people, I took no pleasure in hearing those who had a lot to say, but only those who taught the truth, and not those who recalled commandments from strangers, but only those who recalled the commandments which have been given faithfully by the Lord and

proceed from the truth itself. But whenever someone arrived who had been a companion of one of the elders (*parēkolouthēkōs tis tois presbuterois elthoi*), I would carefully inquire after their words, what Andrew and Peter had said, or what Philip or what Thomas had said, or James or John or Matthew or any of the other disciples of the Lord, and what things Ariston and the elder John, disciples of the Lord, were saying.[39]

Any would-be boundary between the written and the oral is tangled here. Papias is the textualizer of the living voice. Like the writer of the preface to the Gospel according to Luke, Papias thinks of his method as that of *following closely* (*parakoloutheō*). He sifts through the source material and arranges it carefully and in a reasonable order. The description is an *apologia* for his own writing. It comes from his preface and shows how, in his narrative (*exēgēsis*) that follows, he tapped into the best available information. He carefully scrutinizes it and puts it in a literary arrangement that follows closely the expected elements of a narrative.

Eusebius, who claimed to have had access to Papias's five books, provides information about how Papias's comments concerning a figure named Mark fit into this larger project. Eusebius mentions that Papias's writings were "books" (*suggrammata*). They were titled: *Narrative of the Dominical Logia* (*logiōn kuriakōn exēgēsis*). Lexically, the word *exēgēsis* itself could be translated as "interpretation," "narrative," or "statement."[40] The books were numbered 1 through 5. Papias wrote a preface to his books. Thus, the work was coded with several recognizable literary paratextual features. Part of the preface included an explanation about how and where Papias received his source material.[41] Papias was not a disciple of Jesus or of Jesus's apostles. He learned the stories in his books from "the elders" who knew the apostles.

The main body of Papias's five books told stories from the life of Jesus through the activities of early disciples and apostles. Stories about the woman caught in adultery (see John 7:53–8:11), the selection of Matthias (see Acts 1:23–24), and stories about the unnamed daughters of Philip demonstrate the breadth of Papias's work. It appears to have been comparable in both its literary compositional style and its scope to the companion volumes, the Gospel according to Luke and the Acts of the Apostles.

From what Eusebius relates, a significant portion of Papias's preface focuses on his sources, although this was also done in the main body of the work.[42] Thus, Philostratus's treatment of Damis's notebooks in the beginning of book 1 of *Life of Apollonius* is an apt comparison. Ariston, though not an apostle himself, was an important source for Papias. Papias deals with Ariston in his preface.[43] In relation to Ariston, Eusebius remarks

> In the same writing (*tē idia graphē*) he [Papias] also quotes other interpretations of the words of the Lord given by the Ariston mentioned above [3.39.4–7] and traditions of John the presbyter. To them we may dismiss the studious; we are now obliged to append to the words already quoted from him a tradition about Mark who wrote the gospel, which he expounds as follows. . . .[44]

The writing in question here seems to be from Papias's preface mentioned in *Hist. eccl.* 3.39.2–7. The tradition about Mark as textualizer of gospel tradition is categorized along with the traditions ascribed to Ariston and John the Presbyter. Since Papias described Ariston and John the presbyter in his preface, it seems most likely that his comments about Mark also derive from his preface. Alternatively, they could have been one of the sources mentioned in the main body of the books. Either way, his comments about "Mark" were not the main act; they were a supporting act to his main focus: the *logia* of the Lord.

Papias never refers to the Gospel according to Mark or the Gospel according to Matthew or even a or the gospel. It seems such concepts were not (yet) available to him. His aim is not detailing the history of how the gospels were created and why their authorship lends them authority, which is how modern historians tend to read him. Taken on his own terms, Papias makes some opening remarks about how he received the best information, which comes from the living voice of the apostles and thus directly from the Lord. Papias, like the producer of the Gospel according to Luke, continues the textualization of gospel tradition. In such a reading, his comments on the textual tradition we now know as the Gospel according to Mark show Papias demonstrating to his readers exactly how Peter's living voice became textualized in the form of memory aids. His answer is that a certain person named Mark, who is a textualizer of oral tradition and not an "author," textualized Peter's teaching in the form of *apomnēmoneumata*, which in the context is roughly a synonym of *hypomnēmata*.[45] They were a physical extension of Mark's memory of Peter's teaching, and therefore could be thought of as not a book but access, through Mark's notes, to the living voice of Peter, albeit through the medium of textual objects.

Eusebius records Papias's characterization of a textualized tradition associated with Mark's name in *Hist. eccl.* 3.39.15:

And the elder used to say the following: Mark, who was Peter's interpreter, carefully wrote everything he remembered (*hosa emnēmoneusen*) that the Lord had said and done, although he did not add any arrangement to it (*ou mentoi taxei*). For Mark neither heard the Lord nor followed him closely (*parēkolouthēsen autō*), but later, as I mentioned, he followed Peter closely, who used to adopt his teaching to the form of *chreiai* [short punchy anecdotes], and he did not make, as it were, an orderly arrangement (*ouk hōsper suntaxin*) of the dominical *logia*. So, Mark did not make a mistake when he wrote down some of the things he remembered (*apomnēmoneusen*). For Mark only had one goal in mind: to leave nothing out and not to include anything untrue among them.

Again, it is anachronistic to think of Papias in his *Narrative of the Dominical Logia* as archiving the history of how a person named Mark authored his gospel book, since he never refers to a gospel of any kind. Such a question is Eusebius's, and it may be the question of many modern readers of Papias, but it is not Papias's question per se. Rather, he views himself as engaged in the continuation and refashioning of textual traditions about Jesus active in the first two centuries, not unlike what the Gospel according to Luke did with the Gospel according to Mark and what Tatian will later do to several constellations of gospel tradition.

Philostratus's comments on and use of Damis's *hypomnēmata* in his *Vita Apollonii* is a helpful comparandum to Papias's use of the Gospel according to Mark, as is Porphyry's description of Plotinus in *Vita Plotini*, whose disciple, Amelius wrote notes for twenty years, but never "wrote" anything until Amelius later arranged his notes into more than a hundred books, or so Porphyry reports.[46] Mark, in Papias's account, is a text producer, not an author. His textual objects are not books. They lack arrangement, without literary order (*ou mentoi taxei ... ouk hōsper suntaxin*), unfinished. They are not a gospel; they are, nonetheless, the gospel.

Galen's comments on *taxis* prove helpful in understanding what it means to refer to the "order" of texts in antiquity. In his *On the Order (taxeōs) of My Own Books,* Galen begins the small treatise by explaining what he means by "order" (*taxis*):

> I think you had a good idea, Eugenianus, to have demanded a book explaining how properly to utilize my writings (lit. "the order [*taxin*] of my writings"). For they do not all have the same aim (*skopos*), the

same utility (*dynamis*), and the subject matter (*epaggelia*). For some were written, as you know, because my friends asked me for them, being aimed at their particular level of skill. But some others were dictated for beginners. It was neither my aim to pass down information to people nor to preserve [information] for future generations (because I have noticed that few people understand what happened in the past).[47]

He then proceeds to give a taxonomy of his writings, with information about their composition and how to use them. Galen notes that understanding the "order" (*taxis*) of a text is a critical component for understanding it, because its "order" indicates its (1) aim, (2) usefulness, and (3) content. Such information informs how one understands why it was created and consequently how the producer imagined the writing to be used. In this context, Papias notes that the *logia* created by Mark lack a literary organization and polish, and thus have a different aim and utility.

Papias also offers a remark about a textual tradition associated with a person named Matthew. Since both comments are preserved in Eusebius, it is hard to say for certain, owing to their fragmentary preservation, how Papias's comments on the texts produced by figures named "Mark" and "Matthew" related to one another in his *Narrative of the Dominical Logia*, but it seems that Papias offered them as a comparison, likely following immediately on the heels of the comments on the Gospel according to Mark.

> So while Matthew arranged (*sunetaxato*) the *logia* in the Hebrew dialect, every one interpreted (or, "explained") [the *logia*] to the best of his ability.[48]

Papias's comparison between the notes that Mark produced and what Matthew did with the notes is clear, when read in light of ancient writing practices and modes of authorship. Mark did not author a book called the gospel, nor did Matthew create a separate gospel. Matthew took Mark's *logia*, themselves a textualization of Peter's speech, and placed them in an interpretive arrangement.

Chronological arrangement or even literary arrangement (in the modern sense) does not seem to be in question in Papias's comments; arrangement as in a literary compositional form, readily recognizable to an ancient reader seems more likely.[49] As we will see in chapter 6, such an understanding of the term "arrangement" fits Papias's comment better, since the text we now call the Gospel according to Matthew follows the text we now call the Gospel according to Mark (as we have them) in the order of events remarkably closely, at least compared to other ancient texts.[50] As noted, order (*taxis*) was what a writer added to the rough draft (*hypomnēmata*) in order to move it into a more readable, polished, and recognizable form. Thus, the movement is from rough, unordered, unfinished literary raw material toward a more finished and polished text, and an important part of that movement is adding order to the rough draft.[51] Similarly, for Papias, "Mark" wrote unarranged *logia* and "Matthew" adds *taxis* to the *logia*. In this scenario, the texts we now call the Gospel according to Mark constitute the rough draft, and the text we now call the Gospel according to Matthew is the continuation and polishing of the same unfinished work.[52] Papias does not write the history of creation of "the Gospels." Rather, he himself continues the ongoing *project* of textualizing the gospel.[53]

## *Irenaeus on the Gospel according to Mark*

Irenaeus is the earliest extant evidence of the new discourse regarding the gospels as stable, authored, and published books—the discourse which became widespread in the third and fourth centuries CE (at least among elite Christian intellectuals) and the one that remains dominant among historical-critical scholars to the present day. In 3.1.1 of *Against Heresies*, Irenaeus offers insight into a new way of thinking about the textual origins of the gospels.[54]

> Now Matthew published a written gospel among the Hebrews in their own dialect, while Peter and Paul were proclaiming the gospel in Rome and founding the church. After their death, Mark, the disciple and interpreter of Peter, also passed Peter's preaching down to us writtenly (*eggraphōs*). Luke, the follower of Paul, also put the gospel preached by Paul down in a book. Then John, the disciple of the Lord, who reclined on the Lord's breast, he also published the gospel while he was residing in Ephesus of Asia.[55]

Throughout the second century CE there was a wide variety of ways of thinking about the textuality and author(ization) of the gospel. Irenaeus speaks about the provenance of the gospels. In striking contrast to the ways other second-century writers refer to gospel, he marks the time and place of each gospel's creation, treating them as books published and attributed to specific people.

It should not be surprising, then, that Irenaeus also speaks about another aspect of each of the four gospels. He offers the first traces of a discourse of the bibliographic dimensions of the gospels. Not only does the speech genre of gospel become textualized but also they are now full-fledged published and authored books. But not all of them. In a serializing manner, Irenaeus goes through each gospel of his fourfold gospel and talks about their status as published books. But one of the four gospels stands out in comparison with the others.

In his description just given, Irenaeus tells us explicitly that two of the gospels are published. And he uses specific bibliographic terms. In 3.1.1, he says,

> Now Matthew published (*exēnegken*) a written gospel among the Hebrews in their own dialect, while Peter and Paul were proclaiming the gospel in Rome and founding the church. . . . Then John, the disciple of the Lord, who reclined on the Lord's breast, he also published (*exedōken*) the gospel while he was residing in Ephesus of Asia.

The Greek words and their Latin translations use the specific literary compositional terms in both languages to refer to the act of publishing a book. Publication, it must be remembered, was a cultural *habitus* in the ancient world, and the etymology of both the words *ekdidōmi* and *ekpherō* express the essence of publication: it is to give or bring a piece of writing out into a public sphere.[56] The etymology of the Latin verb *edo* is similar, referring to giving something out. When referring to a piece of writing, it means to publish.[57]

The Gospels according to Matthew and John, in Irenaeus's configuration, are not just *biblia*; they are published *biblia*. Irenaeus makes sure the writtenness of the Gospel according to Matthew is not in question. Irenaeus tells us that Matthew published his gospel in the Hebrew dialect. He published his gospel during the time in which Peter and Paul were evangelizing Rome and founding the church there. The Gospel according to John is also identified in a similar manner. Lest anyone be confused about the John to which Irenaeus refers, he tells us the John he has in mind is the one who reclined on the Lord's breast in the upper room. John published his gospel book in Ephesus. To Irenaeus, the specificity of the attribution of who produced what gospel is important, since it is the authority of the source that separates his gospels from the gospels of heretics like Marcion and Valentinus.

Mark and Luke, in comparison with Matthew and John, lack any language about the public nature of their writings. Of the two gospels that are not described as published, Irenaeus labels one of them as a book. He uses the word *biblion*. The other he does not. After their death, Mark, the disciple and interpreter of Peter, also passed Peter's preaching down (*paradedōken*) to us writtenly. Luke, the follower of Paul, also put the gospel preached by Paul down *in a book* (*en bibliō katetheto*).

While Irenaeus does not use technical terms to explicitly describe the Gospel according to Luke as published, it is nonetheless designated as a book (*biblion*). In contrast to Luke, Mark's text is described neither as published nor as a book. In fact, unlike the other three, it is not even called a gospel. Irenaeus says that Luke composed the gospel preached by Paul in a book (*en bibliō katetheto*). *Katatithēmi* is less frequently used to talk about the creation of literature, but *katatithēmi* is used with *biblion* in Demosthenes's *Erotic Essay* 61.1–2.[58] His use of the phrase is insightful as an analogue to Irenaeus's comments on Luke. Demosthenes uses the phrase "put down in a book" (*eis biblion katatheito*) to denote the creation of a proper piece of literature, designed to endure the test of time. He puts proper literary writing in contrast with the kind of writing that records oral speech, which reflects a more everyday use of language.

It is useful to read Demosthenes's phrase "put down in a book" analogically alongside Irenaeus's comments on the gospels, as it throws Irenaeus's comparison of the styles of the Gospel according to Mark and the Gospel according to Luke into clear contrast. In terms of the nature of the texts in question, when Irenaeus uses the phrase *en bibliō katetheto*, he puts Luke's composition on a different literary plane from Mark's with respect to its textuality. Luke writes in a more elaborate style of writing, one designed to come off as more timeless than timely. His book is more literary, more "bookish." Mark's text, by contrast, is governed more by speech genres than literary conventions.

Irenaeus's comments on the textual creation of the Gospel according to Mark confirm this. Neither called a "book" nor labeled as "published," Irenaeus imagines a figure named Mark who passes down the oral tradition of Peter. Without the adverb "writtenly" (*eggraphōs*), we would not even know that the proclamation had been textualized at all. The Gospel according to Mark is not a piece of literature; it is certainly not a book. Rather, it is a speech that happens to have become textual object.

Usually, those who write *hypomnēmata* are people like the Valentinians, not those who wrote "his" gospels. Irenaeus claims that the disciples of Valentinus call their writings *hypomnēmata*.[59] By contrast, Irenaeus's gospels (at least most of them) are polished books. Irenaeus distinguishes not only the content of their writings from those his own but also the textuality of their writings. Nevertheless, when Irenaeus discusses the textuality of the Gospel according to Mark, he describes it in terms akin to *hypomnēmata*.

Thus, we see competing gospel textuality discourses within Irenaeus's framework for thinking about gospel, textuality, and authority. On the one hand, Irenaeus can write of certain gospels as books published by authors. On the other hand, he preserves a tradition about the Gospel according to Mark and its textual production that remembers the Gospel according to Mark as similar to *hypomnēmata* or other textual raw material. In contrast with other gospels of Irenaeus's four-form gospel, Irenaeus presents the Gospel according to Mark as less published, less "bookish," and therefore less finished than the other three gospels.

With Irenaeus, then, the earliest evidence appears of discourse about the gospel as a book published by an author. But such an advent does not mean the disappearance of prior discourses. As I have shown, Origen in the third century and Eusebius in the fourth century preserve the discourse of gospel texts as *hypomnēmata*. Just because a new discourse emerges in the late second and early third century about gospels as books with authors, that does not mean the prior discourses disappear. We need not think in a building-block fashion about discourse development. The emergence of one discourse need not mean the disappearance of another. Discourses rarely die so easily.

## *Clement of Alexandria and Eusebius on the Gospel according to Mark*

As with Irenaeus, we need to read Clement of Alexandria's account of the textuality of the Gospel according to Mark with a sensitivity to disjointed discourses of gospel textuality and authorship. Clement is writing at the end of the second and the beginning of the third century CE. In places, he does refer to books called gospels: one according to Matthew, one according to Mark, one according to Luke, one according to John, one according to the Egyptians, and so forth. Yet, while he has access to a later gospel discourse, he retains reminiscences and traditions from previous discourses of gospel textuality and tradition, the latter which did not assume the concepts of books, authors, or publication. These earlier memories are now reformatted into a third-century discourse on uniquely authored books called gospels.[60]

For instance, consider the concentric circles of citation at play in the anecdote cited in Eusebius's *Hist. eccl.* 2.15. The story comes from an unknown source, but is quoted by Clement of Alexandria. Eusebius then quotes the quotation of Clement. What's more, elsewhere, when Eusebius gives his own account of the textual creation of the Gospel according to Mark in book 6 of his *Ecclessiastical History*, he seems basically to rewrite Clement's quotation of a quotation. But the notion that the Gospel according to Mark was *hypomnēmata* or *apomnēmoneumata* does not originate with Clement. As we have seen, Eusebius knows an earlier tradition that imagines the Gospel according to Mark as unpolished notes, citing Papias. In both Bart Ehrman's and Michael Holmes's editions of the Apostolic Fathers, the following story is categorized under Papias's fragments.[61] According to Eusebius, however, it is not quoted by Papias, but quoted by Clement of Alexandria in his *Outlines*, a work now lost. Clement quotes (*paratetheitai*) the story; Papias agrees with it (*sunepimarturei*).[62] So the story is from Clement, but stands in agreement with Papias's understanding of how the Gospel according to Mark came to be. It is from an anonymous source, quoted by Clement, corroborated by Papias, and reworked by Eusebius.

We must bear in mind that Clement and Eusebius write from within a different, later gospel discourse that assumed more bookish modes of thinking. They remember and redeploy the story, manipulating it in new directions.

> Such a pious light illuminated the minds of those who heard Peter that a single hearing of Peter was not nearly enough nor was the unwritten teaching of his divine proclamation. So, with constant requests they were begging Mark (whose gospel is in circulation), who was a follower of Peter, that he might leave behind for them also a written memory aid (*dia graphēs hypomnēma*) of teaching passed down orally, and they did not leave him alone until they were successful. And it was in this way that they became the cause of the writing that is called *the Gospel According to Mark*. They say the apostle Peter knew what happened because the Spirit had revealed it to him. He was pleased with their eagerness and he authorized (*kurōsai*) the document for use (*eis enteuxin*) among the churches. Clement quotes this story in the sixth book of his *Outlines*. Papias, the bishop of Hieropolis, also corroborates Clement's story.[63]

Clement, from a textual production point of view, labels the Gospel according to Mark as an *hypomnēma*.[64] Clement uses the Platonic idea of *hypomnēmata* as textual objects that are not so much a book or a piece of literature as a physical extension of human memory. A figure called Mark textualized Peter's oral proclamation, but this act of textualization alone does not make it a book or a piece of literature per se.

The *hypomnēma* addresses the need for a memory aid for Peter's auditors in Peter's absence. When his oral teaching was preserved in a textual object, someone could use the notes as memory aids to recall his teaching and to reanimate his voice. The auditors ostensibly could be reilluminated by Peter's voice, even in his absence. So goes the logic of Clement's quotation. A movement occurs from unwritten to written, but in either case, Peter's oral teaching is the point of focus. Who is the authorizer of the textualized tradition—Peter, Mark, or the one who reactualizes the oral tradition of the Gospel according to Mark again by new proclamation through the *hypomnēma*? The answer is unclear.

Peter's approval of the *hypomnēma* lends his authority to the text, but this act does not make it Peter's "book." There is no language about "publication" of a "book." The text has more utilitarian purposes than literary ones. The purpose of the textualization of the teaching is for others to be able to use the notes for their own reading and teaching and preaching among the churches.

Clement's account of the textualization of the Gospel according to Mark sounds similar to Arrian's production of *hypomnēmata* of Epictetus's teachings, to Eucleides's textualization of Socrates's conversation in *Theaetetus*, to Galen's transformation of his own teachings into textual objects for disciples who would be away from him for some time, and to Catius's inscribing of the culinary philosopher's lecture in Horace's *Satires*.[65] In each case, the text in question is not a piece of literature, not even book, just a textualization of tradition. Like Eucleides with Socrates, Mark textualizes Peter's spoken teaching into the Gospel according to Mark, and then the textual objects of the message are shown to the original source, who does not reject them. Unlike Eucleides, the cause of the textualization is an unnamed mass of people, not the one producing the text. In both cases, the source of *auctor* of the teaching is aware his teachings are being written down.

Clement of Alexandria speaks of a book called the Gospel according to Mark, but it seems he also utilizes a tradition that remembers the Gospel according to Mark as textual raw material. Like the other earliest readers of the textual tradition we now call the Gospel according to Mark, he describes it as *hypomnēma*—rough, unfinished, in need of polishing. Papias uses the concept of *apomnēmoneumata*, which George Kennedy argues functions here as variant of *hypomnēmata*.[66] Kennedy's understanding of the terms is corroborated by Eusebius, who sees Clement and Papias as in full agreement about their views of the textual makeup of the Gospel according to Mark. So, paying attention to different archeological layers of knowledge about Gospel textuality and authorship, we find the early readers of the textual tradition we now call the Gospel according to Mark speaking of it as unfinished, unpolished textual raw material.

# 6
## The Earliest Users of the Gospel according to Mark

THERE CLEARLY EXISTS a relationship between the texts we now call the Gospels according to Matthew and Mark—as we presently know them. Most people assume that the Gospel according to Matthew used the Gospel according to Mark, not vice versa. What I query, however, is this: What do we mean by the word *used*? It is a vague word, which leaves much room for anachronism and misunderstanding. In antiquity and late antiquity, there were many different types of use one could make of another's text, work, or book. How can we think in a more textured way about the interaction between the textual traditions behind the Gospels according to Matthew and according to Mark?

I am aware that one cannot distinguish cleanly between readers and users of a text. In some senses, a reader is a user and a user is reader. I retain the distinction here, despite its limitations, as a way to put different types of ancient voices together into heuristic categories. In chapter 5, I grouped together some of the earliest descriptions of the Gospel according to Mark in terms of its textuality. How did readers experience the Gospel according to Mark? Different answers were given that may be grouped into a constellation with some of the distinctive commonalities: the Gospel according to Mark was described as rough, unfinished, less "bookish" notes. In chapter 6, I grouped together examples of ancient "users" who filled in what was lacking in the unfinished and open gospel.

The earliest users of the Gospel according to Mark engaged in different types of revision. Some users reworked and added material throughout the text; other users lengthened the text by adding new endings. By rewriting and continuing the textual tradition we now call the Gospel according to Mark, its early users showed a regard for it as somehow unfinished and plastic, like *hypomnēmata*, designed to be changed, improved, finished (at least provisionally). In so doing, its early users stand alongside its early readers in treating it as raw material available for them to rework and update in new ways.

## *The Gospel according to Matthew as Continuing the Gospel according to Mark*

Artemidorus, the second-century dream interpreter, writes in his book *Onirocritica* that he knew others would be likely to alter his books or steal his ideas.[1] At the end of book 2, in an effort to head off such activity, he writes: "I ask those who read my books not to add or remove anything from their contents. For anyone who would be able to add (*prostheinai*) things to my books could quite easily make one's own (*idia poiēseien*)."[2] Implied in his comments are two things significant for the purposes of this chapter. First, textual revision was prevalent in antiquity. Based on Artemidorus's comments in the prefaces in books 1 and 2, reworking bits and pieces of previous texts was especially prevalent in technical works such as his own.[3] It was an expected fact in the contexts of ancient writing practices and text production.[4] Second, Artemidorus thinks that reworking his book would not have constituted the creation of a new, separate book with a new, distinct author. Whether it involves adding, subtracting, or otherwise altering, changing his text is not *ipso facto* the same thing as creating a new and separate book. For Artemidorus, reworking his existing work and writing another book are two distinct activities. In fact, he says authoring a new book would be easier than reworking his book. For Artemidorus, creating an original and different work requires less of a person than revising an existing work.[5]

If we want to speak about a book finished in the latter half of the first century CE called "Mark" and treat it as a closed, finished work, then the best way to understand "Matthew's" use of it is in the creation of a new, separate book. But if we think of the Gospel according to Mark as an unfinished collection of notes (perhaps even multiple versions of collections of notes, one of which came to be known as the text we call the Gospel according to Mark), then we can imagine a different historical and literary way of thinking about "Matthew's use of Mark."[6] It is a useful project to try to read the Gospel according to Mark as *hypomnēmata* because, when we do so, we can begin to imagine new ways of thinking about what the textual tradition we now call the Gospel according to Mark *was*—before it became a book, a narrative, or a gospel. The objective in what follows is to account for the textual relationship between the Gospel according to Matthew and the Gospel according to Mark in its first- and second-century historical-cultural landscapes. I will look at both the similarities and the differences between the texts of the Gospel according to Matthew and the Gospel according to Mark (as we have them) and then situate those differences in terms of textual revision, writing practices, and modes of authorship in antiquity.

Over the last several decades, redaction critics have noted nearly every difference in words, phrases, sentences, and theological emphases between the Gospel according to Mark and the Gospel according to Matthew. From their work, the impression that these are two rather different documents emerges clearly. The impression is correct, but only within a certain discursive framework—specifically, a third-century (and later) discourse of gospels as stable and published books with author figures.

Viewed from within a different framework, we begin to see another picture. If one assumes the texts we now call the Gospels according to Matthew and Mark are not both part of the same fluid textual tradition, then to my knowledge there are no two works from the ancient world more similar to each other than the Gospel according to Mark and the Gospel according to Matthew, a fact often overlooked.[7] It is important to hold their remarkable similarity in tension with the differences noted by redaction critics.[8] To find two textual traditions as similar as the Gospel according to Mark and the Gospel according to Matthew, the place to look is not two separate but similar works, such as Plato's *Apology* and Xenophon's *Memorabilia*, but to examples of multiple versions of the same text, like the Greek and Hebrew editions of Jeremiah, Hebrew and Greek versions of Esther, recensions A and B of the *Testament of Abraham*, or the various versions of the *Rule of the Community*.

Just how similar are the textual traditions we now call the Gospel according to Mark and the Gospel according to Matthew—as we have them in modern critical editions? It is common to offer up a percentage of similarity, and that varies from 70 to 90 percent of the Gospel according to Mark found in the Gospel according to Matthew.[9] It is not always clear how scholars arrive at these percentages. These statistics function almost at the level of common knowledge and seem to require no citation or support. Clearly there is some relationship between the Gospel according to Mark and the Gospel according to Matthew, but how can we best quantify the extent of their similarity? In traditional historical scholarship, the relationship between the Gospel according to Mark and the Gospel according to Matthew—usually in the form of the Two-/Four-Source Hypothesis—is expressed in a flow chart. Figures 6.1, 6.2 and 6.3 are

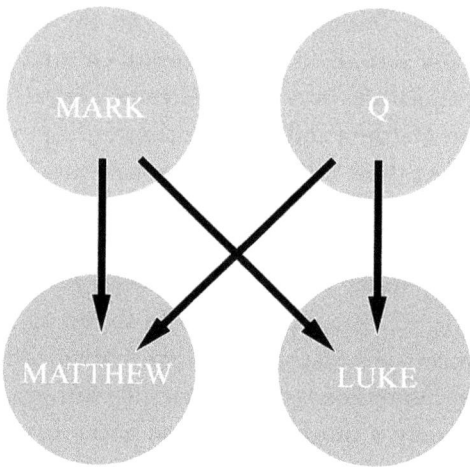

FIGURE 6.1 Two-Source Hypothesis

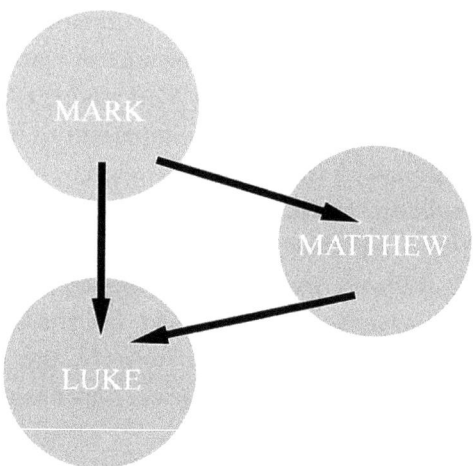

FIGURE 6.2 Farrer Hypothesis

examples, respectively, of the Two-Source Hypothesis, the Farrer Hypothesis, and the Neo-Griesbach Hypothesis.[10]

In all these graphic depictions, each constellation of textualized gospel tradition is represented as its own discrete unit, bounded by lines within a box or a circle or some other shape, with arrows indicating the direction of source relationship and redaction. All of this, however, as should be clear by now, serves to reinforce the third-century and subsequent gospel textuality and authorship discourse, reifying each gospel as an enclosed, separate text with its own unique author. How might we rethink the data?

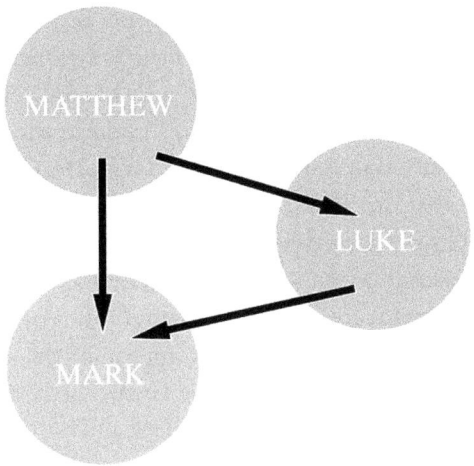

FIGURE 6.3 Neo-Griesbach Hypothesis

There are a few ways that one could go about determining the similarities between the textual traditions we now call the Gospel according to Mark and the Gospel according to Matthew. One could count letters, words, sentences, verses, or stories. Letters are too small a unit of measurement to be helpful. Sentences have the disadvantage of relying on later punctuation marks. Versification was added much later. Those who produced the Gospel according to Matthew and the Gospel according to Luke seemed to view their own alterations of prior iterations of the textual tradition in terms of changing both words and stories, in that they changed words in their revision and swapped stories in and out. The Eusebian canons (or Ammonian sections), which are a system derived in late antiquity by Eusebius to allow readers to compare similar passages in the gospels, corroborates the idea that breaking the gospels down into stories or chunks of text was reasonable to late ancient readers.[11]

I suspect counting words has been a method used by scholars in the past, and it has merit. But the problem with counting words is that one must first be able to establish the text from the manuscript traditions of textual constellation, each of which points in different directions in terms of exact word count. Thus, counting and comparing overlapping stories seems to be the least problematic way and is the approach used here. So as to remove the subjective element in my own counting of stories, I look to the Aland synopsis and its demarcation of stories in each gospel tradition.[12]

Relying on the *Conspectus locorum parallorum evangeliorum* index in the back of the Aland synopsis, I count a total of 115 stories in the Gospel according to Mark and 178 stories in the Gospel according to Matthew.[13] The two overlapping textual constellations have 107 stories in common. The Gospel according to Mark in the Aland synopsis has only eight stories that it does not share with the Gospel according to Matthew; the Gospel according to Matthew has seventy-one stories not shared with the Gospel according to Mark. This means that, in the Aland synopsis index, the Gospel according to Mark and the Gospel according to Matthew share a total of 186 stories. By this count, 93 percent of the stories in the Gospel according to Mark are also found in the Gospel according to Matthew. Only 7 percent of the stories in the Gospel according to Mark do not appear in the Gospel according to Matthew. Moreover, 60.1 percent of the Gospel according to Matthew's stories come from the Gospel according to Mark and only 39.9 percent of the stories in the Gospel according to Matthew are not also found in the Gospel according to Mark.[14] How might one graphically depict this degree of similarity between the textual traditions we now call the Gospel according to Mark and the Gospel according to Matthew?

One helpful way to show the degree of similarity, as well as the degrees of difference, is to use a proportional Venn diagram. To my knowledge, while a not-to-scale Venn diagram has been used to illustrate the relationship of the Synoptic Gospels, a proportional Venn diagram has not been used to illustrate the degree of overlap between the Gospel according to Mark and the Gospel according to Matthew. With the numbers given earlier now plugged in, the overlap of the Gospel according to Mark and the Gospel according to Matthew appears as shown in figure 6.4.

Area B in the middle of figure 6.4 shows the common stories between the Gospel according to Mark and the Gospel according to Matthew (107). Area C on the right represents the stories unique to the Gospel according to Mark (8) and area A on the left the stories unique to the Gospel according to Matthew (71).[15] The advantage of a proportional Venn diagram is that it is less prone to importing the later discourse of gospels as separate books made by different human authors. There are no clear black lines separating out discrete gospels from one another. Another advantage is that it shows the remarkable similarity between the textual traditions. Now, consider the Venn diagram alongside the comments in chapter 3 from Martial and Ovid. Martial says that he revised an already published version of his *Epigram* 10, republished the new edition, and that the reader would find that over half of the new edition was new.[16] Ovid reports that his first version of his *Amores* had five books, but Ovid cut them down to three books in a later version.[17] We do not know enough about the textual differences of the various versions of their

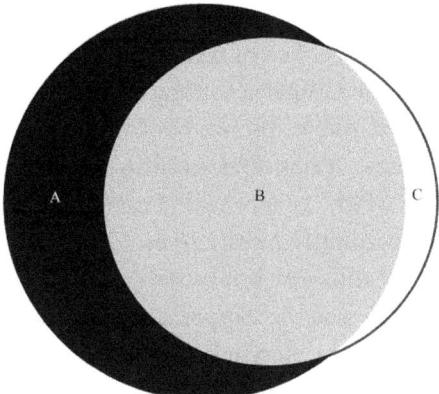

FIGURE 6.4 Proportional Venn Diagram of Overlap Between the Gospels of Mark and Matthew
Source: Graphic created by A. Seth Reese. Used with permission of the artist.

works, but the overlap between the textual traditions we know as the Gospel according to Mark and the Gospel according to Matthew fits well within the growth of the single-fluid textual tradition in light of ancient writing practices among Roman writers.

Similarly, the Greek and Hebrew versions of Jeremiah and the different versions of the *Rule of the Community* are best considered within the same framework of overlapping, growing textual traditions. Their comparison with the Gospel according to Mark and the Gospel according to Matthew is insightful. That is, the Greek version of Jeremiah is shorter by about one-sixth.[18] It reorganizes material in a way not unlike the Gospel according to Mark and the Gospel according to Matthew. Moreover, the Greek version of Jeremiah adds Baruch and the epistle of Jeremiah to the end of Jeremiah. If one takes such additions into account, a proportional Venn diagram appears that is not unlike the one for the Gospel according to Mark and the Gospel according to Matthew. Additionally, the versions of the *Rule of the Community* differ from one another. The fragmentary nature of the scrolls makes it difficult to produce a proportional Venn diagram with any kind of precision, based on words, units, or otherwise. Nevertheless, it appears that columns I to IV and the latter part of X and all of XI were not a part of the earlier regional iterations of some version of the *Rule*.[19] If six out of eleven columns were potentially part of the textual growth of the *Rule*, then it may be roughly estimated that about 50 percent of the documents overlap one another.

These are rough estimates, of course. Nonetheless, placing the proportional Venn diagram of the Gospel according to Mark and the Gospel according to Matthew in comparison with Roman and Jewish comparanda makes at least one thing clear. The sheer fact of textual differences between the Gospel according to Mark and the Gospel according to Matthew alone—apart from first hypothesizing a final, stable, discrete book with a human author—hardly merits the conclusion that seems obvious to so many readers: "Matthew" is one gospel book and "Mark" is another.[20] From a twenty-first-century perspective, the Gospel according to Mark and the Gospel according to Matthew may well be considered different books with unique authors. Even in the third century CE, many viewed the Gospel according to Mark and the Gospel according to Matthew as two different books. Yet, when considered in a first- or second-century context, the textual difference and overlap between the two textual constellations fit comfortably within the framework of finishing, continuing, or otherwise altering the same unfinished and still fluid textual tradition.

There is no "natural" or obvious point of textual difference at which one fluid text becomes two different works. Determining whether textual difference constitutes a different version of the same text or the creation of a new text is a social assignment done by readers. It is a question of reader expectations and reading *habitus*. Imagine hypothetical readers in the late first or early second century with manuscripts before them of the texts we now call the Gospel according to Mark and the Gospel according to Matthew. Based on how Gospel discourse worked throughout the late first and most of the second century, it seems highly unlikely that readers would have thought of these manuscripts as two different "books," especially if they lacked a title or an ascribed author. Rather, the manuscripts of the gospel texts would fall well within the range of expected textual fluidity and difference of the same work.

How do the Gospel according to Mark and the Gospel according to Matthew differ? As we saw in chapter 5, early readers differentiated the Gospel according to Mark and the Gospel according to Matthew by noting that the Gospel according to Mark lacked "order" (*taxis*) and the Gospel according to Matthew provided order to the textual tradition.[21] Yet the order of events in the Gospel according to Mark and the Gospel according to Matthew are conspicuously similar. The different narrative order hardly seems the most notable difference. Matthew 3:1–4:22 follows the order of Mark 1:2–20 fairly closely and Matthew 12:22–28:8 follows the basic order of Mark 3:20–16:8, with (relative to historically relevant comparanda) minor additions,[22] subtractions,[23] and rearrangement.[24] The Gospel according to Matthew does reconfigure the Gospel according to Mark's order in 1:40 through 3:19, yet given the degree to which a text could be revised from one version to the next in the ancient writing practices, the Gospel according to Matthew's revision of the order of the Gospel according to Mark is relatively light.

If the order of events in the Gospel according to Mark and the Gospel according to Matthew is so similar, is there another way to think about the difference in *taxis* between the Gospel according to Mark and the Gospel according to Matthew? Lucian's *How to Write History* may prove helpful. Lucian offers his approach to writing. In context, he speaks in reference to history writing, but it also seems more or less applicable to other forms of writing.

> After the writer has collected everything, or nearly everything, let the writer first weave together from them a rough draft (*hypomnēma ti sunuphainetō*) and make a text that is still unadorned and disjointed. Then, after the writer has put it in proper arrangement (*tēn taxin*), let the writer bring in beauty, give it a touch of style, shape it, and bring it to order.[25]

*Hypomnēmata* lack "order" (*taxis*) and are unfinished, unpolished, and uncorrected. It is one of their characteristics, and not a flaw. Adding order to notes is an integral part of turning them into polished pieces of writing. Lucian uses three different words that reflect adding proper shape to a rough draft: "proper arrangement . . . let [the writer] shape it and bring it to order" (*taxin . . . schēmatizetō kai rhuthmizetō*). For Lucian, adding organization to a rough draft involves more than just the simple question of which particular story goes where in the whole narrative. It looks at the expected overall literary arrangement of a piece of writing, and it is a question not only of what is supposed to be in a text but also what different parts are supposed to go where. It is a question of meeting reader expectations in a pleasing way as much as it is about narrative chronology. The quote from Lucian on *taxis* adds texture to the understanding of *taxis* expressed in Galen's *On the Order of My Own Books*, who there describes *taxis* as about the purposes and utility of a work.

For a narrative about a person, the Gospel according to Mark contains much information about Jesus in a few of the expected areas, especially his actions and death. Topics such as parentage, birth, childhood, speech, and things after death, however, are noticeably missing. The Gospel according to Matthew mostly adds to the Gospel according to Mark, supplementing expected yet missing elements. Matthew 1–2 describes Jesus's lineage, his birth, and his childhood. Matthew 28:9–20 fills out what happened after Jesus's death, not least his resurrection. Matthew 4:24–7:29 (the Sermon on the Mount), 10:1–39 (the Mission Discourse), 11:1–30 (the Discourse on John the Baptist and Jesus), 18:10–35 (the Community Discipline Discourse), and 24:37–25:46 (the Olivet Discourse) fill out Jesus's speech. Matthew 13:24–52, along with 20:1–16, 21:28–32, and 22:1–14, provides new expansions of parabolic teachings, fleshing out parables already in the Gospel according to Mark. In this way, it adds arrangement or order to the gospel.

All these additions begin to conform to the textual tradition we now call the Gospel according to Mark to expected forms of narrative about a person in the ancient world. The additions account for sixty-two of the seventy-one stories in the Gospel according to Matthew not found in the Gospel according to Mark; 87.3 percent of those stories fill in missing yet expected in elements in historical biographies or narratives about individuals. Only seven other stories do not fill in expected but lacking elements in the Gospel according to Mark, as defined by Theon and Nicolaus of Damascus.[26] The Gospel according to Matthew seems to correct missing elements, as well as continue and "finish" the gospel as found in the text we now call the Gospel according to Mark, rather than write a "new and separate book."[27]

Which stories does the textual tradition we now the Gospel according to Matthew omit from the one we call Gospel according to Mark? Only eight: Mark 1:21–22 (Jesus teaching in the synagogue at Capernaum), 1:23–28 (Jesus heals the demoniac in Capernaum synagogue), 1:35–38 (Jesus departs Capernaum to pray in the wilderness and Simon comes to find him); 3:20–21 (Jesus's family accuse him of being out of his mind); 4:26–29 (the parable of seed growing secretly); 8:22–26 (Jesus has to try twice in order to heal a blind man); 11:18–19 (the chief priests and scribes plot to kill Jesus); and 12:41–44 (the story of the widow's small temple offering). It is easy to understand why most of these stories drop out as the textual tradition of the gospel grew. Almost all the omitted stories fall into three categories: repetitive, potentially embarrassing, and/or confusing. The story of the widow sharing her two copper coins worth about a penny is the possible exception.[28] The other seven stories either repeat things mentioned elsewhere, like the theme of seed growing right after the parable of the sower or the healing of the demoniac or the conspiring of the chief priests and scribes to kill Jesus, or are potentially embarrassing, as when Jesus's family calls him crazy, or simply confusing, and as when Jesus apparently botches a healing and has to try again in Mark 8:22–26.

Of course, the Gospel according to Matthew does more than just add missing content to the unfinished Gospel according to Mark and remove some unnecessary or nettlesome stories. The Gospel according to Matthew also alters and rewrites stories found in the Gospel according to Mark. Ever since Günther Bornkamm's famous 1963 article "The Stilling the Storm in Matthew," redaction criticism has been an active field of study, noting the changes between earlier and later gospels and drawing conclusions about the theologies and perspectives of each gospel author.[29] I suspect it is obvious by now that, in my approach, redaction criticism cannot be comfortably situated within the earliest discourses of gospel textuality and authorship, since concepts like author and stable text—so necessary for the establishment of redaction criticism as a tool of historical study—were missing. In earliest discourses, in which gospel *qua* textual object was fluid and lacked a human author figure, the foundational assumptions and questions of redaction criticism should be rethought.[30]

In what other ways can one describe the textual alterations between the textual traditions we now call the Gospel according to Matthew and the Gospel according to Mark? Is there a framework for thinking about textual alteration in the ancient world that fits well within the earliest discourses of gospel textuality and authorship? Chapter 2 looked at Galen's reading of unfinished aphorisms of Hippocrates. Galen not only noted the unfinished quality of some of Hippocrates's writings, which were meant for the writer himself or a smaller circle of users of the text. As we saw, Galen on occasion even went so far as to finish Hippocrates's unfinished aphorisms. Let us return to the passages and look at what Galen reworks, consider for what reason, and see how he finishes them. Take, for example, the Hippocratic aphorism from *Epidemics* 6.2.25.[31]

> Because in a warmer place, more solid, on the right-hand side and dark because of this and the veins are rather on the outside [and with more bile].[32]

This is the last note in section 2 of book 6. The previous note does not clarify the comparatives used in the aphorism, and the comparatives demand some kind of contextualization. Right side of what? Warmer than what? Darker than what? It is an irksome aphorism to interpret without more contextual information.[33] It assumes a close relationship between writer and reader, one in which a good deal of common knowledge can be assumed. Someone without such proximity would easily misread or misunderstand Hippocrates's comment.

Galen picks up on all this ambiguity. For him, the ambiguity clues him into the fact that the text was rough, unfinished notes, and not meant for public consumption. If Hippocrates had intended to finish and polish the text into a publishable form, Galen says, he would have added clarifying information (*prosethēke ta ephexēs*), so that the reader would not be misled or confused. Then—and this is where it potentially becomes insightful vis-à-vis the textual traditions we now call the Gospels according to Matthew and of Mark —Galen goes on to alter the comment into a more finished form. As we saw in chapter 2, when Galen finishes the aphorism of Hippocrates, he provides us with an example of how an ancient reader might finish someone else's unfinished and unpublished text. Galen clarifies what is left ambiguous in Hippocrates's unfinished comment, which he sees as meant only for Hippocrates's personal use or use by his close associates. Without Galen, it is hardly clear that Hippocrates speaks about fetuses, gender, the womb, and gestation. With Galen's comment, however, the potential for misreading the text diminishes. Hippocrates's aphorism simply assumes that the reader—whether himself or his close associates—already knew fetuses, gender, womb, and gestation were the topics in question. Thus, when Galen finishes Hippocrates's unfinished aphorism, he supplies the necessary, assumed information that limits the possible range of interpretations of the aphorism and diminishes the opportunity to "misread" the aphorism.

Another example from Galen's commentary on Hippocrates's *Epidemics* shows the need for clarification in the textual finishing process. The Hippocratic comment in question is from the first comment in section 3 of book 6: "Watch for the sign of purification at the same time of day."[34] The context leaves the meaning of the phrase ambiguous. It is modified by "because it comes down suddenly." The exact time of day and the exact sign of purification (from what?) are left unclear. Galen observes the problem of the ambiguity and says the following:

> It is not unclear that this sentence goes with what was written before, where he was teaching how one should effect the purification. And so that we can know if we have got the right amount for it, he now writes the sign. But the text is unclear to us because, as I have already said several times, this book was not written for publication but as an outline sketch and draft for himself. If he were writing for publication he would have said everything he needed to say, specifically what time of day we should watch for the sign of the purification.[35]

What Galen makes clear is that the lack of clarity concerning the time of day would be a problem for a reader outside Hippocrates's circle. Without knowledge specifying exactly what time of day to watch for the sign of purification, Hippocrates's guidance does not help much, if at all. One cannot be watchful at the right time if one does not know what time is the "same time." Galen explains that Hippocrates did not write for an anonymous public. On the contrary, he wrote an outline sketch and draft for himself. If Hippocrates had gone through the text to prepare it for public readership, he would have clarified what he meant by "the same time of day." The ambiguity in some of Hippocrates's writings is, for Galen, a dead giveaway that the text is rough, unpolished, unfinished, and meant for its personal utility to Hippocrates.

The interaction between the overlapping textual traditions we now call the Gospel according to Matthew and the Gospel according to Mark (as we have them) shows a similar pattern to Galen's interaction with Hippocrates's unfinished aphorisms. The Gospel according to Matthew aims to narrow ambiguities in the Gospel according to Mark and direct the reader by limiting the number of possible meanings of a story or anecdote, supplying essential yet previously unspecified information. Where the Gospel according to Mark often assumes a shared knowledge and close proximity with the reader, the Gospel according to Matthew provides the necessary information to make sense of the passage. Where the Gospel according to Mark permits potentially dangerous ambiguity within a story, the Gospel according to Matthew typically reduces the ambiguity and clarifies the story.

In what follows, I do not detail every example, nor even most; I point out a few illustrative cases. An obvious example of the Gospel according to Matthew's clarification of ambiguity is found at Mark 13:14–17:

> Whenever you see "the desecration that makes desolate" standing where it shouldn't be standing (let the reader understand), then those in Judea must flee into the mountains, [and] the one on the roof must not go down or go into his house to take something out, and the one in the field must not return to get his garment. Those days will be wretched for women who are pregnant or nursing.

Important bits of the text are left ambiguous in Mark 13:14–17. From the context, it is not clear what "desecration that makes desolate" is. Furthermore, it is clear that the "desecration that makes desolate" is forbidden to stand somewhere, but exactly where is left unstated. The text assumes the reader knows who or what "the desecration that makes desolate" is, as well as where it is not supposed to stand. The narrator knows what the reader will know and assumes what the reader will be able to assume. It is as if the text offers a knowing wink to the one who reads the text aloud to auditors.

The expansion happening between the texts we now call the Gospel according to Matthew and the Gospel according to Mark bears similarities less to the creation of new, discrete book and more to Galen's treatment of Hippocrates in his sixth book of *Epidemics*. Matthew 24:15–22, which reworks Mark 13:14–17, reads as follows:

> So whenever you see "the desecration that makes desolate" standing in the holy place (the one mentioned by the prophet Daniel, let the reader understand), then those in Judea must flee to the mountains. The one on the roof must not go down to his house to take things out, and the one in the field must not return to get his garment. Those days will be wretched for women who are pregnant or nursing.

Matthew 24:16–19 follows Mark 13:15–17 almost exactly to the word, but Matthew 24:15 reworks Mark 13:14 in important ways. As with Hippocrates and Galen, two assumed pieces of knowledge in the Gospel according to Mark are filled out in the Gospel according to Matthew. First, the identity of "the desecration that makes desolate" is positively identified as coming from the prophet Daniel. Second, the "place where [the desecration that makes desolate] is not supposed to stand" is clarified as the holy place: the temple. With these two clarifications, Matthew 24:15 moves the comment in Mark 13:14 from remarks among close associates, said with a wink and a nudge, to a less ambiguous comment discernable to a more public audience.

*Hypomnēmata* were textual objects with a specific purpose. At their root, they are about remembering the already known, not informing about the not yet known. They seek to capture the already said, to collect what has already been heard.[36] "They constituted a material memory of things read, heard, thought, . . . offering these as an accumulated treasure for rereading and later meditation. They also formed raw material for the writing of more systematic treatises."[37]

I do not wish to weigh in on the debate about "Matthew's" *intentions* or make an argument about how "Matthew" *felt* about "Mark."[38] My objective is simply to show that, as was customary for *hypomnēmata* and for those reworking *hypomnēmata*, the textual tradition we now call the Gospel according to Mark makes assumptions, lacks clarity, and contains potentially ambiguous statements, and that the one we call the Gospel according to Matthew continues the text by seeking to clarify the gospel and remove its ambiguities.

Consider other examples: Mark 6:5 contains the information that Jesus "was unable to do any mighty deed [in his hometown of Nazareth] (*kai ouk edunato ekei poiēsai oudemian dunamin*)." Matthew 13:58, however, clarifies what was unclear in Mark 6:5: that his inability to do a miracle was not a question of Jesus's power but of Jesus's response to his hometown's unbelief (*ouk epoiēsen ekei dunameis pollas dia tēn apistian autōn*). The Gospel according to Matthew precludes any implication that Jesus lacked power. Ancient readers could well have supposed that the textual tradition we now call the Gospel according to Matthew is the same work—the same gospel—as the one we call the Gospel according to Mark, just with some clarification.

Similarly, Mark 10:18 mentions a response of Jesus to the rich ruler, "Why do you call me good? No one is good except god (*ti me legeis agathon; oudeis agathon ei mē heis ho theos*)." Matthew 19:17 then reworks and hones Jesus's answer by shifting the focus away from God and toward the oneness of the good, saying "Why do ask me about *the good*? There is only one who is good" (*ti me epōtas peri tou agathou; heis estin ho agathos*)." It was not that Jesus was not God, as the Gospel according to Mark is most easily read to claim, but that Jesus is making a rhetorical and philosophical comment about the singularity of the good. Jesus shifts from a non-divine Jewish figure to a philosopher debating the nature of the good.

The Gospel according to Mark concludes its story of Jesus walking on the water in 6:46–52 with the strangely ambiguous and seemingly non sequitur remark, "and they were completely shocked among themselves because they had not gained an understanding into the bread, but their heart was hardened." Nothing in the story is about bread, so the comment hangs there without explanation. The textual tradition we now call the Gospel according to Matthew reworks the walking on the water story by doing two things: removing the odd and ambiguous reference to misunderstood bread and adding a story about Peter also walking (with mixed results) on the water. While the punchline in the Gospel according to Mark is obscure, the Gospel according to Matthew removes the ambiguities and clarifies a purpose of the story. The Gospel according to Matthew makes clear the tale about a church struggling to survive amid troubled times.[39]

Of course, many more examples could be trotted out, but these four show in broad strokes the ways the Gospel according to Matthew continues the same fluid textual tradition found in the Gospel according to Mark by removing potential problems and ambiguities. In summary, when one approaches the Gospel according to Mark and the Gospel according to Matthew within a framework of ancient writing practices and modes of authorship and conceptions of publication, the two overlapping textual constellations of what modern readers call the Gospel according to Mark and the Gospel according to Matthew should not be viewed as separate books. Simply because they differ does not mean they are different "books." Especially if, as most critical scholars assume, the Gospel according to Mark and the Gospel according to Matthew originally circulated without titles or ascribed authors, it seems most reasonable to think of the textual tradition we call the Gospel according to Matthew as continuing the same unfinished textual tradition of "the gospel" more broadly understood, adding stories to a textual tradition that help that tradition conform better to ancient readers' expectations about what should be in a story about an individual.[40] The alterations of stories often fit well within the framework of a person's clarifying potentially ambiguous or misleading elements in an unfinished draft.

## *The Many Endings of the Incomplete Gospel according to Mark*

Porphyry describes a critic and poet named Zoticus engaging in the act of polishing and improving a text.[41] Zoticus found a piece of writing and revised it, likely because he considered it unfinished yet full of potential. He corrected it where it was unpolished. He altered the shape of the poem. He produced *The Atlanticos*. It would surely be reductive of a modern critical scholar to label as forgery or adulteration what Porphyry himself regards as a sign of artistry by a skilled critic and poet. Similarly, as we saw in chapter 2, Hirtius added another book to Caesar's unfinished *commentarii* about his war in Gaul because he knew the genre of *commentarii/hypomnēmata* invited such revision and because he thought Caesar's notes needed a better conclusion. The different versions of Esther show how a fluid tradition can grow and evolve, both textually and ideologically.[42] Irene Peirano Garrison notes persuasively how Servius often preferred the "better" or "improved" text of Virgil, emended by later editors and correctors, over the "original" unfinished one left by Virgil himself.[43]

The Gospel according to Matthew was not the only attempt to fill in what was lacking in the Gospel according to Mark. In fact, if we acknowledge the openness of the Gospel according to Mark, it should come as no surprise that the manuscript tradition contains a wide variety of options for how the story ends. The different endings of the Gospel according to Mark illustrate the openness of the textual tradition and offer a variety of examples to maintain vitality in the gospel tradition by expanding the text with new endings.[44]

Most text critics think the Gospel according to Mark "originally" ended at 16:8 with these words about the women at the tomb:[45]

> And after they went out, they fled from the tomb, for trembling and entrancement (*ekstasis*) had taken hold of them. They did not say anything to anyone, for they were terrified (*ephobounto gar*).

No doubt this constitutes a highly unusual conclusion. In addition to the unusual content, it is also linguistically strange, as the Greek text "ends" with a postpositive conjunction, "for" (*gar*). While it was rare, though not impossible, to end a narrative with the conjunction "for," it was certainly a bit bizarre.[46] Moreover, while the Gospel according to Mark anticipates Jesus's post-resurrection appearance in Galilee, the event never actually transpires in the so-called original ending.[47] In some ways, one might say that the Gospel according to Mark does not really have an ending. In the ancient Greek literary contexts in which revision of unfinished texts occurred, it seems likely that someone would have experienced the Gospel according to Mark as crying out for an ending. Several people did, and in fact gave it new endings.

In addition to the so-called original ending of the Gospel according to Mark that leaves the reader with terrified women, a dangling *gar*, and no appearance of Jesus, the manuscript tradition bears witness to three additional endings.

*The Shorter Ending*[48]
They [the women who were at the tomb] reported briefly to those around Peter everything that they had been commanded. Afterwards, Jesus himself sent out through them from the east to the west the holy and imperishable proclamation of eternal salvation. Amen.

*The Longer Ending*
16:9. After Jesus rose early on the first day of the week, he appeared first to Mary Magdalene, from whom he had cast seven demons. 16:10. She went out and announced to those who had been with him, while they were mourning and weeping. 16:11. Even when they heard that he was alive and had been seen by her, they did not believe. 16:12. After these things, Jesus appeared in another form to two of them who were walking out into the country. 16:13. And these [two] went out and brought news to the rest, but they did not believe them. 16:14. But later Jesus appeared to the eleven while they were reclining at table

and he reprimanded their unbelief and hardheartedness, because they had not believed those who had seen him after he had been raised. 16:15. Jesus said to them: go out into the whole world and announce the good news to the whole creation. 16:16. The person who believes and is baptized will be saved, but the one who does not believe will be condemned. 16:17. Now these signs will accompany those who believe: they will cast out demons in my name, they will speak in new languages, 16:18. and they will pick up snakes [with their hands], and even if they drink some deadly poison, it will in no way harm them, they will lay hands on the sick and they will be made well. 16:19. So then Lord Jesus, after he had spoken to them, was taken up into heaven and sat down at the right hand of God. 16:20. They went out and proclaimed everywhere, while the Lord worked with them and confirmed their message through the accompanying signs. [Amen.][49]

*The Longer Ending with the Freer Logion*
(inserted between verses 14 and 15 of the longer ending)
 And they defended themselves by saying "this age of lawlessness and unbelief is under the control of Satan, who does not allow the truth and power of God to overtake the unclean things produced by the spirits. That's why we ask you to reveal your righteousness right away." They said this to Christ, and Christ addressed them, "The years of Satan's authority are up, but other awful things are coming near. It was on behalf of those who have sinned that I have been handed over to death, in order that they might turn back to the truth and not sin any more, in order that they might inherit the spiritual and uncorrupted heavenly glory of righteousness."

From a certain perspective, it makes sense to speak about four possible endings to the Gospel according to Mark. Yet from the perspective of material philology, which attends to manuscripts not as witnesses to a lost "original" but as textual objects in their own right, the number of endings would be far higher. As we shall see, each individual manuscript might pick and choose from the variety of endings, and might pick more than one possibility. If paratextual notes are taken into account, the number of possibilities of how to end the Gospel according to Mark increase greatly, as each note may give readers a different piece of advice, which in turn the reader may or may not take.

In addition to the four endings just discussed, Codex Bobiensis (*k*) may also be regarded as yet another ending. While it not typically categorized as a "fifth ending" to the Gospel according to Mark, it does not neatly map onto the reading of any of the other endings. Codex Bobiensis was copied in the fourth century and is the oldest surviving Latin gospel book.[50] The Latin text to which it attested, however, comes from earlier than the fourth century and may derive from North Africa at a time before Cyprian of Carthage in the third century CE.[51] It is the only surviving manuscript that contains the shorter ending of the Gospel according to Mark without also supplying the longer ending.[52] Additionally, however, much of the ending of the Gospel according to Mark in Codex Bobiensis does not match other Greek or Latin manuscripts. Appendix B presents the text of Codex Bobiensis without grammatical or spelling corrections compared with the Nestle-Aland 28th edition of the Greek New Testament and the Latin Vulgate in parallel synopsis.

Codex Bobiensis differs significantly from the Latin Vulgate and other Latin manuscripts. At times, it appears to be a divergent translation of similar underlying Greek. Yet at other times, it appears to deal with a Greek text that differs from early Greek manuscripts and from the Greek source text behind the Vulgate. As noted, it is the only manuscript that moves directly from the fleeing women at the tomb to the shorter ending without any notation of textual problems. Furthermore, Codex Bobiensis adds in 16:4 a fascinating, otherwise-unattested addition (33 Latin words) to the Gospel according to Mark about the moment of resurrection itself:

> But suddenly at the third hour of the day darkness came over the whole world and angels from heaven descended and, as he was rising in the brightness of the living God, at the same time they [the angels] ascended with him and immediately there was light.

For the most part, I follow the text established by John Wordsworth, but I also follow the conjectural emendation suggested by Bruce Metzger, changing *surgent* ("they will arise") to *surgente eo* ("and as he was rising").[53] The reading of Mark 16 in Codex Bobiensis provides details not found in other manuscripts of the Gospel according to Mark about what happened *inside* the tomb.[54] Angels are given meaningful agency: the act of resurrecting Jesus from the dead. The resurrection is associated with brightness and light. Moreover, in this reading Jesus ascends right away with the angels, and it would appear this ascension is to heaven, from which the angels had come in the first place. Thus, the ascension happens immediately after the resurrection.

All translation is interpretation, and as such, there is no naturally occurring line between what constitutes a translation and what constitutes a new version of a work. In fact, the line is always blurred.[55] Nonetheless, Codex Bobiensis contains enough new additions and textual variance that it may be regarded, at least from a certain perspective, as a fifth, different ending to the Gospel according to Mark.

The variety of possible endings, by their very existence, demonstrates a few things. First, when we focus on these manuscripts as evidence of readers and practice, they demonstrate moments of people or communities who found the Gospel according to Mark useful. That is, evidently people were using the textual tradition we now call the Gospel according to Mark in some fashion, whether in liturgy, teaching, preaching, or otherwise. If no one used it, it never would have received new endings. Second, while they found the textual tradition we now call the Gospel according to Mark useful, the versions reveal instances of readers regarding the gospel as incomplete and lacking a sufficient ending. Third, they confirm evidence of early readers regarding the textual tradition we now call the Gospel according to Mark not only as unfinished but also as open, and therefore able to be further reworked. Like Hirtius, the producers of the three longer endings show people treating it as *hypomnēmata* or otherwise unfinished.

The shorter ending is reasonably short, adding only two rather ornate sentences, and basically covering just enough ground to have Jesus appear and give his disciples a commission to evangelize the world. Its language is more grandiose than the rest of the Gospel according to Mark. The shorter ending also concludes in some manuscripts with an "amen," which reflects liturgical use. The longer ending recapitulates the resurrection appearances from other gospel traditions and adds passages about signs to accompany Jesus's disciples, which will validate the authenticity of their message.

The Freer Logion is found in Codex Washingtonianus (W), which dates to the fourth or fifth century CE.[56] In terms of reading and using the Gospel according to Mark, it does to the longer ending of the Gospel according to Mark what the longer ending does to the shortest ending: it fills in gaps. It is a growth of tradition within a growth of tradition. The Freer Logion clarifies ambiguities and lingering questions created by the longer ending. It offers an *apologia* from the disciples about why in the longer ending they cannot seem to believe, even after Mary Magdalene and the other two disciples tell them about Jesus's resurrection: the current age is under the power of Satan and is blinded to God's true power. Just as the producers of the longer ending perceived unfinishedness within the Gospel according to Mark, so also the producers of the Freer Logion perceived the longer ending to be lacking and incomplete. Thus, the Freer Logion illustrates that textual unfinishedness is not unanimously agreed upon nor is it static. Readers are the ones who determine textual unfinishedness, and that changes from time to time, place to place, and reader to reader. Unfinishedness is discursive, negotiated in each particular context, and not uniform among readers. As long as there are questions to ask and gaps to fill, textual unfinishedness remains a possibility.

Several manuscripts contain multiple, different endings.[57] For instance, Codex Regius (L; eighth century) and Codex Athous Laurae (Ψ; ninth or tenth century) offer both shorter and longer endings.[58] In such manuscripts, readers find themselves in a choose-your-own-adventure approach to the ending of the textual tradition we now call the Gospel according to Mark. Readers have the opportunity to collapse the divide between themselves and the textual tradition and to insert themselves into the production of the story. That the resurrected Jesus appeared to his disciples is clear in these manuscripts. How the resurrection appearances occurred is a question open to readers, who are left with more than one option, and therefore must choose for themselves. Moreover, many manuscripts provide readers' notes with information about how to negotiate the textual pluriformity. For instance, in two manuscripts of family 1 (1 and 1582) one finds the following note recorded between 16:1–8 and 16:9–20: "While in some copies the evangelist stopped here, the place in which Eusebius Pamphili also made his canons, but in most copies [vv. 9–20] are also present."[59] These two manuscripts offer both the longer ending (16:9–20) and the shortest ending (stopping in 16:8), but then provide readers with notes to support both readings and guide them in their decision. Manuscript 1582 also has a marginal note next to the text of Mark 16:19, written in a downward triangular shape, "Irenaeus, who [lived] close to [the time of] the apostles, in the third book of his *Against Heresies*, attributed this statement as being in Mark."[60] Thus, in manuscript 1582, the reader is confronted with multiple voices from the past as informants, though the reader is ultimately the one who is left to make meaning of the endings of the Gospel according to Mark.

The longer ending of the Gospel according to Mark, which is the story represented by the Majority Text, is found in 16:9–20 in many critical editions of the New Testament. James Kelhoffer has argued that the author of Mark 16:9–20 created an ending that was an amalgamation of the resurrection appearances in the other gospels and Acts.[61] He argues that the author of the longer ending of the Gospel according to Mark (16:9–20) shows respect for the four canonical gospels and that "this author, like the author of Mark's shorter ending, considered the Gospel according to Mark valuable enough to be improved in order to meet the needs of his and future generations."[62] But then Kelhoffer labels the shorter and longer endings of the Gospel according to Mark forgeries.[63] Yet he never clearly defines "forgery."[64] He seems to assume that his ancient and modern audiences would share the same conceptions of forgery.[65] His comparison of the longer ending of the

Gospel according to Mark with the *Epistle to the Laodiceans* is unhelpful, since the *Epistle to the Laodiceans* is a new, separate literary creation, whereas the longer ending of the Gospel according to Mark is the reworking of the same already existing text.[66] If, as I have argued, we take the Gospel according to Mark as an unfinished note collection, new perspectives on the multitude of options for ending the textual tradition we now call the Gospel according to Mark emerge. We may imagine that, as was often the case with unfinished texts, the various new endings constitute an acceptable act of continuing and improving an open text. Forgeries fabricate an authentic writing, or perhaps make false authorial claims about a well-known person; adding to an unfinished text, rather, improves upon a text perceived to be open and in some way ambiguous or lacking.[67] All the new endings of the textual tradition of the Gospel according to Mark may be better understood in the latter category, because they attempt to rework the text we now call the Gospel according to Mark by adding (what was perceived to be) a much-needed proper ending—complete with a resurrected Jesus and all. Stated simply, adding an ending to an unfinished text would be regarded as a proper response to such a text.

## *Conclusion*

The Gospel according to Mark has been read as both beautiful and brutish, like a powerful lion. Narrative critics often point to the power and intricacy of "Mark's" story; historical critics occasionally malign "Mark" as a clumsy editor with bad Greek and poor theological sensibilities. Both these arguments have been based to one degree or another on the assumption that the Gospel according to Mark is a finished and fully authored book of some sort.

The interaction between the textual traditions we now call the Gospels according to Matthew and Mark, as well as the variety of ways of ending the Gospel according to Mark, are concrete data points that demonstrate early readers' attempts to revise and polish existing *hypomnēmata*, thus improving the Gospel according to Mark's rough yet powerful text. That is to say, perhaps there is a way to understand the text we now call the Gospel according to Mark as a powerful text that was not "finished" until the tradition we now call the Gospel according to Matthew took it up and continued it by reworking it, until the various longer endings of the Gospel according to Mark added proper resurrection narratives, until later prologues were added, until the different gospel traditions were gathered together into a fourfold gospel, until commentators made meaning of the text, until modern narrative critics supply readers with nuanced readings, and so on.

# 7

# *Reading Mark as Unfinished*

IN 2016, THE Metropolitan Museum of Art in New York City offered an exhibit called "Unfinished."[1] It had collected and curated unfinished works of art in order to ask the question: When is a work finished? It presented two types of unfinished works: works that just happened to be left in an unfinished state and works that seem to have been intentionally left unfinished by the artist. One type represents the accidents of history; for instance, one painting in the exhibit was left unfinished because the sitter left for the Vietnam War and never returned to sit for the rest of the painting.[2] The other type represents a crafted, self-conscious attempt to leave a work open and in a state of liminal unresolvedness. Intentionally unfinished works of art are treated differently, and have received the designation of a *non finito* work of art. In the end, however, it is not always easy to distinguish cleanly between the two types of unfinished works. It is often easier to speak from the point of view of reception, reader or viewer expectations, and cultural *habitus*.

Briefly, a word about what I mean by the term "unfinishedness." One should not assume a state of perfect finishedness as its binary. It is misleading to think that all texts must be categorized as either unfinished or finished. Strictly speaking, no work or text is ever perfectly, completely, irreversibly finished. The works of art selected by the curators of the "Unfinished" exhibit showcase well the complicated and social nature of unfinishedness. On one hand, the works in the exhibit were selected because they were experienced as unfinished. But on the other hand, the very act of their placement in the exhibit has something of a finishing effect on the work. They are "finished" as an exhibition of unfinished works of art. Yet, from a different perspective, it is also conceivable that the original artist, another artist, or—frankly—any attendee at the exhibit could pick up a brush or a trowel and alter the work yet again. At issue is what Mikhail Bakhtin calls "unfinalizability": the idea that a work, text, dialogue, relationship, or even one's approach to the world is open, incomplete, fluid, interactive, social, and oriented toward the future.³ So long as a work is being encountered by readers and communities, degrees of unfinishedness are socially negotiated, again and again. By "unfinishedness," then, I refer to the posture with which one interacts with or receives a text.

Unfinished written texts are not limited only to pre-printing press, premodern contexts. Ernest Mandel notes that Karl Marx's second and third volumes of *Capital* were left unfinished at the time of Marx's death, and their unfinishedness, he insists, must impact one's reading of each volume.⁴ Similarly, Walter Benjamin's *The Arcade Project* attracts attention not despite but because it is an unfinished collection of notes.⁵ Moving to the ancient world, Sean Gurd draws attention to several ancient Greek literary papyri left still in the process of revision. He notes that the order and even purpose of the revision can often be determined, and the revision process is not necessarily a linear one.⁶ *P.Oxy.* 2070 exhibits doodling and notes that seem to reflect a work that is still open or otherwise in progress.⁷ Naturally, unfinished works were less frequently copied, and thus relatively few unfinished works survive from antiquity into the present. Select examples, however, can be found.

I do not wish to speculate here about the intentions of the producer(s) of the Gospel according to Mark. That is, I do not argue that the Gospel according to Mark was intentionally crafted to be an unfinished text, a *non finito* work of art. My claim is more modest: the Gospel according to Mark was regularly described and received by its earliest readers and users as less finished, more rough, open, revisable, unpublished, and not very "bookish." My question is not what the Gospel according to Mark is but what it was to its earliest readers. I argue it is productive to read the Gospel according to Mark as unfinished notes (*hypomnēmata*). When we do, we begin to envision a way of experiencing it that is native to first- and second-century readers, long before it became a "gospel," "narrative," or a "biography," as it certainly did in later centuries.

Reading the Gospel according to Mark as an unfinished collection of notes poses new questions regarding the text. For instance, if one assumes the Gospel according to Mark is a book with an author weaving a coherent narrative, then one would try to understand how each particular story fits into the whole narrative, from beginning to end, creating a unified portrait or trajectory. The assumption of an author producing a coherent narrative underwrites the practice of reading one passage in light of another seemingly contradictory passage. It assures the reader that each passage plays a part in the same story, viewpoint, or ideology. That is, if an author produced a book, one can reasonably try to discern the "mind of the author" by reading each passage in light of the whole. It is sort of like solving a puzzle or opening a safe; the interpreter must find the right code, so that all will fall into place.

If, however, one treats the Gospel according to Mark as an unfinished collection of notes, different possibilities emerge. It is not about how an author would craft an individual story to fit within a larger monological narrative but, rather, how a person or community would collect stories in a useful and logical manner. One need no longer necessarily picture an authorial genius weaving an intricate tapestry designed to convey a meaning or moral. When we dispense with the metaphor of the book and an authorial genius as its creator, different options become available. With respect to the Gospel according to Mark and its earliest readers, I suggest the image of a person or persons compiling textual records of stories from a wide variety of sources, rewriting them for later rereading, liturgical recitation, or teaching. The issue is less about polish, pleasure, and elegance and more about utility. Thus, understanding the textual tradition we now call the Gospel according to Mark as a collection of unfinished notes reconfigures the way one understands the kind of unity the text has.

## Understanding the Order and Logic of Unfinished Notes

Up to this point, one may have resisted the idea of labeling the text we call the Gospel according to Mark (as we have its text constructed in critical editions) as *hypomnēmata*, because one senses a logic in the organization of the text, and it is assumed that such unfinished note collections would lack such order. Texts like *hypomnēmata*, however, do have a logic to their organization, but the logic of unfinished notes differs from the logic of a finished book or an episodic narrative. *Hypomnēmata* are meant to be practical resources, usually for known or limited audiences, but they are helpful only if the notes contain an order or textual organization readily accessible to its users. At issue is producing a text to meet reader expectations, even if the producer happens to be the same person as the reader.

As a narrative is expected to have a particular literary arrangement (*taxis, suntaxis*), an unfinished note collection would also be expected have its own type of order or organization. Consider the following example from recension B of the *Testament of Abraham* in which a collection of notes appears. The scene picks up as the archangel Michael takes Abraham into paradise to see the process of human judgment.

Then Michael took Abraham upon a cloud, and led him into Paradise. And when he came to the place where the judge was, the angel came and gave that soul to the judge. And the soul said: "Lord have mercy on me." And the judge said: "How will I have mercy upon you, when you had no mercy upon your daughter which you had, the fruit of your womb? Why did you slay her?" It answered: "No, Lord, slaughter has not been done by me, but my daughter has lied against me." But the judge commanded him to come that wrote down the records (*ton ta hypomnēmata graphonta*). And behold, cherubim (were) carrying two books (*biblia duo*).... And the man had in his hand a golden pen, and the judge said to him: "Exhibit the sin of this soul." And that man, opening one of the books of the cherubim, sought out (*anezētēsen*) the sin of the woman's soul and found it (*heuren*). And the judge said: "O wretched soul, why do say that you have not committed murder? "Did you not, after the death of your husband, go and commit adultery with your daughter's husband, and kill her?" And he convicted her also of her other sins, whatsoever she had done from her youth.[8]

In the story, a huge man is constantly making *hypomnēmata*, producing textual records of human deeds. The man's *hypomnēmata* are then collected into two books, which cherubim bring to the scene of judgment. The books are archived in such a way that one is able to navigate them quickly, which given their function, must have been truly huge (see the parallel scene in recension A; *T.Ab.* 12.7). In this instance, one could imagine an arrangement by person and in chronological order or by type of sinful action, or both.[9] That is, it would be something like Person A, Year A, Sin $A_1$; Person A, Year A, Sin $A_2$; Person A, Year A, Sin $B_1$, and so forth.

In *Flacc.* 131, discussed in chapter 2, Philo also makes the point that *hypomnēmata* often had a form of *taxis*. Flaccus stands near the rulers and takes notes (*hypomnēmata*) on the cases he hears. He then creates a system of organization for filing his notes on cases (*eisagōn hōs echōn taxin*). The organization allows Flaccus to return easily to a certain case and erase, interpolate, or rewrite the notes as was most politically and economically expedient for him. The organization of the *hypomnēmata* demonstrates a kind of arrangement (*taxis*), but the arrangement differed from the arrangement of a piece of literature.

People who intend to go back and use their notes usually arrange them in some sort of a memorable and useful way. The logic of the order depends on the intended use of the notes. Sometimes the order of the notes can be highly nuanced. Benjamin, for instance, described his *Arcade Project* as a collage or montage of thirty-six sections that he called "convolutes." David Ferris explains the work: "Each convolute is dominated by quotations removed from their contexts and placed in montage-like relations to each other. Interspersed amongst these are notes and observations made by Benjamin. Beyond this organization, it is difficult to say precisely what Benjamin had in mind for the final form of the work."[10] Michel Foucault notes the logic of creation, preservation, and use of *hypomnēmata*:

> One wrote down quotes in them, extracts from books, examples, and actions that one had witnessed or read about, reflections or reasonings that one had heard or that had come to mind. They constituted a material record of things read, heard, or thought, thus offering them up as a kind of accumulated treasure for subsequent rereading and meditation. They also formed a raw material for the drafting of more systematic treatises, in which one presented arguments and means for struggling against some weakness (such as anger, envy, gossip, flattery) or for overcoming some difficult circumstance (a grief, an exile, ruin, disgrace).... These *hypomnemata* should not be thought of simply as a memory support, which might be consulted from time to time, as occasion arose; they are not meant to be substituted for a recollection that may fail. They constitute, rather, a material and a framework for exercises to be carried out frequently: reading, rereading, meditating, conversing with oneself and with others.[11]

Those who organize notes do not do so with the same logic as one would a narrative. They place ideas in juxtaposition with one another, with the whole being greater than the sum of its parts. The collection is designed to produce and enable rereading, reflection, rewriting, reworking, and reuse. Though some general principles may apply, each set of notes would be organized to fit its particular function. If we take clues from the earliest readers and users of the Gospel according to Mark, are we able to read the textual tradition we call the Gospel according to Mark as *hypomnēmata*? That is, does the Gospel according to Mark bear signs of being organized like *hypomnēmata*?

## *Ancient Organization of Notes*

Collecting notes by topic or keyword was common in antiquity, as it is still today. In chapter 2, we saw Plutarch was pressed for time and grabbed his set of notes on the topic of tranquillity of the soul and sent them to Paccius. This suggests that Plutarch perhaps had filed notes together on the topic of tranquillity of the soul. A. Locher and R. C. A. Rottländer argue that Pliny the Elder read, took notes, and arranged them by keywords (*Schlüsselwörter*), probably on wooden tablets not unlike the Vindolanda tablets.[12] Tiziano Dorandi has shown in *P.Herc* 1021 an example of how an ancient writer (in this case, Philodemus) might arrange notes and then later reuse them in producing a composition.[13] The back of the text contains arranged excerpts and thoughts, while the front of the text puts the notes into a more literary arrangement and prose. Aulus Gellius refers to his *Attic Nights* as *commentarii* and describes their arrangement.

> But in the arrangement of my material I have adopted the same haphazard order that I had previously followed in collecting it. For whenever I had taken in hand any Greek or Latin book, or had heard anything worth remembering, I used to jot down whatever took my fancy, of any and every kind, without any definite plan or order; and such notes I would lay away as an aid to my memory, like a kind of literary storehouse, so that when the need arose of a subject or a word (*aut rei aut verbi*) which I chanced for the moment to have forgotten, and the books from which I had taken it were not at hand, I could readily find and produce it.[14]

Like the other examples mentioned, Gellius arranged his notes (*commentarii*) by subject and word (*aut rei aut verbi*). Ironically, while *Attic Nights* itself possesses a highly nuanced style, Gellius taps into a culturally recognizable practice of note organization to present his work as not really a polished piece of literature so much as some notes he "just happened" to have thrown together. Moreover, while *Attic Nights* is "narrative," it nonetheless presents itself as notes. The ostensible purpose of the arrangement of his "literary storehouse" (*litterarum penus*) in an order arranged by word and subject was so that he could access them easily at some later point. They are designed, he claims, for utility, not for serious literary consumption. Annewies van den Hoek notes a similar method of note-taking and arrangement in the writings of Clement of Alexandria.[15]

While arrangement by keyword or subject was common, it was not the only way to maintain and arrange an evolving note collection. As mentioned earlier, the *Testament of Abraham* seems to envision an archive arranged either by person or chronology or both. Similarly, Lorenzo Perilli has made a case that at Epidaurus an archive of individual patients' files may have been recorded for subsequent reference (in a fashion similar to Strabo and Pliny the Elder).[16] There is not one right way to collect notes or records. Arranging notes (*hypomnēmata*) by keyword and subject was one way, but in order for records to be readily accessible and beneficial, one would order the texts with a logic befitting the material and its particular uses.

## *The Logic and Structure of the Gospel according to Mark as Unfinished Collection of Notes*

If we take the earliest readers and users seriously in their characterization of the Gospel according to Mark as *hypomnēmata*, we might expect to find an arrangement more suited to the logic of unfinished note collections than episodic narrative structure. The outline of the Gospel according to Mark has presented problems to interpreters. It is commonplace in Markan scholarship to mention Martin Kähler's aphorism: the Gospel according to Mark is a passion narrative with an extended introduction.[17] Many have found Kähler's comment amusing, since in such a framework the introduction would be significantly longer than the main topic. Labeling everything up to the passion narrative "an extended introduction" was a clever way of saying that all the stories from the beginning of the text to the passion do not hang together in any kind of an obvious narrative way. The famed afterlife of Kähler's comment likely comes both from its wit and from the fact that many intuitively recognize some truth in it.

Many different and competing attempts have been made to "outline" the Gospel according to Mark, though I will not describe them here.[18] It seems clear that Mark did not write an "episodic narrative, one in which episodes . . . follow each other according to the laws of inevitability or even of probability."[19] Despite the many attempts to describe Mark's narrative structure, no clear consensus exists. For example, after entertaining a topographical and a topical outline structure (favoring the topical over the topographical), Robert Gundry concludes that no outline structure really works and that the Gospel according to Mark is more of a collage than anything else.[20] Adela Yarbro Collins avoids the word *outline*, but writes of the composition and structure of the Gospel according to Mark, addressing narrative unity in smaller chunks throughout her commentary (for example, 1:16–45), rather than offering her own overall narrative structure in her introduction.[21] Building on these observations, I note a different kind of structure, one that does not presuppose the logic of monological authorial genius, but one that is in keeping with the organization of *hypomnēmata*.

In a similar though not identical manner to other arrangements of *hypomnēmata*, the Gospel according to Mark also groups stories together by topic and keyword.[22] Moreover, the Gospel according to Mark brackets each set of notes with parallel stories. In addition to an introduction, the Gospel according to Mark contains five sets of notes.[23] Within each set are other groupings, such as a group of parables, groups of miracles, and so forth. The structure of each set of notes differs from one another.

The people in the first centuries of the Common Era who used and produced the stories in the textual tradition we now call the Gospel according to Mark did so in a wide variety of places and contexts, and for a variety of reasons. We should think of notes as open, in progress, and thus changing all the time. Some of the producer(s) may have heard preached and later textualized and altered. Others the producer(s) may have found already textualized, read them, and rewrote them in the note collection to use them again later. Still others the producer(s) may have invented themselves, perhaps while reading a Psalm or passages from the Hebrew Bible, or reflecting on it in a preaching or didactic context. For instance, Mark 4:35–41 may have emerged in connection with meditation on Psalm 107:25–30 and the Book of Jonah.[24] The producer(s) wrote down each story in his(their) own writing style, though influenced by the language he(they) received. Some recurring themes, such as the messianic secret or suffering, and certain linguistic "ticks," such as the frequent use of the word *immediately* (*euthus/eutheias/eutheōs*; 42 times), appear throughout the text, yet their sheer repetition does not constitute a narrative unity. Each set of notes and the overall structure of various sets of notes within the Gospel according to Mark suggest rereading, meditating, and reworking of stories, especially the intercalation of stories—one of the more "finished" aspects of the Gospel according to Mark.

Some aspects of the keyword and bracketing structure have already been noted by Markan scholars, although without appreciating the historical textual and writing practices behind it—namely, the production and collection of *hypomnēmata*. Many scholars treat Mark 8:22–10:52 (or 8:27–10:45) as a unit, observing that it begins and ends with a healing of a blind person, repeats the phrase "on the way" (or "beside the way" or "in the way") several times, and has three passion predictions.[25] I argue, however, that the structure of 8:22–10:52 is similar to *hypomnēmata* or *commentarii*, as described by other ancient writers. Often such collections of notes were grouped together by keyword and topic. The topic is Jesus's journey to Jerusalem to suffer. "On the way" (*en tē hodō*) is a repeated key phrase, but there are also others. Seeing properly is also a key theme. Seeing, in its various cognate forms, appears eleven times in 8:22–10:52.²⁶ While the execution of Jesus looms over the whole Gospel according to Mark, the necessity of the "Son of Man" to suffer comes through in the 8:22–10:52 set of notes, as seeing Jesus clearly means following Jesus on the way to suffering in Jerusalem. The bracketing of a set of keywords and ideas with parallel stories is unique to the Gospel according to Mark, to my knowledge, when compared to other *hypomnēmata*, but it fits well with the logic of grouping stories and anecdotes by keywords and themes for later use and meditation. It is a practical way of setting off the notes in 8:22–10:52 from other sets.

This note-like structure of the Gospel according to Mark does not just appear in 8:22–10:52; it can be seen throughout the text. When one looks for keywords and topics bracketed by parallel stories, five sets of notes emerge, as shown in table 7.1.

Having discussed 8:22–10:52, let us look at the other sets of notes. Mark 1:21–3:6 contains a set of notes organized under the keywords of Jesus's activity in synagogues on the Sabbath. *Sabbath* (*sabbaton*) occurs eight times and

Table 7.1 Structure of Note Collections in the Gospel according to Mark

| Chapters & Verses | Keywords | Topics | Bracketing Stories |
| --- | --- | --- | --- |
| 1:21–3:6 | Sabbath, synagogue | Mighty deeds and opposition | Exorcism in synagogue on the Sabbath (1:21–28) and healing in a synagogue on the Sabbath (3:1–6) |
| 3:7–6:30 | twelve, sending | Hearing and doing; the sea and discipleship | The making of the twelve (3:7–19) and the sending of the twelve (6:6b–30) |
| 6:31–8:21 | bread, eating | Eating with insiders and outsiders | Feeding of the five thousand (6:31–45) and feeding of the four thousand (and debriefing) (8:1–21) |
| 8:22–10:52 | "on the way," seeing | Seeing clearly, following Jesus, and suffering | Healing the blind man twice (8:22–26) and healing Blind Bartimaeus (10:46–52) |
| 11:1–16:8 | temple, Jerusalem | Jesus's death and the fate of the temple | Jesus's entry into Jerusalem (11:1–11) ad Jesus's exit from Jerusalem (15:40–16:8) |

*synagogue* (*sunagōgē*) occurs five times.²⁷ Cognates of *sunagōgē*—*sunagō* and *episunagō*—also appear in Mark 1:33 and 2:2. The words *Sabbath* and *synagogue* (and its cognates) occur in almost every passage (1:21–22, 23–28; 29–38; 38–45; 2:1–12; 23–29; 3:1–6).²⁸ The themes are mighty deeds and opposition to Jesus's action for not observing ritual boundaries of food, time, and place. Two stories of Jesus performing mighty deeds in a synagogue on the Sabbath bracket the set of notes (1:21–28; 3:1–6). In Mark 1:21–28, Jesus exorcises a demon in a synagogue and the people greet him with excitement. In Mark 3:1–6, Jesus heals a man's hand and Jewish religious leaders plot to kill him. The text says that Jesus operated in Capernaum and the surrounding area of Galilee (1:21, 35, 39, 45; 2:1), although oftentimes it is not clear where Jesus is. The space of the synagogue seems more important than Jesus's precise geographical location.

Within the set of notes collected in 1:21–3:6 are other groupings of stories. Joanna Dewey notes the stories of 2:1–3:6 go together as a cohesive unit.²⁹ While I remain skeptical, I think it is possible that the producer(s) of the Gospel according to Mark received these stories from another source as a unit. Yet if we read the Gospel according to Mark as an unfinished note collection, the question is not *how* "Mark" the author crafted such stories but *where* the "note writer(s)" (*hypomnēmatographos*) of the text we now call the Gospel according to Mark grouped the stories within the overall note collection. The answer is the producer(s) placed the stories within the set of stories in 1:21–3:6 because they address issues of mighty deeds, synagogues, and Sabbath activity. Thus, they belong bracketed within the synagogue and Sabbath controversy set of notes.

There is, however, a narrative progression within the set of notes collected in 1:21–3:6. In 1:21–45, Jesus performs mighty deeds, by and large, without opposition (at least direct human opposition). His mighty deeds are met with eager response. In 2:1–3:6, however, Jesus performs similar mighty deeds, but faces opposition from Jewish religious leaders. Within the note-like organization of 1:21–3:6, one also finds narrative structures, which allow for rereading, preaching, and teaching. Thus, the question of narrative versus note structure is neither binary nor zero-sum.

The second set of notes (3:7–6:30) is organized around the making, preparing, and sending of the twelve as apostles. The calling of the twelve in 3:7–19 and their sending in 6:6b–30 bracket this set of notes, each of which is paired with another story.

> And he appointed twelve, whom he also named apostles, to be with him, and to be sent out to proclaim the message, and to have authority to cast out demons. (Mark 3:14–15; NRSV)

He called the twelve and began to send them out two by two, and gave them authority over the unclean spirits (Mark 6:7; NRSV).

Between these bracketing stories, the focus of the set of notes is on the disciples' hearing Jesus teach and watching Jesus do mighty deeds, so that the disciples themselves may also go preach and do mighty deeds. There are two pairs of keywords around which 3:7–6:30 is organized: the *twelve* (*dōdeka*) and *sending* (*apostellō*).[30] Other sets of keywords, *sea* (*thalassa*) and *boat* (*ploion*), are also collected into the set of notes. The word *twelve* appears six times and *sending* appears seven times; *sea* appears nine times and *boat* ten times (including the diminutive *ploiarion* in Mark 3:9). Every story in the set of notes in 3:7–6:31 has a keyword in it, often more than one, and often used more than once.[31] "Being with Jesus" also joins the stories of 3:7–19 and the exorcism of the Gerasene demoniac in 5:1–20 (see 5:18).

Within the set of notes, smaller groupings of notes can be seen. Collections of parables are grouped side by side in 3:20–4:34.

And Jesus called them and began to speak to them in parables, ... (Mark 3:23)

And he was teaching them many things in parables and he began to say this teaching to them.... (Mark 4:2; see also 4:10, 11, 13, 30, 33, 34)

Along with Jesus speaking in parables, proper "hearing" is also a major theme, as the verb *akouō* and its cognates occurs twenty-five times in these chapters, and in almost every story. Hearing first and then doing is another topic in the 3:7–6:30 set of notes. The disciples hear Jesus teach in 3:20–4:34, then see him doing mighty deeds in 4:35–5:43, and then they preach and do mighty deeds themselves in 6:6b–31, following Jesus's example.

Moreover, stories about daughters or little girls are brought together and interpolated toward the end of the set of notes. The words *daughter* (*thugatēr; thugatrion*) and *little girl* (*korasion*) appear nine times in 5:23–6:28. Two stories involving daughters and little girls, each twelve (*dōdeka*) years old, are sandwiched together in 5:21–43, and a story about Herodias's daughter is interpolated in the story of the sending and return of the twelve (*dōdeka*) in 6:6b–31. So, the structure of the note collection is not haphazard, like a disorderly filing cabinet, but shows careful organization and interpolation, perhaps designed for later reflection, teaching, and preaching.

Perhaps the most easily discernable example of the Gospel according to Mark being organized like *hypomnēmata* comes from the third set of notes in Mark 6:31–8:21, which is bracketed by the feeding of the five thousand in 6:31–45 and the feeding of the four thousand (along with a debrief with Jesus and the disciples on the feeding) in 8:1–21. Moreover, every story in the set of notes, except for one (7:31–37), mentions bread and/or eating. Read in succession, the stories do not hang together tightly from the perspective of an episodic narrative, with each pericope leading seemingly into the next. Rather it is the bracketed stories and keywords of *bread* and *eating* that hold the collection of stories together. Taken as a collection, the set of notes in 6:32–8:21 selects otherwise heterogeneous stories and arranges them to create a place for reflecting upon or teaching about Jesus's action, table fellowship, and social boundaries. There is, however, also a logic in their progression. As one reads through and meditates upon the set of notes, Jesus moves farther into Gentile territory and, as he goes, the resistance to sharing bread grows among Jewish religious leaders.

I have already mentioned the fourth set of notes found in Mark 8:22–10:52, so I move on to the fifth and final set of notes, Mark 11:1–16:8. Jesus's entrance into Jerusalem from Galilee and Jesus's removal from the city and return to Galilee (announced but not realized) bracket the set of notes. Not surprisingly, the keywords *Jerusalem* and *temple* (both *hieron* and *naos*) occur in most stories throughout the set of notes and thus serve as keywords. The themes uniting the set of notes is the destruction of the temple and its connection with Jesus's impending death. As with other sets of notes in the Gospel according to Mark, various subsets of notes can be seen, many of which possibly existed as a group prior to their being archived in the Gospel according to Mark. The rhetorical showdowns between Jesus and the various Jewish religious leaders in 11:27–12:44 and the apocalyptic discourse in Mark 13:1–37 are two examples that may have had a history prior to being incorporated into the textual tradition we now call the Gospel according to Mark. Adela Yarbro Collins (and others) has argued that much of Mark 14–15 existed as a pre-Markan passion narrative.[32] Moreover, the stories of challenge and riposte, and the discourse about the temple in 11:27–12:44 and the apocalyptic reflection in Mark 13:1–37, could have conceivably had a prior life disconnected from the context of Jesus's looming execution. Yet the producer(s) of the Gospel according to Mark seems(seem) to have taken these elements, recorded them in a collection, reworked them, and sandwiched them in between Jesus's entrance to Jerusalem and his suffering and death in Jerusalem. The purpose of the sandwich likely serves to allow the user to meditate upon the interrelatedness of Jesus's death and the destruction of the temple or to preach or teach on the topic.

Seeing 11:1–16:8 as a set of notes allows a new perspective on one of the endings of the Gospel according to Mark that is perceived to be odd: the terrified silent women in 16:8. Scholars debate whether "Mark" intended to finish his narrative in such a strange way. Some say he did; others say that he did not and must have died before he could finish his story; still others say that the "original" ending of the Gospel according to Mark, which would have continued after 16:8 with a resurrection appearance, has been lost. In order to argue that "Mark" intended to finish his narrative with the conjunction *gar* and with scared women running away from the tomb, some literary critics offer explanations arguing that the Gospel according to Mark is a fine-tuned, brilliantly interwoven, nuanced narrative.[33] The scared, silent women were intended to have a haunting and suggestive impact upon readers. Usually such critics understand the ending in 16:8 as encouraging readers or those listening to the text to go tell the message of resurrection themselves.

While I am sympathetic to the view that the Gospel according to Mark was never finished, approaching the Gospel according to Mark as fluid collection of notes arranged by keywords, themes, and bracketing structure provides a new understanding of Mark 16:8. It is not that "Mark" never finished his narrative but that, when we read the Gospel according to Mark as an unfinished collection of notes (*hypomnēmata*), it is not a narrative, biography, or history (at least not yet).

Thus, the ending of 16:8 serves well as the bracketing story of Jesus leaving the city of Jerusalem and returning to Galilee. It productively ends a set of notes that began with Jesus's entry into Jerusalem more than it concludes a narrative. The set of notes begins with Jesus entering Jerusalem and pronouncing destruction upon the temple. The set ends with Jesus's death, the temple veil tearing from top to bottom, Jesus's burial, and the claim that he will meet the disciples back in Galilee. The story of 16:1–8 is strange, if one presupposes a narrative logic and structure, because in such a context 16:8 must serve as a conclusion to a story. In fact, it can be argued that it serves as an ineffective *dénouement*—if the Gospel according to Mark is taken as a narrative.[34]

But if the Gospel according to Mark has a different logic and is not a finished or polished "biography" (*bios*) or "narrative" (*diēgēsis*), then the oddness of the story of 16:1–8 diminishes. It is a bad conclusion to a narrative. It is a good closing bracket to a set of notes about Jesus in Jerusalem, his death, and the temple, because it tells of Jesus returning from Jerusalem to Galilee, without assuming that the end of the text is the end of a book.

Of course, while a note-like organization pervades the text, the Gospel according to Mark does in fact have some narrative logic to it. That is, while it lacks the narrative elements present in the Gospel according to Matthew, and especially the Gospel according to Luke, like stories about parents, childhood, teaching, things after death, and so forth (see chapters 5 and 6), it nonetheless has a clear beginning and a middle and an end. Jesus's death is foreshadowed early in the text (2:20; 3:6) and Jesus's impending execution remains a recurring theme from 8:31 onward.[35] In fact, it has concentric circles of narrative logic, with each set of notes having its own narrative logic, and the five sets of notes possessing a narrative logic. So, while the Gospel according to Mark is not a narrative (*diēgēsis*), it does have narrative logic to it. One need not think in binary terms. It is not the case that it is *either* a narrative without any note collections *or* a collection of notes with no narrative structure whatsoever. Rather, it *is* an unfinished collection of notes *with* narrative logic.

Can we say anything about how the Gospel according to Mark was used as *hypomnēmata*? *Hypomnēmata* have different textual functions for different contexts. A philosopher's notes would differ in organization and structure from a doctor's or historian's notes. The Gospel according to Mark is structured into units by topic and keyword, and the units seem to be structured to teach and preach about Jesus. One could imagine an early church leader using the Gospel according to Mark as a script for a five-part series teaching the life and death of Jesus.

Many times, the Gospel according to Mark makes clear that the context that gave rise to a miracle (or some other kind of story) was Jesus's teaching or preaching.[36] The words *teaching* (*didaskō*) and *preaching* (*kērussō*) occur thirty-one times in the Gospel according to Mark, and twelve times Jesus is called "teacher" (*didaskolos*). The centrality of the theme of teaching and preaching within the text itself, especially in stories in which the context of teaching is not critical to a story, may provide a clue as to its use as a teacher's guide, with the context of the story and the context of the text coalescing. The Gospel according to Mark, read from the perspective of hypothetical readers in the first few centuries CE, then, looks not like a finished, authored, published book but more like a teacher's script for teaching or preaching the good news, with a set of notes for each unit of teaching.

The community rules found at Qumran, discussed in chapter 4, provide a helpful analogue to the utility and textual function of early gospel texts like the one we now call the Gospel according to Mark. Each local leader and teacher would be the primary user of the text. They are not its author per se but, rather, its authorizers and, thus, would have the authority to alter their own texts as fits their context and needs. The main way an average Jesus follower in first centuries of the Common Era would have experienced the text was through the reoralizing of the textualized script of the gospel. Moreover, the textual pluriformity of the community rules found in the caves of Qumran mirror the textual evolution of gospel texts in the first few centuries of the Common Era.[37] The scripts are performed and remain open and fluid. They are texts authorized and altered by local users and teachers, but they are not books with human authors. While not in content or genre, the textual function and pluriformity of the two traditions show some parallels.

To sum up, the structure of the textual tradition we now call the Gospel according to Mark (as we now have it) demonstrates a structure that coheres with ancient writing practices of creating and compiling *hypomnēmata*. It invites readers, both ancient and modern, to meditate on collections of stories within bracketed sets of stories. An entire book would be needed to do a closer reading of the whole Gospel according to Mark from the perspective of an unfinished note collection. But for the present it is sufficient to note that once one is dislodged from presupposing narrative logic as the only possible form of organization, a different kind of logic emerges within the Gospel according to Mark.

## *Unfinished Notes and Voices in Tension*

What are the implications for readers of approaching the Gospel according to Mark not as a finished book with an author figure but as a collection of *hypomnēmata* geared toward practical use? Mikhail Bakhtin's treatment of Dostoevsky's novels may prove an insightful analogue. In the opening chapter of *Problems of Dostoevsky's Poetics*, Bakhtin surveys the field of critical literature on Dostoevsky's novels. He concludes that an erroneous assumption has led Dostoevsky's critics to misunderstand his works. All of Dostoevsky's critics, according to Bakhtin, have assumed a book or a novel written by an author must possess a monological unity of meaning. "Everyone interprets in his own way Dostoevsky's *ultimate word*, but all equally interpret it as a *single* word, a *single* voice, a *single* accent, and therein lies their fundamental mistake."[38] What Bakhtin critiques as a fundamental flaw of Dostoevsky's interpreters is the desire to see his novels as "cut from a single piece, polished and monolithic."[39] Bakhtin then spends the rest of his book showing how Dostoevsky's novels possess a polyphonic and dialogical unity—they do not have *a* meaning; they have multiple *meanings*. Within the same work exists a whole host of competing voices. Dostoevsky's genius, for Bakhtin, is that he does *not* merge all the voices into one. Unlike Tolstoy, Bakhtin does not understand Dostoevsky to allow one word or one perspective to win in the end, with the goal of making a moral, political, or social point.[40] The dialogical tension is not the problem; it is the point.

Within a dialogical viewpoint, unlike a monological one, an idea is not always presented for the purpose of asserting its truthfulness or mendacity. That is, one does not necessarily present an idea as true, nor does one present a false idea for the sole purpose of tearing it down.[41] The assumption and logic of a single, monological consciousness is the thing that authorizes such interpretive moves. Bakhtin's point, however, is that such presuppositions close off and finalize elements that do not fit on the Procrustean bed.[42] Without the idea of an authorial genius producing a monological narrative, a different approach is possible—one that allows for competing voices and ideas to remain in tension, even in the "final" form of a work. Contradictory elements are not flaws but, rather, assets.

Of course, one need not assume that author figures *only* produce monological writings and writers of unfinished texts *only* produce polyphonic texts. In Bakhtin's reading, Dostoevsky is an author, but his novels are polyphonic. Conversely, one can imagine an unfinished text with a relatively monological message. Thus, when one acknowledges the limitations of author figures and monological unity, unfinished texts with dialogical tension are not the only alternatives.

I find Bakhtin's analysis helpful not because I believe "Mark" produced a dialogical, polyphonic novel *avant la lettre* but because Bakhtin illuminates the connections between the authorial genius, monological unity, and the assumptions of modern interpreters. The presumption of an author figure is what leads an interpreter to read two seemingly contradictory passages in light of one another, making one, upon further analysis, agree with the other after all. Without the assumption of a monological viewpoint, there is no reason why passage A must be made to cohere with passage B. The validity of a hermeneutical Procrustean bed arises from the idea of monological unity, and monological unity arises from the assumption of an author and a monological authorial genius. Thus, losing the author of the Gospel according to Mark allows us to move beyond the quest for his unified literary (or theological) vision and entertain new possibilities.

When one approaches the textual tradition we now call the Gospel according to Mark as *hypomnēmata*, as an unfinished collection of notes, a new hermeneutical perspective comes into play. The idea of an author "finishing" and publishing a book has led readers to seek, and consequently to "find," a unified message within a gospel.[43] What allows some critics, then, to weave the "multilayered" and mutually "subverting" elements of the Gospel according to Mark into a christological unity is the idea of an author figure.[44]

Étienne Trocmé wrote an essay called "Is There a Markan Christology?"[45] Trocmé presents a picture of an author "Mark" who took a rather liberal approach to christology within the social and theological landscape of early Christianity. After surveying and showing the flaws of a wide variety of Markan christologies, Trocmé argues that Mark felt "A fairly elaborate christology was . . . one of the obstacles he met among the church leaders" in their evangelizing responsibilities. Here Trocmé presents a "Mark" who wants to allow all the various voices a place at the table of the early Jesus movement. For Trocmé's Mark, an elaborate christology limits Christianity. Thus, he argues for a simple and plain christology.

I would like to adopt yet rework Trocmé's question, not by asking "Is there *a* Markan Christology?" but, rather, "Are there *christologies* in the textual tradition we now call the Gospel according to Mark?" In fact, within the text we now call the Gospel according to Mark, without the prior assumption of an authorial and authorizing unity of textual meaning, one finds multiple competing christologies in dialogical tension with one another. I am not convinced that the producer(s) of the Gospel according to Mark sought in the end to merge these voices into one winning perspective on christology. Moreover, similar claims can be made about the messianic secret, Jesus's perspective on family and gender, his ability to do mighty deeds, the extent of Jesus's knowledge, and so forth.

Even a casual reading of the Gospel according to Mark shows different and incompatible pictures of Jesus. William R. Telford captures well the kaleidoscopic portrait of Jesus in the Gospel according to Mark with the following quote.

> In reading the Gospel according to Mark from beginning to end, one is immediately struck by the number of narrative images by which its central figure is characterized. He appears as an authoritative teacher (1.21–2), a charismatic prophet (8.27–8) and a popular healer and exorcist (1.32–4). He is described as the "Nazarene" (10.47) and addressed as "Teacher" (4.38), "Rabbi" (9.5), or "Lord" (7:28). He is acclaimed as the "Holy One of God" (1.24), greeted as the "Son of David" (10:47) and confessed as "Christ" (8.29) or "Son of God" (15.39). He speaks of himself, however, as the "Son of Man" and defines his role as that of a servant (10.45). Given the multifaceted representation, how then do

we determine Mark's Christology, his understanding of the person of Jesus?[46]

Telford has succinctly described the many characterizations of Jesus in the Gospel according to Mark. In my approach, however, he has incorrectly presupposed an author figure, "Mark," especially a "Mark" who is primarily concerned with theological correctness and theological errors. In back-to-back passages in the Gospel according to Mark, the perspectives on Jesus can shift dramatically. In 7:1–23, for instance, Jesus comes off as a radical Jewish teacher debating the application of the Torah in relation to food and purity, even going so far as to declare all foods clean. Then in 7:24–30, Jesus appears as a Jewish exorcist who must be convinced to offer help to a Gentile female and her daughter. In 7:31–36, Jesus would be best characterized as a magician using incantations (*ephphatha*; 7:34) and saliva to restore a man's speech and hearing.

Contradictory images of Jesus vis-à-vis the divine occur throughout the Gospel according to Mark. In some stories, Jesus does things that many first-century Jewish readers would have associated with activity of the God of Israel alone; in others, Jesus flatly denies his divinity. For instance, 6:45–52 describes Jesus as walking on the water.

> Immediately he made his disciples get into the boat and go on ahead to the other side, to Bethsaida, while he dismissed the crowd. After saying farewell to them, he went up on the mountain to pray. When evening came, the boat was out on the sea, and he was alone on the land. When he saw that they were straining at the oars against an adverse wind, he came towards them early in the morning, walking on the sea. He intended to pass them by. But when they saw him walking on the sea, they thought it was a ghost and cried out; for they all saw him and were terrified. But immediately he spoke to them and said, "Take heart, it is I; do not be afraid." Then he got into the boat with them and the wind ceased. And they were utterly astounded, for they did not understand about the loaves, but their hearts were hardened. (Mark 6:45–52; NRSV)

The act of walking on water, taken out of a context, could have meant a variety of things to a variety of ancient audiences. Jesus's walking on the water, however, seems to have a specific emplotment in this passage. Jesus not only walks on the sea (*peripatōn epi tēs thalassēs*); he also wishes to pass by his disciples (*ēthelen parelthein autous*).⁴⁷ The language of wishing to pass by would have led many Jewish readers to think about or reread passages in the Septuagint about a theophany of the Lord. As Adela Yarbro Collins notes, "The language of 'passing by' suggests that Jesus appears to his disciples in a way analogous to the appearance of God to Moses and Elijah."⁴⁸ Moreover, the words Jesus speaks to his disciples, "Have courage, I am, do not be afraid" (*tharseite, ego eimi, mē phobeisthe*), would have directed knowledgeable Jewish readers or listeners to think of the name of the Lord in Exodus, where the name of the God of Israel is revealed as "I am" (*ego eimi*).⁴⁹ Taken together, Jesus does and says in 6:45–52 what the God of Israel alone does and says in the Hebrew Bible.

While Mark 6:45–52 does not make any kind of metaphysical claims about Jesus's ontology, and later Nicene reflections on Jesus's divine nature must be set aside, the story of Jesus walking on the water reflects a tradition that treats Jesus as functioning as a divine figure, at least for Jewish readers, if not also for other types of readers. Similar kinds of statements could be made about Jesus functioning in a divine manner in 4:35–41; when Jesus takes command of the violent sea, as Yahweh does in Psalm 107:25–30; and in 6:32–44, when Jesus miraculously feeds a multitude in the desert, as the God of Israel does with the wilderness generation in Exodus and Numbers.

Mark 10:17–22, however, presents a Jesus who flatly denies he is divine. The Gospel according to Mark relates the following exchange between Jesus and someone running up to him along the way to Jerusalem:

> While [Jesus] was setting out on the road, someone ran up to him, knelt down, and asked him, "Good teacher, what must I do to inherit eternal life?" But Jesus said to him, "Why do you call me good? There is only one who is good and that is God (*oudeis agathos ei mē heis ho theos*). You know the commandments: Do not murder. Do not commit adultery. Do not steal. Do not bear false witness. Do not rob. Honor your father and mother." Then he said, "Teacher, I have kept all these commandments from my youth."

The striking part of the story is when Jesus tells the man that only God is good, and therefore the rich man ought not to call Jesus good. The most straightforward implication of the story is that Jesus claims that he is not God.

The same Greek phrase occurs in Mark 2:7, *ei mē heis ho theos*. There it is on the lips of scribes rather than Jesus. The scribes say only God can forgive sins. In Mark 2:1–12, however, Jesus performs an action to prove that he can forgive sins, thereby showing himself performing actions that only god can perform (as in 4:39 and 6:45–52).⁵⁰ Mark 10:17–22, however, records Jesus using the same phrase to say explicitly that he should not be treated as divine. The man learns his lesson and next time calls him only teacher. Moreover, in 10:23–31, the disciples react with shock to Jesus's interaction with the rich man. Only they are not surprised by Jesus's claim not to be divine, but by his claim about the difficulty of entering the kingdom of God. To put it in theological terms, they marvel not at the christology expressed in the exchange between Jesus and the rich man but at the soteriology: if you must give up great riches to inherit eternal life, and if it is extremely hard for a rich person to enter the kingdom of God, then who can be saved? So not only does the story in 10:17–22 offer a contradictory christology to passages like 6:45–52, but Jesus's disciples in the story do not seem to think christology is the most confusing part of the exchange.

Unless one wants to make the case that an author figure named "Mark" was making a nuanced distinction in his book between functional and metaphysical aspects of christology (which seems incommensurate with the style, language, and structure of the Gospel according to Mark), the most straightforward solution seems to be that the Gospel according to Mark preserved contradictory viewpoints on Jesus and the divine, both reflecting voices of the early Jesus movement. The advantage of approaching the Gospel according to Mark as an unfinished collection of notes is that it allows interpreters to read both 6:45–52 and 10:17–22 in a straightforward manner. There is no authorial genius providing monological unity of meaning. There is no "Mark" who also happens to be a theologian interested in threading a needle between the finer niceties of christology. There are multiple approaches to thinking about Jesus deemed worthy of being preserved and collected together within the same text. Many other examples could be offered of diverging perspectives on Jesus and christology, but the passages discussed here demonstrate the point. That is to say, the Gospel according to Mark does not, strictly speaking, have *a* christology; it has *christologies*. It is multiple voices, reflecting different traditions of early Jesus movement, speaking against each other within the same text.

Jesus's knowledge and his ability to do mighty deeds are also contested questions within the textual space of the Gospel according to Mark. Sometimes Jesus can do tremendous miracles and is aware of his power. Other times, though, the text is clear that he is not able to do miracles. Yet, still other times Jesus comes off as confused about the specifics of how or for whom he has performed a miracle. All these viewpoints are present within the textual tradition of "Mark" with no apparent attempt to massage them all into one unitary meaning. In 5:21–6:6a, three stories about Jesus's ability to do mighty deeds are spliced together, and each story stands as an exemplar of a different perspective on Jesus's power and self-knowledge. In the story in Mark 5:21–24 and 5:35–43, on the one hand, Jesus overcomes not only the doubt and ridicule of those present but even death when he raises the little girl. Before Jesus arrives at the house of the dead girl, he foretells his ability to save her. The mourners laugh at Jesus and mock him for his claims about the temporary nature of the girl's condition. Nonetheless, despite their lack of belief, Jesus raises her from the dead. In this story, their doubt seems to have no effect on Jesus.

Yet, on the other hand, in 6:1–6a, the doubt and contempt of those around Jesus diminish his ability to do miracles. The text even goes so far as to report that because of the lack of faith of the people of Jesus's hometown "he was *unable* to do any mighty deeds there" (*ouk edunato ekei poiēsai oudemian dunamin*).[51] The text then clarifies that Jesus did lay his hands on a few people in his hometown and heal them in 6:5b. The doubt of those around Jesus in 6:1–6a does not totally nullify Jesus's power, but it greatly weakens it. In any case, the function of the doubt of those around Jesus in 6:1–6a stands in almost incompatible contrast to the doubt and ridicule of those around Jesus in 5:35–43. The Gospel according to Mark makes no attempt to explain why doubt in one context has such an impact on Jesus, but in another context it does not. The contradiction lies in unresolved tension.

A third story adds further tension to the contrasting collage of perspectives related to Jesus's power. Sandwiched in the story of the raising of Jairus's daughter is a story of Jesus's performing another mighty deed. In 5:25–34, Jesus heals a woman who has had a flow of blood for twelve years. She had previously spent much money on doctors, but the medical treatments of the doctors left her in worse condition. Unlike many people in the surrounding stories (5:21–24, 35–43; 6:1–6a), the woman with the health issue has faith in Jesus's power to heal her. Because of her secrecy, no one else around Jesus had the opportunity to express doubt or faith in his abilities to heal. She kept repeating the mantra to herself, "If I can only touch his clothes, I will be healed" (5:28). She sneaks up behind Jesus, touches his clothes, and is healed. But here is where the portrait of Jesus's power to do miracles gets interesting. The Gospel according to Mark relates that, after the healing occurred, Jesus does not understand what happened. He is aware that power has leaked out of him, but he does not know what miracle he performed or at least he does not know who benefited from his power. He keeps asking the crowd "Who touched my clothes? (*tis mou hēpsato tōn himatiōn*)."[52] His repeated looking around and questioning finally leads the woman to confess. In the surrounding story of raising Jairus's daughter, Jesus controls the flow of power from his body. Now the woman's uncontrollable flow of blood is healed, but it is Jesus whose body leaks power.[53]

Another place where one finds clashing messages within the Gospel according to Mark is in relation to Jesus's desire to have his identity and power known. Ever since William Wrede's 1901 publication of *Das Messiasgeheimnis in den Evangelien*, the "messianic secret" has remained one of the most well-known and widely discussed features of the Gospel according to Mark.[54] The provocative thesis remains a debated point. Some passages show a desire on the part of Jesus to keep his identity secret—some almost irrationally so. For instance, Mark 5:35–43 has Jesus suggesting that the witnesses in the house to his raising a girl from the dead should not let the funeral mourners outside know what happened. Thus, his command to silence about his powerful deed is unreasonable and almost comical. How could those inside possibly keep her raising a secret from those attending her funeral?

In reality, however, not all of the Gospel according to Mark is privy to the "messianic secret." Some passages show a tendency to hide Jesus's identity; others reflect an eagerness to make Jesus's identity known to a wide audience during his own lifetime. In reality, there is not one but several different types of "messianic secrets" in the Gospel according to Mark.[55] Jesus often tells demons to be silent because they know who he is (1:25; 3:11–12). In other cases, Jesus urges the recently healed or witnesses to a healing not to tell others about Jesus's action (5:43). Sometimes Jesus urges people not to tell, but then the more he urges, the more they tell (7:36). In still other cases, Jesus asks his disciples not to share his identity as messiah until after his resurrection (9:9).

Yet other times, Jesus explicitly tells the beneficiaries of a miracle to go tell an entire region about everything that he has done (5:19–20). Still other times, Jesus demands that a man healed of leprosy go show himself to the priests, but the man disobediently spreads the news of Jesus's action to a broad audience (1:44–45). Perhaps the clearest example of an anti-messianic secret viewpoint comes in Mark 6:6b–31. There two interpolated stories show Jesus sending out twelve apostles to preach and do mighty deeds. They do the same kinds of miracles that Jesus had done and they preach about the kingdom of God, as Jesus had also done. As a result of their proclamation, Jesus gains a widespread reputation. Even King Herod hears the report about Jesus, his mission, message, and its eschatological tenor.[56]

How is one to make sense of the contradictory gestures of the Gospel according to Mark regarding whether or not Jesus wished to make his identify known? That is, is there a messianic secret in the Gospel according to Mark? Or is there not a messianic secret? The answer to both questions is yes. If one presupposes an author publishing a book called the Gospel according to Mark, then one may feel obligated to make a decision. One must read, say, Mark 5:19–20 to portray a message symbiotic with Mark 5:43. Or one must at least imagine a nuanced level of thought not reflected in the structure, style, and language of the rest of the text.

Yet if one does not need to think about the textual tradition we now call the Gospel according to Mark (at least as we have in in the earliest and best manuscripts) emerging through the work of an author figure producing a finished book with a unified meaning, one is not pushed into such a decision, and a variety of other options open up. If one approaches the Gospel according to Mark as its earliest readers approached it—as *hypomnēmata*—one is freed to acknowledge that the text possesses ambiguities, gaps, and inconsistencies, and that it holds together a dialogue of viewpoints, all of which suggests that creating a singular and unified message regarding issues of christology or the public proclamation of Jesus's identity was not of primary importance to the producer(s) of the Gospel according to Mark. Again, the Gospel according to Mark, taken at face value, does not have *a* christology; it has *christologies*. It does not promote the agenda of a messianic secret but, rather, messianic secrets. It also promotes the opposite: an agenda of messianic proclamation. In both issues, the priority of collecting stories into a useful and memorable arrangement takes priority over presenting a monologically unified narrative and message.

Such dialogical voices appear throughout the Gospel according to Mark on a variety of topics. Regarding soteriology, at times the Gospel according to Mark presents a picture of Jesus speaking self-consciously of his own death as a ransom for many (*lutron anti pollōn*; 10:45). Similarly, in Mark 14:24, Jesus makes mention of his blood being spilled on behalf of many (*hyper pollōn*) in connection with his impending death. Mark 1:40–45 may be read as Jesus substituting his own position for that of the leper's position as an outsider, since in the end Jesus is left out in deserted places, which is where the leper was, and the former leper spreads the message about Jesus in population centers. Yet at other times, the Gospel according to Mark has Jesus teaching that one achieves eternal life by keeping Torah and giving alms to the poor (10:17–22). To add further tension, Mark 7:1–23 offers a picture of Jesus, if not undoing, at least significantly reinterpreting and diminishing literal obedience to the Torah's food and purity codes.

Regarding Jesus's estimation of the value of family, Jesus does several miracles in the context of family. He heals Jairus's daughter, he exorcizes the daughter of a Syrophonecian mother in 7:24–30 and the son of a father in 9:14–29, and he upholds the command to honor one's father and mother in 10:19, all of which show Jesus working within and seemingly supporting existing family structures. Yet at other times, Jesus forsakes and essentially disowns his own family in favor of a new eschatological family (3:20–21, 30–35) and calls on others to do the same (10:28–31). Moreover, Jesus points to an androgynous and seemingly family-less future for the resurrected people of God (12:18–27), who will become like angels in heaven.

Making *hypomnēmata* is an act of unifying the disparate. Foucault put it this way: "[Writing *hypomnēmata*] is a selecting of heterogeneous elements. In this, it contrasts with the work of the grammarian, who tries to get to know an entire work or all the works of an author; it also conflicts with the teaching of professional philosophers who subscribe to the doctrinal unity of a school."[57] The goal of producing *hypomnēmata* was not so much to teach a coherent truth or to propagate unified doctrines as to collect a set of notes for later rereading, reworking, reflection, meditation, use, teaching, and preaching. Such seems to be the chief unifying logic of the text of the Gospel according to Mark. Read in this way, the Gospels according to Matthew and Luke are not separate gospel books from the Gospel according to Mark but, rather, the development of the open, unfinished, and tensive textual tradition of the gospel.

My approach reconfigures the way we think about the production, use, and experience of gospels (and especially the one we now call the Gospel according to Mark) in the first couple centuries of the Common Era. It does not vindicate thinking of "Mark" as an author in any kind of modern, bourgeois, or (to use the term of Eva Mroczek) Miltonian sense of the term.[58] Moreover, there does not appear to have been an author named "Mark" who was a systematic theologian, weaving together a consistent structure of theological truths. He was not even a theologian, if by theologian we mean that "Mark" was explicitly concerned with imparting *a* correct christology, soteriology, and so forth. The Gospel according to Mark is, of course, quite christological in the way it arranges and preserves its *hypomnēmata*, as the identity of Jesus and his looming execution are ongoing themes. The aim of the producer(s) seems(seem) to have been more about creating a collage of useful images of Jesus more than crafting a seemless narrative (*diēgēsis*) or a biography (*bios*) or teaching a particular set of dogmas. Thus, not only is the Gospel according to Mark a *hypomnematic* script for teachers to use, but it is one in which the teacher must navigate and make meaning out of an open dialogue of multiple, unresolved, competing voices.

Of course, gesturing to French poststructuralist thinkers such as Roland Barthes and Jacques Derrida, many would say the same is true of all texts.[59] Of course, they are right: all texts may be read as open. Yet even Roland Barthes theorizes a difference between what he calls writerly (*texte scriptible*) and readerly (*texts lisible*) texts. Readerly texts are those works, such as classics and traditional novels, that readers consume. Writerly texts, however, are those works that "make the reader no longer a consumer, but a producer of the text."[60] Reader engagement with a work ultimately determines whether the work is received as readerly or writerly. While I worry about the possibility of creating a false binary (as well as other cautions), Barthes offers productive terminology.

I argue that modern scholars and readers of the gospels, on the one hand, have treated them as texts to be consumed and decoded, *as readerly texts*. By using the tools of a cultural historian of antiquity, I have shown that the earliest readers and users of the Gospel according to Mark, on the other hand, approached it as a work to be used and produced, *as writerly texts*. Such a claim is not only true in interpretation but also in actually reworking the text: filling in gaps, reworking inconsistencies, dealing with ambiguities, erasing elements they do not like, supplying new endings, and so forth.

# *Epilogue*

I ACKNOWLEDGE THAT many people sense a nuanced structure and strategy within the Gospel according to Mark. Many see in "Mark" an author who designed an intricate, multilayered, and self-subverting narrative about Jesus as the Christ and as Son of God. And I do not contend that they are reading this against the grain of the Gospel according to Mark or "misusing" the Gospel according to Mark. Rather, they are treating the text of the Gospel according to Mark exactly as its earliest readers and users did: cooperating in the construction of the meaning of Jesus and his movement.

I contend that they do not *discover* such structure and nuance within the Gospel according to Mark; they *produce* it. But this production is not "eisegesis," or wrongly reading meaning into a text that was not originally there based on one's perspectives, agendas, and biases. In fact, I am not sure what it would look like to do "eisegesis" of a collection of unpolished notes, if the notes are not an end in and of themselves. The producer(s) of the textual tradition we now call the Gospel according to Mark seems (seem) to have collected sets of notes to be meditated upon, to be reread, to be rewritten, to be used, to be taught and preached. When approached as an unfinished collection of notes, the Gospel according to Mark becomes precisely the kind of text with which one expects to cooperate in the production of meaning. Meaning lies not within but beyond the text.

## *The Gospel according to Mark, the Interpreter, and the Unfinalizable Future*

The text is a script and it is the users who create the performance. And in making something out of the text, readers are not acting in some "postmodern" or "transgressive" manner *against* the text. They are doing with the text, from a historical point of view of ancient reading practices, exactly what the earliest readers and users of the gospel did: making *kerygmatic* meaning out of the collected notes for the benefit of the users and hearers. This does not diminish the role of readers or literary critics. Rather, it enhances it, grants them real agency, and gives them a creative and constructive role in the process. When they write about the genius of the narrative structure of the Gospel according to Mark, I am not saying they are reading something "into the text" that was not there. Rather, the genius they find is—at least partially—their own.

In my approach, literary critics are treating the Gospel according to Mark in essentially the same way as the textual traditions we now call the Gospel according to Matthew and Luke treat it. They take the unfinished collection of notes we now call the Gospel according to Mark and attempt to make something meaningful and helpful in their present contexts. I collapse the role of the reader into that of the tradition. There is also no longer any clear line between scripture and tradition. In the open and fluid framework I propose, it may prove unhelpful to distinguish between textual production and "reception history." Production is reception, and vice versa. The modern literary critic and commentator are themselves part of the tradition.[1] Just as the endings of the Gospel according to Mark look to add what is lacking in the text, so also readers of the unfinished Gospel according to Mark must fill in gaps and make meaning. In this way, the gap between the reader and the writer shrinks, if not collapses. What modern scholars and readers do with the Gospel according to Mark is analogous to what "Matthew," "Luke," and the continuators of the Gospel according to Mark did with it: fill in gaps, rework the text, clarify ambiguities, resolve tensions, or enjoy them. In writing a book on the text we now call the Gospel according to Mark, it is not lost on me that I (Matthew Larsen) also play a productive role in the same ongoing process of the making of "Mark," in a way quite similar to what "Matthew" (the gospel) did with "Mark" so many years ago. I contend such an understanding is both less historically anachronistic and more productive for modern readers of the gospels.

My reading situates the textual tradition we have come to know as the Gospel according to Mark in a moment in the first centuries CE when the gospel is still primarily a speech genre. This gospel is, however, already textualized. But it is also still oral, still pliable, still open. It is a living and fluid textual tradition. The goals of the textualization were more about practicality and usefulness than about the production of fine literature. Early gospel texts fit well with what Kathryn Tanner, speaking from a theological frame of reference, has called "Scripture as Popular Text."[2] By text, though, we must not import later printing-press notions of finalization or completion.[3] The textualization of the gospel is an ongoing process, an energy, and a developing idea. The reader is both the ending and the "perpetual present" of the Gospel according to Mark.[4] Whether or not the textual tradition we now call the Gospel according to Mark was produced as an intentionally unfinished work of art, modern readers may treat it as such, if they wish.[5]

## Paths for Future Work on Gospel Writing

The goal of the present book has been to reimagine at a fundamental level how we think about gospels as textual objects from the first few centuries of early Christianity. My hope is to create outward spiraling problems and inspire new frameworks for thinking about textualized gospel in the early Jesus movement—ones that do not rely on anachronistic ideas and metaphors such as book, author, publication, and textual finality. In pursuit of such a goal, I have pointed out some fundamental problems inherent in the historical study of the gospels throughout the modern period. One cannot distinguish between the fundamental tools of traditional historical criticism of the gospels such as redaction, source, and textual criticism without ideas like book, author, and publication. Yet all such ideas are foreign to the earliest centuries of the Common Era.

I have also explored some previously underappreciated aspects of ancient writing practices and reading *habitus* that I contend have bearing on our understanding of how the gospel came to be textualized. I have argued it is productive to approach the text we now call the Gospel according to Mark in a way analogous to the way its earliest readers and users approached it—as an unfinished note collection. Based on my historical investigation, it is highly unlikely that the current scholarly framework of book, author, and textual finality expresses accurately the realities of the first centuries. I suggest my framework would be much more discernible to a first- and second-century reader or user of the gospels. Additionally, such an approach opens up new and exciting possibilities about how to think about what the gospels were before the book.

There are a couple places, however, where I feel further work remains to be done. First, I have taken as a test case the textual tradition we now call the Gospel according to Mark, but it is clear that the issues of textual unfinishedness also have bearing on other textual traditions of the gospel in the first few centuries. I chose the Gospel according to Mark (and its relation to the Gospels according to Matthew and Luke) because the tradition of its earliest readers and users so clearly treats the textual tradition as unfinished note collections. Yet this is not meant to imply that other gospels were always regarded as fully finished books published by human authors. My framework has implications for any gospel text in the first few centuries, as the claim that there is no evidence of anyone using concepts of book, author, or publication to think about the gospel prior to Irenaeus has an impact far beyond just the textual tradition we now call the Gospel according to Mark.

Work remains to be done to think about how my framework applies to other textual traditions of the gospel as experienced by earliest readers and users. For instance, the case that the Gospel according to Thomas was *hypomnēmata* is as strong, and perhaps even stronger, at least from an internal point of view, as the case I have made about the Gospel according to Mark.[6] Additionally, Celsus, the second-century opponent of Christianity, represents an important and underappreciated viewpoint of the gospel at work at that time. Origen preserves his comment in *Cels.* 2.27: "[Celsus] says that some believers, as if in a drunken brawl with one another, alter and remodel *the* gospel from its initial written form (*metacharattein ek tēs prōtēs graphēs to euaggelion . . . metaplattein*)—three times, four times, many times—so that they might be able to give a rebuttal in the face of critical accusations." Celsus participates in and reproduces an active discourse about the gospel that views it as textualized, yet still open, fluid, and in a constant state of flux. For him, the gospel is written, but it is not a stable, containing book. Nor is it attributed to an author. I suspect he represents a fairly common view held among readers of gospel texts in the first few centuries.

Second, there is the issue of timing and development. Since I make much of Irenaeus's comments in *Haer.* 3.1.1 about the gospels as books published by authors, my presentation could potentially be misread as implying that a clean, unilateral, and universal shift happened at the time of Irenaeus (ca. 180–190 CE). While it is the case that Irenaeus is the first-known evidence of someone using concepts of book, author, and publication to describe the gospels, it is not the case that all Christians around the ancient Mediterranean basin "got the memo" at the same time and subsequently shifted their thinking about the gospel. People did not abandon the idea of gospel as open and fluid textual constellation(s) after Irenaeus simply because he said so. I have mentioned how Origen in the third century and Eusebius in the fourth describe gospels, and not just the Gospel according to Mark, as *hypomnēmata*.[7]

Even as late as the fifth century, the *Acts of Timothy* preserves a tradition of the earliest gospel texts as disordered notes—unarranged sheets of papyrus—in the hands of followers of the disciples of the Lord (Jesus). The followers of the disciples come to John in Ephesus with papyri in their possession—loose notes about Jesus scattered here and there (*tous par' autōn sporadēn suntagentas chartas*). They did not know how to organize (*ouk egnōkotes suntheinai*) the loose collection of notes.[8] John takes it upon himself to rework and arrange the loose notes, and entitles them the Gospels of Matthew, Mark, and Luke (*entheis kata taxin Matthiou kai Markou kai Louka apegrapseto*). John then writes another gospel to fill in the parts not mentioned by the other notes. Thus, as late as the fifth century, the notion of early gospel texts as fluid, revisable, unfinished notes about Jesus is preserved.

Third, there is the issue of naming. There was no "Gospel according to [Name]" in the first century or most of the second. I have occasionally in the present book used the longer phrase "the textual tradition we now call the Gospel according to [Name]," but have commonly used "the Gospel according to [Name]" for the sake of convenience for the reader. The former is more accurate, the latter makes for better prose. Yet, in reality, both problematically rely on a system of thinking about textualized gospel and the naming of individualized and separated books unknown to the earliest discourses of the gospel. In a previous draft of this book, I developed a system of naming the various constellations of textualized gospel tradition that does not use names. In the end, I retained the phrase "the Gospel according to [Name]" because I concluded the present book is about pointing out several faulty yet operative, foundational assumptions in the modern historical study of the gospels. I decided the issue of constructing a new system for describing the constellations of textualized gospel tradition is best left to future work.

Similarly, while some may take some modern edition of the Greek New Testament to represent the "original" or first-century form of the text of a gospel, the reality is we do not have access to the textual tradition we now call the Gospel according to Mark as it existed in the first century. The manuscripts do not allow us to speak with confidence about the precise state of the text of any gospel in the earliest centuries of the Common Era.[9] Moreover, I have argued that the Gospel according to Mark was unfinished, fluid, and prone to alteration. In fact, based on the five different endings, we know for a fact that the textual tradition we now call the Gospel according to Mark existed in multiple forms throughout the first few centuries. Thus, it is unwise to assume that a modern critical edition represents a word-for-word representation of a gospel as it existed in the first century. Rather, it represents a construction of texts based on traditional textual criticism done on the existing manuscripts of the gospel. They give us not *the* text but, rather, a construction of a text that stands in some degree of continuity with prior, now-lost iterations of the gospel. When I used the NA28 to compare the Gospels according to Matthew and Mark, I did not do so because I believe I am comparing *the definitive, first-century* text of each gospel, but because I wanted to show that the textual traditions we now call the Gospels according to Matthew and Mark, as we now have them, appear more like two versions of the same, open work than like two discrete books with different authors. As with the names, I chose to identify the problem but not to address it fully in the present book, as my goal was (1) to identify fundamental problems in the way scholars have produced knowledge about the gospels throughout the modern era, and (2) to gesture toward new, productive ways of describing gospel writing in the first few centuries, which do not import anachronistic concepts such as book, author, and publication.

One interesting model for discussing open, divergent traditions of the same story is Robert Darnton's way of thinking about peasant tales in early modern Europe. He develops a theory of how to talk about stories like "Little Red Riding Hood" that are not the sole property of any one author, though they clearly had currency and eventually came to be attached to different named collections. Focused on the cultural and mental worlds of French peasants, he writes, "To reject folktales because they cannot be dated and situated with precision like other historical documents is to turn one's back on one of the few points of entry into the mental world of peasants under the Old Regime."[10] In the face of ever-changing, unprovenanced stories, which seem to have been used widely, he proposes, "Given these uncertainties, it seem unwise to build an interpretation on a single version of a single tale, and more hazardous still to base symbolic analysis on details—riding hoods and hunters—that may not have occurred in the peasant versions."[11] For the peasant teller of the tale, "Texts are not rigidly fixed for him as they are for readers of the printed page. He creates the text as he goes, picking new routes through old themes."[12] Recognizing that there is no definitive version, and that versions diverge to the point of contradiction, and that the whole process is ongoing and experienced through performance, Darnton proposes, "By studying the entire corpus of them [the folk tales] and comparing them with corresponding tales in other traditions, one can see this general dimension of meaning expressed in characteristic narrative devices—ways of framing stories, setting tone, combining motifs, and inflecting plots."[13]

There are, of course, critical differences between the shape of French folk tales and early Christian gospel textualization. Yet the way Darnton discusses "authorless" and open traditions may provide examples that are productive for gospel scholars to consider. It allows for both macro analysis of the shape of the whole gospel tradition and fine-grained analysis that does not rely on author figures and books. Darnton's use of the folk tales to study cultural history may also provide a useful point of comparison for how gospel scholars can study early Christian communities and the mutable gospel textual tradition. When talking about the gospel, one refers, then, to the whole, unbounded, moving, growing textual constellation. When noting the fine differences between traditions, one notes not the difference in perspectives of different books by different authors, but the cultural history of individual communities and how users made, remade, and coped with their world through stories.[14]

Furthermore, digital humanities help us to begin the work of creating a new framework for describing gospel and gospel textualization in the first few centuries. First, the digital turn in textual studies offers interesting parallels with how textuality worked in the premodern world. In describing my work on gospels "before the book" to people who work in the tech world, many of them have noted the similarity of the open gospel text and the software-development process called "source control," specifically the software Git. There are many platforms built on top of Git, but an interesting implementation has been social software development, of which GitHub is preeminent. Social development is the process of collaborative creation of a singular application or library. Developers can write code and add it to the shared repository on GitHub and allow others to rework the code so as to improve it, although the question of improving is often a subjective one. Each modification, or commit, builds upon an initial commit and series of commits, yet the repository is alive and ever-changing to address new problems. Developers can also take the code and start a new branch that reflects a series of alterations. The new branch is tied to the initial developer and the one who opened up the reworked branch. It would be insightful to upload a translation of the Gospel according to Mark and allow users to rewrite the gospel. Eventually people would likely start new branches of the gospel text. The text would always be there, yet it would never arrive at a finished form. The data compiled from such an experiment could provide both an interesting view of the modern religious experience and a useful comparandum for scholars of antiquity and late antiquity to go about the project of redescribing gospel writing.[15]

Second, the proportional Venn diagram I presented in chapter 6 could also be done with other extant traditions of textualized gospel, such as the textual traditions we now call the Gospels according to John, Thomas, Peter, the Diatessaron, and so forth. Once the Venn diagrams are made for each textual tradition, rough dates of creation could be attached, then a "time lapse" video representation could be made of the growth of textualized gospel in the first few centuries. Each year could be given a half second of time in the video.

For instance, the video could start in 70 CE with the emergence of the textual tradition we now call the Gospel according to Mark, then five seconds later, in 80 CE, the textual tradition we now call the Gospel according to Matthew could grow into the shape represented by the Venn diagram. In 85 CE, the Venn diagram of the textual tradition we now call the Gospel according to Luke could be included, and shown to develop upon the Gospels according to Matthew and Mark. In 90 CE, the textual traditions we call the Gospels according to John and Thomas could be added, and the Gospel according to Peter and the Diatessaron could then be added in the second century. And so forth. I imagine a three-dimensional video representation, showing a rhizomatic, bulbous growth over a nearly two-hundred-year period. Each textual tradition could be represented by a different color. Readers with ample knowledge of early Christian gospels can likely visualize the process in their mind already. The video would provide an important step in helping gospel scholars visualize and reimagine the growth of the gospel tradition in the first few centuries.

For those who have found my presentation persuasive, it will be clear that a host of new questions will surface. It is my hope that readers will agree that, while some questions may have reached a dead end, much new work remains to be done. New theories and frameworks must be developed that take textual fluidity seriously and do not rely on notions like author, book, or finished versions of text. I view this not as a problem or a closure but as an exciting opportunity, opening up new chances for dialogue. Given my focus on unfinishedness in this book, I trust I have not had the final word on the matter.

## APPENDIX A

# A Side-by-Side Comparison of Selections of Philodemus's On Rhetoric Book III as Found in P.Herc. 1506 and P.Herc. 1426

| PHerc. 1506[1] | PHerc. 1426 |
|---|---|
| καὶ ἐν δή[μοις] <u>καὶ ἐν [δι]καστη[ρίοις</u> καὶ [ἐν ἐκ κλησίαις][2] | καὶ ἐν δήμ[οι]ς καὶ ἐν ἐκκλησίαις[3] |
| εἰ μὴ τὸ δημηγορεῖν [<u>ἢ</u>] δικολογεῖν[4] | εἰ μὴ τὸ δημηγ[ορ]εῖν <u>καὶ</u> δικολογεῖν[5] |
| πῶς γὰρ ἡ μὴ συγχωρουμένη περιποιεῖν τὴν πολιτικὴν ἐμπεριειλη[φ]έναι κατὰ τὴν πρόληψιν δοθήσεται τὴν πολιτικὴν <u>τῷ γε τεκμη[ρίῳ αὐτῶν]</u>[6] | πῶς γὰρ ἡ μὴ συγχωρουμένη περιποιεῖν τὴν πολιτικὴν ἐμπεριειλη[φ]έναι κατὰ τὴν πρόληψ[ι]ν δοθήσεται τὴν πολι[τ]ικὴν[7] |
| τὸν μέντοι νῦν <u>σχολαστικὸν</u> ῥήτορα πῶς ἂν λέγοιμεν καθόσον ῥήτωρ ἀγαθὸν ἂν γενέσθαι πολιτικὸν[8] | τὸν μέντοι νῦν <u>διατριβικὸν</u> ῥήτορα πῶς ἂν λέγοιμεν καθόσον ῥήτωρ ἀγαθὸν ἂν γενέσθαι πολιτικὸν[9] |
| μὲν γὰρ κατὰ τὴν ἐμπ[ει]ρίαν[10] | μὲν γὰρ κατὰ <u>αὐτὴν</u> τὴν ἐμπειρίαν[11] |
| ἐκωλύετο δ' ἂν εἰ <u>καὶ</u> ὁ ῥήτωρ ἀγαθὸς ὤφειλεν εἶναι[12] | ἐκωλύετο δ' ἂν εἰ <u>καθ</u> ὁ ῥήτωρ ἀγαθὸς ὤφειλεν εἶναι[13] |
| τοῖς δὲ κεκτημένοις ἔστιν ὅτε πλείω τῶν ἐν ἰδιωτείαι <u>μὴ κωλύειν ἔχειν</u> [...] <u>αν ἐν τίνι δὲ τρόπ[ῳ] ῥηθήσε[ται] καὶ παραιτίαν τοῦ πλ[.] ... ἀγαθὰ ἔχειν πολλὰ κακὰ πλεί[ω] παραιτ[ί]αν</u> καὶ τούτοις αὐτὸν οἰόμεθα τὸν βίον μαρτυρεῖν. καὶ νὴ τὸν Δί' ἄ<καὶ>ν <εἰ>τις οἷς εἴπαμεν προσβάλλων λέγῃ δεῖν τὸν ἀγαθὸν πολιτικὸν [<u>ἢ ἀγαθὸν ῥήτορα</u> πολλὰς ἔχειν ἀρετὰς καὶ σῴζεσθ[α]ι τὰς πόλεις οὐκ ὑπὸ τῶν ῥητόρων ἢ πολιτικῶν, ἀλλὰ ὑπὸ τῶν ἀγαθῶν, ὀρθῶς ἐρεῖ.[14] | τοῖς δὲ κεκτημένοις ἔστιν ὅτε πλείω τῶν ἐν ἰδ[ι]ωτείαι <u>πολλάκις δὲ</u> κ[α]κὰ πλείω καὶ τούτοις αὐτὸν οἰόμεθα τὸν βίον μαρτυρεῖν. καὶ νὴ τὸν Δί' ἄν τις οἷς εἴπαμεν προσβάλλων λέγῃ δεῖν τὸν ἀγαθὸν πολιτικὸν πολλὰς ἔχειν ἀρετὰς καὶ σῴζεσθαι τὰς πόλεις οὐκ ὑπὸ τῶν ῥητόρων ἢ πολιτικῶν, ἀλλὰ ὑπὸ τῶν ἀγαθῶν, ὀρθῶς {λ}ἐ<γ>ρεῖ[15] |

# APPENDIX B

## Codex Bobiensis of Mark 16 with "Shorter Ending" in Parallel Columns with the NA28 Greek Edition and the Latin Vulgate

| Codex Bobiensis (k) | NA28 | Latin Vulgate |
|---|---|---|
| 16:1 Et sabbato exacto abierunt et adtulerunt aromata ut eum unguerent | 16:1 Καὶ διαγενομένου τοῦ σαββάτου Μαρία ἡ Μαγδαληνὴ καὶ Μαρία ἡ [τοῦ] Ἰακώβου καὶ Σαλώμη ἠγόρασαν ἀρώματα ἵνα ἐλθοῦσαι ἀλείψωσιν αὐτόν. | 16:1 et cum transisset sabbatum Maria Magdalene et Maria Iacobi et Salome emerunt aromata ut venientes unguerent eum |
| 16:2 et venerent prima sabbati mane | 16:2 καὶ λίαν πρωῒ τῇ μιᾷ τῶν σαββάτων ἔρχονται ἐπὶ τὸ μνημεῖον ἀνατείλαντος τοῦ ἡλίου. | 16:2 et valde mane una sabbatorum veniunt ad monumentum orto iam sole |
| 16:3 dicentes quis nobis revolvet lapidem ab osteo | 16:3 καὶ ἔλεγον πρὸς ἑαυτάς· τίς ἀποκυλίσει ἡμῖν τὸν λίθον ἐκ τῆς θύρας τοῦ μνημείου; | 16:3 et dicebant ad invicem quis revolvet nobis lapidem ab ostio monumenti |
| 16:4 subito autem ad horam tertium tenebrae diei factae sunt per totum orbem terrae et descenderunt de caelis angeli et surgent in claritate vivi dei simul ascenderunt cum eo et continuo lux facta est Tunc illae accesserunt ad monumentum et vident revolutum lapidem fuit enim magnus nimis | 16:4 καὶ ἀναβλέψασαι θεωροῦσιν ὅτι ἀποκεκύλισται ὁ λίθος· ἦν γὰρ μέγας σφόδρα. | 16:4 et respicientes vident revolutum lapidem erat quippe magnus valde |

| Codex Bobiensis (k) | NA28 | Latin Vulgate |
| --- | --- | --- |
| 16:5 et cum intro introissent viderunt iuvenem in dextra sedentem indutum stolam albam et hebetes factae sunt | 16:5 Καὶ εἰσελθοῦσαι εἰς τὸ μνημεῖον εἶδον νεανίσκον καθήμενον ἐν τοῖς δεξιοῖς περιβεβλημένον στολὴν λευκήν, καὶ ἐξεθαμβήθησαν. | 16:5 et introeuntes in monumento viderunt iuvenem sedentem in dextris coopertum stola candida et obstipuerunt |
| 16:6 ille autem didit ad illas quit stupetis ihⁿ illu crucifixum .... nazoraeum quaeritis surrexit...... ecce locus illius ubi fuit positus | 16:6 ὁ δὲ λέγει αὐταῖς· μὴ ἐκθαμβεῖσθε· Ἰησοῦν ζητεῖτε τὸν Ναζαρηνὸν τὸν ἐσταυρωμένον· ἠγέρθη, οὐκ ἔστιν ὧδε· ἴδε ὁ τόπος ὅπου ἔθηκαν αὐτόν. | 16:6 qui dicit illis nolite expavescere Iesum quaeritis Nazarenum crucifixum surrexit non est hic ecce locus ubi posuerunt eum |
| 16:7 Sed ite et dicite discipulis et petro praecedo vos in galileam illic me videbitis sicut vobis dixi | 16:7 ἀλλ' ὑπάγετε εἴπατε τοῖς μαθηταῖς αὐτοῦ καὶ τῷ Πέτρῳ ὅτι προάγει ὑμᾶς εἰς τὴν Γαλιλαίαν· ἐκεῖ αὐτὸν ὄψεσθε, καθὼς εἶπεν ὑμῖν. | 16:7 sed ite et dicite discipulis eius et Petro quia praecedit vos in Galilaeam ibi eum videbitis sicut dixit vobis |
| 16:8 illae autem cum* cum exirent a monumeto fugerent tenebat enim illas tremor et pauor propter timore [*praedicationis] | 16:8 Καὶ ἐξελθοῦσαι ἔφυγον ἀπὸ τοῦ μνημείου, εἶχεν γὰρ αὐτὰς τρόμος καὶ ἔκστασις· καὶ οὐδενὶ οὐδὲν εἶπαν· ἐφοβοῦντο γάρ. | 16:8 at illae exeuntes fugerunt de monumento invaserat enim eas tremor et pavor et nemini quicquam dixerunt timebant enim |
| 16:9 omnia autem quaecumque praecepta erant breviter exposuerunt posthaec et ipse hi adparuit et ab oriente usque usque in orientem misit per illos sanctam et incorruptum ha salutis aeterae amen¹ | [the NA28 then offers both the shorter and longer endings] | 16:9 surgens autem mane prima sabbati apparuit primo Mariae Magdalenae de qua eiecerat septem daemonia [continues with the longer ending through 16:20] |

# *Notes*

PREFACE

1. See Giorgio Tagliaferro, "A New Agony in the Garden by Titian and His Collaborators, and the Problem of Originality in Late Titian," *Artibus et Historiae* 72 (2015): 107–126.

CHAPTER 1

1. See, for example, Adela Yarbro Collins, *Mark: A Commentary* (Minneapolis, MN: Fortress Press, 2009), 6: "In this commentary, 'Mark' will be used as a designation of the author of the second Gospel, as shorthand for 'the author of the Gospel known as the Gospel according to Mark.' The expression 'Mark' will also be used for the text of the Gospel. It should be clear from the context which referent is intended." Retaining the name "Mark," however, encourages the idea of an author figure. See Michel Foucault, "What Is an Author?," in *The Foucault Reader*, ed. Paul Rabinow (New York: Pantheon, 1984), 101–20; Friedrich Nietzsche, "Homer und die klassische Philologie" (1869) *KGW* 2.1: 248–69; Hindy Najman, *Seconding Sinai: The Development of Mosaic Discourse in Second Temple Judaism* (Leiden/Boston: Brill, 2009); Hindy Najman, "The Vitality of Scripture Within and Beyond the Canon," *JSJ* 43 (2012): 497–518. As we shall see, author function has important and anachronistic implications for the study of a text, including gospel texts.
2. For shortly before 70 CE, see Collins, *Mark*, 14; Willi Marxsen, *Introduction to the New Testament*, trans. G. Buswell (Philadelphia: Fortress Press, 1968), 142–43; James R. Edwards, *The Gospel According to Mark* (Grand Rapids: Eerdmans, 2002). For shortly after 70 CE, see Rudolf Pesch, *Das Markusevangelium, 1. Teil: Einleitung und Kommentar zu Kap. 1,1–8,26* (Freiburg: Herder, 1976), 14; W. R. Telford, *The Theology of the Gospel of Mark* (New York: Cambridge University Press, 1999), 9–15; Morna D. Hooker, *The Gospel According to Mark* (Peabody, MA: Hendrickson, 1991), 5–8. For an agnostic stance between before or

after 70 CE, see Joel Marcus, *Mark 1–8: A New Translation with Introduction and Commentary* (New York: Doubleday, 2000), 39.

3. Irenaeus, *Haer.* 3.1.1; Eusebius, *Hist. eccl.* 6.14.6–7. On Rome as the traditional view, see, for example, Raymond Brown, *An Introduction to the New Testament* (New Haven, CT: Yale University Press, 1997), 127. See also Brian Incigneri, *The Gospel to the Romans: The Setting and Rhetoric of Mark's Gospel* (Leiden/Boston: Brill, 2003).

4. See Marcus, *Mark 1–8*, 33–37. For helpful review of the literature up to 1992, see John R. Donahue, "The Quest for the Community of Mark's Gospel," in *The Four Gospels 1992: Festschrift Frans Neirynck*, ed. F. Van Segbroeck et al. (Leuven: Leuven University Press, 1992), 823–28, 832–35. See also Collins, *Mark*, 7–10, 96–102; Brown, *Introduction*, 127.

5. Discussed in detail in chapter 5.

6. Irenaeus, *Haer.* 3.1.1 will be discussed in detail in chapter 5.

7. See, for example, Origen, *Cels.* 2.27; Justin Martyr, *Dial.* 101.3; 106.4 et al.; Theophilus, *Autol.* 3.13–14; Did. 8.2 et al.; 2 Clem. 8.5.

8. Gilles Deleuze and Félix Guatarri, *A Thousand Plateaus: Capitalism and Schizophrenia 2*, trans. Brian Massumi (Minneapolis: University of Minnesota, 1987), 15: "We're tired of trees. We should stop believing in trees, roots, and radicles. They've made us suffer too much. All of arborescent culture is founded on them, from biology to linguistics. Nothing is beautiful or loving or political aside from underground stems and aerial root, adventitious growths and rhizomes."

9. After I had done my own research, written my book, and while I was in the final stages of manuscript preparation, I became aware of Francis Watson's recent work on the survival of the Gospel according to Mark. See Francis Watson, "How Did Mark Survive?," in *Matthew and Mark Across Perspectives: Essays in Honor of Stephen C. Barton and William R. Telford*, ed. Kristian A. Bendoraitis and Nijay K. Gupta (New York: T&T Clark, 2016), 1–17. Watson claims that the Gospel according to Mark was experienced as not final, not definitive, unfinished, open, fluid, and work in progress. I have argued along similar (though also rather different) lines, using the same terms, in various venues from 2013 to 2015 at Yale and other places. Watson takes his argument in a rather different direction from where I do (and would be willing to do). His is a more theological than historical treatment. As I have come across his work on the Gospel according to Mark as unfinished only in the final stages of manuscript preparation, I am unable to engage fully in his thinking at this point. Yet I note Watson's work to illustrate that others are already beginning to think along the lines of my project in the field of gospel studies.

10. See Eva Mroczek, *The Literary Imagination in Jewish Antiquity* (New York: Oxford University Press, 2016). Drawing inspiration from her work, I apply similar questions to early gospel texts.

11. Mroczek, *Literary Imagination*, 9–11.

12. Mroczek, *Literary Imagination*, 89.

13. Mroczek, *Literary Imagination*, 106. Citing Brennen W. Breed, *The Nomadic Text: A Theory of Biblical Reception*, Indiana Studies in Biblical Literature (Bloomington: Indiana University Press, 2014), 203.

14. Mroczek, *Literary Imagination*, 113.
15. I will often use some variant of the formula "in the textual tradition behind the text we now call the Gospel according to [Name]" or "in the text of the Gospel according to [Name] as we have it," as opposed to simpler and more common formulas like "[Name]'s Gospel" or even just "[Name]." I do so for several reasons. First, in the first century and likely most of the second, there was no such thing as the Gospel according to [Name]. There was just the gospel. Second, we cannot be certain of the state of their texts during that time. The manuscript tradition does not allow us to speak with a high level of certainty about the text of any gospel before the fourth century (on recent work redating several important manuscripts, see Brent Nongbri, *Constructing God's Library* [New Haven, CT: Yale University Press, in press]). Third, "according to [Name]" did not signify authorship in antiquity. It denoted a corrector or editor of an open textual tradition (see Matthew D. C. Larsen, "Correcting the Gospel: Putting the Titles of the Gospels in their Historical-Literary Context," in *Rethinking 'Authority' in Late Antiquity: Authorship, Law, and Transmission in Jewish and Christian Tradition*, ed. Mark Letteney and A. J. Berkowitz, London: Routledge, forthcoming. Such lengthy phrases will no doubt become nettlesome to the reader, but I hope the benefit of the reminders will outweigh the cost.
16. On the claim that the gospels were not the kinds of texts that would have had originals, see David C. Parker, *The Living Text of the Gospels* (New York: Cambridge University Press, 1997), 7. See also Parker, *Living Text of the Gospels*, 93: "any writer who crystallizes a point in a changing tradition (which he thereby also changes) must accept that his writing may also be liable to alteration by somebody else. And once this is acknowledged, then the concept of a Gospel that is fixed in shape, authoritative, and final as a piece of literature has to be abandoned."
17. Thanks to Greg Given for this suggestion.
18. I will also capitalize "Synoptic Gospels."
19. See Malcolm X and Alex Haley, *The Autobiography of Malcolm X as Told to Alex Haley* (New York: Grove Press, 1965).
20. I return to the question of naming in the epilogue, where I note problems and possible ways forward. Such work, however, lies beyond the scope of my book.
21. Bernard A. van Groningen, "ΕΚΔΟΣΙΣ," *Mnemosyne* 16 (1963): 1–17.
22. van Groningen, "ΕΚΔΟΣΙΣ," 5.
23. Raymond Starr, "The Circulation of Literary Texts in the Roman World," *ClQ* 37 (1987): 213–23.
24. Starr, "Circulation of Literary Texts," 213–14. "To trace the circulation of a Roman literary work, we shall use a schematic model to follow a literary text from its initial conception through the widening circles through which it moved [i.e., inner circle of the author's friends to the outermost circle of strangers].... The work remained entirely in the control of the author, who could decide whether it would ever reach a wider public either in further recitations or in written form. For the purposes of my discussion, I shall assume that the text is now polished and in its final form, although, obviously, the testing and revision of a work could go on indefinitely."

25. Both van Groningen and Starr are not wrong to make such distinctions, but I worry that their theories may give the impression of a stable, and overly simplified approach to the issue of publication in the ancient world.
26. Tiziano Dorandi, *Le stylet et la tablette: dans le secret des auteurs antiques* (Paris: Les Belle Lettres, 2000), 104. Here Dorandi quotes H. I. Marrou, "La technique de l'édition à l'époque patristique," *VC* 3 (1949): 209. The French is "ayant arrêté le texte définitif de son manuscrit, prend la decision (spontanée ou sollicitée, peu importe) de mettre son œuvre à la portée du public" (translation mine).
27. Harry A. Gamble, *Books and Readers in the Early Church* (New Haven, CT: Yale University Press, 1997), 82–143.
28. Gamble, *Books and Readers*, 84.
29. On publication in the ancient world, see also William Johnson, *Readers and Reading Culture in the High Roman Empire: A Study of Elite Communities* (New York: Oxford University Press, 2010); W. A. Johnson and H. N. Parker, eds., *Ancient Literacies: The Culture of Reading in Greece and Rome* (New York: Oxford University Press, 2009); Jaap Mansfield, *Prolegomena: Questions to be Settled before the Study of an Author or a Text* (Philosophia Antiqua; Leiden: Brill, 1997); W. Speyer, *Die literarische Fälschung im heidnischen und christlichen Altertum: Ein Versuch ihrer Deutung* (Handbuch der Altertumwissenschaft; Munich: Beck, 1971); Theodore Birt, *Das antike Buchwesen in seinem Verhältniss zur Litteratur* (Berlin: Hertz, 1882).
30. A potentially interesting modern comparandum might be Joan Didion, *South and West* (New York: Knopf, 2017). It is previously unpublished notebooks and drafts of a roadtrip she took in 1970.
31. John Bryant, *The Fluid Text: A Theory of Revision and Editing for Book and Screen* (Ann Arbor: University of Michigan Press, 2002), 1.
32. Bryant, *The Fluid Text*, 1.
33. Bryant, *The Fluid Text*, 11.
34. Foucault, "What Is an Author?," 107–8.

CHAPTER 2

1. On *commentarii*, see Andrew Riggsby, "Formal Questions," in his *Caesar in Gaul and Rome: War in Words* (Austin: University of Texas Press, 2006), 133–55. On *hypomnēmata*, see Dorandi, *Le stylet et la tablette*, 27–50, 86–101; A. van den Hoek, "Techniques of Quotation in Clement of Alexandria: A View of Ancient Literary Working Methods," *VC* 50 (1996): 223–43.
2. Christina Shuttleworth Kraus, "Hair, History, and Hegemony: Caesar's Style and its Earliest Critics," in *Aspects of the Language of Latin Prose*, ed. Tobias Reinhardt et al. (New York: Oxford University Press, 2005), 97–98.
3. Riggsby, "Formal Questions," 134.
4. See the discussion of Lucian, *How to Write History*, that follows.
5. Riggsby, "Formal Questions," 134–35.

6. Augustine, *Conf.* 3.4.7.
7. Cicero, *Fam.* 5.12.
8. Cicero, *Fam.* 5.12.8–9.
9. Cicero, *Att.* 1.19. All translations, unless noted otherwise, are mine.
10. Riggby, "Formal Questions," 133–55. One usually finds *hypomnēmata* in the plural, but occasionally—as in here and a couple other examples considered—also in the singular. The singular seems to function in many of these texts in more or less the same way as the plural. When I use the word in this book, I tend to use the plural.
11. Lucian, *How to Write History* 48.
12. Cicero, *Att.* 2.1.
13. Cicero, *Att.* 2.1.
14. Cicero, *Att.* 2.1: *nostrum illud* ὑπόμνημα.
15. Cicero, *Att.* 2.1.
16. Mroczek, *Literary Imagination*, 105.
17. Mroczek, *Literary Imagination*, 107.
18. See also Matthew Leigh, "Epic and Historiography in Rome," in *Companion to Greek and Roman Historiography*, ed. J. Marincola (Chichester: Blackwell, 2007), 484.
19. Josephus, in *Life* 358, translates the name of Caesar's text into Greek as τὰ Καίσαρος . . . ὑπομνήματα, which shows the rough equivalence of the terms *commentarii* and *hypomnēmata*.
20. He also wrote *commentarii* of his civil war against Pompey. Suetonius reports that he was aware of other *commentarii* of Julius Caesar's campaigns in Alexandria, Africa, and Spain, but he says no one knows who authored them, perhaps Oppius or Hirtius. See Suetonius, *Jul.* 56.
21. In the use of the phrase, "nude, erect, sexy," I follow the suggestion of Christina Shuttleworth Kraus, "Hair, History, and Hegemony," 112.
22. Cicero, *Brut.* 262.
23. Kraus, "Hair, History, and Hegemony," 109–15.
24. See Sean A. Gurd, *A Work in Progress: Literary Revision as Social Performance* (New York: Oxford University Press, 2012), 56–66. Gurd has drawn the connection to Cicero's desire for a literary Republic of perpetual collaborative revision and Caesar's literary autocracy.
25. There is a problem with the text of Hirtius's preface. For the details, see Lindsay J. H. Hall, "Hirtius and the *Bellum Alexandrinum*," *ClQ* 46 (1996): 411–15. The variation of text does not affect my reading of the preface.
26. Hall, "Hirtius and the *Bellum Alexandrinum*," 411–15.
27. *Bell. gall.* 8.*praef.*
28. See also Suetonius's reported speech of Asinius Pollio about Caesar's compositions in *Jul.* 56.
29. Bryant, *The Fluid Text*, 11.
30. On plausible deniability, see Andrew Riggsby, "Memoir and Autobiography in Republican Rome," in *Companion to Greek and Roman Historiography*, ed. J. Marincola (Chichester: Blackwell, 2007), 266–74.

31. Not all *hypomnēmata* and *commentarii* were intentionally created to be rewritten and authored by someone else.
32. See A. van den Hoek, "Techniques of Quotation in Clement of Alexandria," 223; A. N. Sherwin-White, *The Letters of Pliny: A Historical and Social Commentary* (Oxford: Clarendon, 1966), 219. See, however, Scott McGill, *Plagiarism in Latin Antiquity* (New York: Cambridge University Press, 2012), 53n68. McGill does comment on the financial aspects of the passage.
33. On the economics of book production and distribution in the ancient Rome world, see Roger S. Bagnall, *Early Christian Books in Egypt* (Princeton, NJ: Princeton University Press, 2009), 50–69; Charles W. Hedrick Jr., "Literature and Communication," in *The Oxford Handbook of Social Relations in the Roman World*, ed. Michael Peachin (New York: Oxford University Press, 2011), 167–90.
34. One difference in the modern analogy is that, if the one who reworked and published the deceased author were "caught," the person would likely be charged with forgery or plagiarism. In antiquity, concepts of forgery and plagiarism worked differently.
35. Plato, *Phaedr.* 275d.
36. Plato, *Phaedr.* 275e. See Jacques Derrida, "Plato's Pharmacy," in his *Dissemination*, trans. Barbara Johnson (Chicago, IL: University of Chicago Press, 1981), 61–119.
37. Plato, *Phaedr.* 278a.
38. Plato, *Phaedr.* 276d.
39. Plato, *Pol.* 295b–c.
40. Plato, *Pol.* 295c–e (Fowler, LCL).
41. From one point of view all texts in antiquity, not just ὑπομνήματα, were fluid (per discussion of John Bryant's work in chapter 1). Yet I am attending to reading practices vis-à-vis textuality, as well as writers' and readers' *habitus* regarding what one can do with different types of texts.
42. See also Galen, *On Anat. Proc.* 1.1, 2.1.
43. On this passage and the role of social revision and collaboration, see Gurd, *Work in Progress*, 11, 23, 32–39.
44. Gurd, *Work in Progress*, 11, 23, 32–39.
45. While her entire book is relevant to this discussion, see especially her chapters on the "Book" of the Psalms, Davidic attribution, and Ben Sira. Mroczek, *Literary Imagination*, 19–50, 51–85, 86–113.
46. See, for instance, Philo, *Heir* 176; *Virt.* 20; *Leg.* 2.146, 160; *Leg.* 1.150.
47. See Philo, *Fug.* 4. See also Philo, *Abr.* 5, in which the lives of the ancient are called *hypomnēmata*.
48. Philo, *Somn.* 2.268.
49. Philo, *Mos.* 2.48.
50. Philo, *Leg.* 4.162. See Galen on Hippocrates's writings and the potential ambiguity of hypomnēmata in the next chapter.
51. Lucian, *How to Write History*, 16.
52. Philo, *Flacc.* 131.

53. On Caligula as "Bootikins," see Mary Beard, *SPQR: A History of Ancient Rome* (New York: W. W. Norton, 2015), 390.
54. Philo, *Legat.* 165.
55. On Roman perception of daybooks, see Elizabeth Meyer, *Legitimacy and Law in the Roman World: Tabulae in Roman Belief and Practice* (New York: Cambridge University Press, 2004), 216–49.
56. Frank Cole Babbit, Introduction to *Moralia, Vol. 1*, by Plutarch, trans. Frank Cole Babbit (Cambridge, MA: Harvard University Press, 2000), ix.
57. Plutarch, *Tranq. an.* 464e–f.
58. There is also, perhaps, a playful tension between urgency and contentment in the preface: Plutarch selects reading materials on contentment in a hurry so that someone named Eros can rush him something on which to meditate.
59. See Christopher Pelling, "Plutarch's Method of Work in the Roman Lives," *Journal of Hellenic Studies* 99 (1979): 74–96; Luc van der Stockt, "A Plutarchan Hypomnema on Self-Love," *AJP* 120 (1999): 575–99; Luc van der Stockt, "Plutarch in Plutarch: The Problem of the Hypomnemata," in *La Biblioteca di Plutarco, Atti del IX Convegno plutarcheo Pavia, 13–15 giugno*, ed. Italo Gallo (Naples: D'Auria. 2004), 331–40.
60. See, for example, van der Stockt, "Plutarchan Hypomnema," 575–77.
61. See van der Stockt, "Plutarchan Hypomnema," 580.
62. See, for example, Sophia A. Xenophontos, "Plutarch's Compositional Technique in the *An seni respublica gerenda sit*," *AJP* 133 (2012): 61–91.
63. Plutarch, *Sull.* 6.5, 6.6; 14.2, 14.6; 17.1; 23.2; 37.1. See H. Behr, *Die Selbstdarstellung Sullas: ein aristokratischer Politiker zwischen persönlichem Führungsanspruch und Standessolidarität* (Frankfurt am Main: Peter Lang, 1993).
64. Plutarch, *Sull.* 37.1. See also 17.1.
65. Plutarch, *Sull.* 6.6.
66. γέγραφεν in Plutarch, *Sull.* 6.5; γέγραφε in 17.1; γράφων 37.1.
67. παραινεῖ in Plutarch, *Sull.* 6.6; λέγει in 14.2 and φησιν in 14.6; ἀπολογεῖται in 23.2.
68. Plutarch, *Sull.* 14.6.
69. Galen, *Lib. Prop. prol.* (19a.9K).
70. Galen, *Lib. Prop. prol.* (19a.10K).
71. Galen, *Lib. Prop. prol.* (19a.10–11K).
72. See Galen, *Lib. Prop. prol.* (19a:22–23K).
73. Galen, *Avoiding Distress*, 29. Translation taken from Vivian Nutton, *Avoiding Distress*," in *Galen: Psychological Writings*, ed. P. N. Singer (New York: Cambridge University Press, 2014), 86–87. See also Clare K. Rothschild and Trevor W. Thompson, "Galen's *On the Avoidance of Grief*: The Question of a Library at Antium," *CP* 107 (2012): 131–45.
74. Galen seems to have a category of texts or literature that are useful and uses the words χρεία or χρήσιμος. Galen, *Avoiding Distress*, 24b, 29.
75. Translation from Charles Singer, *Galen On Anatomical Procedures: Translation of the Surviving Books with Introduction and Notes* (New York: Oxford University Press, 1956), 1–2.
76. Translation from Singer, *Galen, On Anatomical Procedures*, 31–32.

77. On the notion of word usage and family resemblances, see Ludwig Wittgenstein, *Philosophical Investigations* §67–77. See Ludwig Wittgenstein, *Philosophische Untersuchungen-Philosophical Investigations*, 4th ed., trans. G. E. M. Anscombe, P. M. S. Hacker, and Joachim Schulte (Malden, MA: Wiley-Blackwell, 2009), 36–41.
78. On the Greek text, translation, and the point about discerning lack of finish in Hippocrates's writings, see Sean Gurd, "Galen on ἔκδοσις," in *Regards sur la Seconde Sophistique et son époque—Perceptions of the Second Sophistic and its Times*, ed. Thomas Schmidt and Pascale Fleury (Toronto: University of Toronto Press, 2011), 172, 182.
79. 17b.13K. See Sean Gurd, "Galen on ἔκδοσις," 172, 182; translations taken from Gurd.
80. 17a.1001K. See Sean Gurd, "Galen on ἔκδοσις," 172, 182; translation of Galen and Hippocrates taken from Gurd.
81. Philostratus, *Vit. Apoll.* 1.3.
82. Philostratus, *Vit. Apoll.* 1.3. Here I follow the translation of Christopher P. Jones, *Philostratus: The Life of Apollonius of Tyana, Books I–IV* (LCL 16; Cambridge, MA: Harvard University Press, 2005), 38–39, except that I opt to translate the phrase μεταγράψαι . . . τὰς διατριβὰς ταύτας as "alter these discourses" rather than "transcribe these works," as Jones does, because Philostratus seems to present himself as changing the text of Damis, not merely transcribing, and because τὰς διατριβὰς refers more to a speech genre than a written work.
83. See Jones, *Life of Apollonius*, 5–6; Edvard Meyer, "Apollonius von Tyana und die Biographie des Philostratos," *Hermes* 52 (1917): 317–424; E. L. Bowie, "Apollonius of Tyana: Tradition and Reality," *ANRW* 16, no. 2 (1978): 1652–99. See also Maria Dzielska, *Apollonius of Tyana in Legend and History* (Rome: L'Erma Bretschneide, 1986), 19–50.
84. See Raffaella Cribiore, *Gymnastics of the Mind: Greek Education in Hellenistic and Roman Egypt* (Princeton, NJ: Princeton University Press, 2001), 127–59.
85. See, for example, Quintillian, *Inst.* 10.3.30–32. See also Alan Millard, *Reading and Writing in the Time of Jesus* (Sheffield: Sheffield Academic Press, 2000), 63.
86. Philostratus, *Vit. Apoll.* 1.19 (Jones, *Life of Apollonius*, 77).
87. See *LSJ*, ἐκφάτνισμα I.
88. As will be clear by now, to "author" something in antiquity is itself a fluid configuration of authorization, origination, and ownership of a text.

CHAPTER 3

1. On *habitus*, see Pierre Bourdieu, *Outlines of a Theory of Practice*, trans. Richard Nice (Cambridge: Cambridge University Press, 1977). See also the helpful summary of Louise Hitchcock, *Theory for Classics: A Student's Guide* (New York: Routledge, 2008), 90.
2. Quintilian, *Inst.* 10.7.30–31. For an interesting comparandum, see Ann E. Hanson, "Memorandum and Speech of an Advocate," *ZPE* 8 (1971): 15–27.
3. Quintilian, *Inst.* 10.7.30–31.

4. Quintilian, *Inst.* 4.1.69
5. See, for example, Cicero, *De or.* 1.21.94.
6. Cicero, *Att.* 3.15; Katherine A. Geffcken, *Comedy in Pro Caelio: With an Appendix on the* In Clodium et Curionem (Waukunda, IL: Bolchazy and Carducci, 1995), 64.
7. See Jane W. Crawford, *M. Tullius Cicero: The Lost and Unpublished Orations* (Göttingen: Vandenhoeck und Ruprecht, 1984), 107; Giulio Puccioni, *Frammenti delle orazioni perdute* (Milan: A. Mondadori, 1971), 117–27; Richard Gustav Beck, *Einleitung und Disposition zu Ciceros fragmentarisch erhaltener Rede in Clodium et curionem* (Zwickau: Druck von Zückler, 1886).
8. See, for example, the elder Seneca, *Contraversiae* 4.5, in which a doctor is able to heal his father but not his mother-in-law because the cause of his father's sickness was grief.
9. Cicero, *Att.* 1.10.
10. Cicero, *Att.* 14.3.
11. Cicero, *Att.* 12.6; 13.44.
12. A comparable activity in antiquity would be *damnatio memoriae*, in which people attempted to remove the memory of despised persons, usually a ruler, by scratching out their names from coins, monuments, and other forms of texts.
13. In general, I try to avoid the term "pseudipigraphy," as it brings in a modern value judgment on ancient texts. I use the term "pseudepigraphon" because Cicero himself uses the concept.
14. On Cicero and collective literary revision, see Gurd, *Work in Progress*, 49–76.
15. Diodorus is mentioned in the tenth-century encyclopedia, the *Suda*, though there are obvious problems with its entry on Diodorus in constructing historical information about him.
16. Diodorus, *Library of History* 1.4.1. On travel in antiquity, especially vis-à-vis the apostle Paul, see Timothy Luckritz Marquis, *The Transient Apostle: Paul, Travel, and the Rhetoric of Empire* (New Haven, CT: Yale University Press, 2013).
17. Diodorus, *Library of History* 1.4.1.
18. Diodorus, *Library of History* 40.8.
19. I am aware that such claims of prolonged revision may be more a rhetorical ploy than a reflection of historical realities. The historical situation is less important to me than the *habitus* of ancient reading and writing reflected in Diodorus.
20. Sean Gurd has argued that every new draft of a work functioned provisionally as a final draft—until someone, whether the author or someone else, decided to rework it again, in which case the newer text became the final draft. See Sean Gurd, "Revision in Greek Literary Papyri," in *Probabilities, Hypotheticals, and Counterfactuals in Ancient Greek Thought*, ed. Victoria Wohl (New York: Cambridge University Press, 2014), 160–84, esp. 162. See also R. W. McCutcheon, "Silent Reading in Antiquity and the Future History of the Book," *Book History* 18 (2015): 1–32. See also Ann Ellis Hanson, "Galen: Author and Critic," in *Editing Texts-Texte edieren,* ed. Glenn Most (Göttingen: Vandenhoeck und Ruprecht, 1998), 22–53.

21. Diodorus, *Library of History* 1.5.2. *LSJ*, διασκευάζω, A.IV.1 lists this usage in Diodorus and defines the word in that context as "*revise* or *edit* a work *for publication*."
22. Of course, it seems possible that someone making or circulating a pirated copy would have simply not copied Diodorus's outline.
23. I borrow the phrase about an historically disciplined use of the imagination from Loveday Alexander, "Ancient Book Production and the Circulation of the Gospels," in *The Gospels for All Christians*, ed. Richard Bauckham (Grand Rapids, MI: Eerdmans, 1998), 71.
24. Horace, *Sat.* 2.4. Translation taken from Niall Rudd, *Horace: Satires and Epistles* (New York: Penguin, 2005), 56–57.
25. I am intentionally avoiding the word *pseudepigraphy* here, which implies falseness and therefore somehow a problem to be solved, rather than a complication to be analyzed and relished. See Irene Peirano, *The Rhetoric of the Roman Fake: Latin Pseudapigrapha in Context* (Cambridge: Cambridge University Press, 2012). See also the many works of Hindy Najman, but especially *Seconding Sinai*; and Hindy Najman, Itamar Manoff, and Eva Mroczek, "How to Make Sense of a Pseudonymous Attribution: The Cases of *4 Ezra* and *2 Baruch*," in *A Companion to Biblical Interpretation in Early Judaism*, ed. Matthias Henze (Grand Rapids, MI: Eerdmans, 2012), 308–36.
26. See Hindy Najman, "How Should We Contextualize Pseudepigrapha? Imitation and Emulation in *4 Ezra*," in *Flores Florentino: Dead Sea Scrolls and Other Early Jewish Studies in Honor of Florentino García Martínez*, ed. Anthony Hilhorst et al. (Leiden: Brill, 2007), 529–36.
27. Ps-Plato, *Epistles* 2.310a, 314 (Bury, LCL).
28. See, for instance, Col. 4:16; 2 Tim. 4:13.
29. See, for instance, Hindy Najman, "Traditionary Processes and Textual Unity in *4 Ezra*," in *Fourth Ezra and Second Baruch: Reconstruction After the Fall*, ed. Matthias Henze and Gabriele Boccaccini (Leiden/Boston: Brill, 2013), 112–13; Hindy Najman, "Configuring the Text in Biblical Studies," in *A Teacher for All Generation: Essays in Honor of James C. VanderKam*, ed. Eric F. Mason et al. (Leiden/Boston: Brill, 2012), 3–22, esp. 13–18. Najman notes that Ezra is described in *4 Ezra* 14 as a Moses-like figure both in his authority and the authority of the texts he produces. See also Jacob M. Myers, *I and II Esdras: Introduction, Translation, and Commentary* (Garden City, NY: Doubleday, 1974), 324–26; Michael Edward Stone, *Fourth Ezra: A Commentary on the Book of Fourth Ezra* (Hermeneia; Minneapolis, MN: Fortress, 1990), 418–19, 431–32, 441. See also Elliott R. Wolfson, "Gazing Beneath the Veil: Apocalyptic Envisioning the End," in *Reinterpreting Revelation and Tradition: Jews and Christians in Conversation*, ed. John Pawlikowski and Hayim Goren Perelmuter (Franklin, WI: Sheed and Ward, 2000), 80–83. Stephen Pfann does introduce some of the material elements of writing and writing in esoteric script in "The Use of Cryptographic and Esoteric

Scripts in Second Temple Judaism and Surrounding Cultures," in *Interpreting 4 Ezra and 2 Baruch: International Studies*, ed. Gabriele Boccaccini and Jason M. Zurawski (New York: T&T Clark, 2015), 173–96.

30. *4 Ezra* 14.23–26.
31. *4 Ezra* 14.44–46.
32. Quintilian, *Inst.* 10.3.31–33.
33. Cribiore, *Gymnastics of the Mind*, 127–59.
34. Dorandi also lists ἐπεκδιδόναι, προεκδιδόναι, προέκδοσις, ἀνέκδοσις, *publicare, emittere, divulgare, pervulgare, proferre*, and *foras dare* as Greek and Latin words to express publication. See Dorandi, *Le stylet et la tablette*, 103–104.
35. See *Oxford Latin Dictionary*. Edited by P.G.W. Glare. Oxford [Oxfordshire]: Clarendon Press (New York: Oxford University Press, 1982), s.v. 2.a.
36. I thank Olivia Stewart Lester for bringing this observation to my attention.
37. Epictetus, *Diatr.* [Arrian, *Epict. diss.*] praef. 1–8.
38. See Louis Hay, "Genetic Criticism: Origins and Perspectives," in *Genetic Criticism: Texts and Avant-textes*, ed. Jed Deppman et al. (Philadelphia: University of Pennsylvania Press, 2004), 17–27.
39. See Karen King, "What Is an Author?: Ancient Author-Function in the *Apocryphon of John* and the *Apocryphon of James*," in *"A Share in All Good Things": Essays in Honour of John S. Kloppenborg*, ed. William Arnal et al. (BETL; Leuven: Peeters, in press). King distinguishes three types of author function in antiquity: "to indicate the source of the work's contents, to guarantee stable transmission, and to situate the work within some broader context." Arrian participates in (at least) the first and third.
40. Here I am influenced by the work of Hindy Najman, especially her book *Seconding Sinai*, and Michel Foucault's foundational essay, "What Is an Author?"
41. A clear example of this distinction is the Aesopic tradition. In the preface to his collection, Phaedrus, a freedman of Augustus, says explicitly that he is the polisher (*ego polivi*) and Aesop is the author, or source (*Aesopus auctor*). Babrius similarly says he adorns the fables but he attributes the content to Aesop. Though such is not always the case; authenticity, attribution, and authority need not be so neatly linked. See Mark Letteney, "Authenticity and Authority: The Case for Dismantling a Dubious Correlation," in *Rethinking 'Authority' in Late Antiquity: Authorship, Law, and Transmission in Jewish and Christian Tradition*, edited by Mark Letteney and A. J. Berkowitz. London: Routledge, forthcoming.
42. Martial, *Epigram* 10.1.1–2.4. Gurd, *Work in Progress*, 108–113, esp. 111.
43. Ovid, *Am.* 1.1. See Gurd, *Work in Progress*, 15.
44. Horace, *Ars* 390. See Dorandi, *Le stylet et la tablette*, 129–54.
45. Here he quotes Terence, *Haut.* 75.
46. Aristophanes used the Greek phrase Περικλέης οὐλύμπιος ἤστραπτ' ἐβρόντα ξυνεκύκα τὴν Ἑλλάδα.
47. The Teubner and Oxford Classical Texts editions of Cicero's *Orator* read "*ab Aristophane*" and make no mention of other variants. See Dorandi, *Le stylet et la*

*tablette*, 119. It was Dorandi's book that initially brought this passage and the existence of only corrected manuscripts to my attention.
48. Cicero, *Att.* 13.44.
49. Cicero, *Lig.* 33 (Watts, LCL).
50. Josephus, *Ag. Ap.* 1.46.
51. Josephus, *Ag. Ap.* 1.48
52. Josephus, *Ag. Ap.* 1.49–50.
53. On the use of rough draft material, see Lucian, *How to Write History* 48. See also Shaye J. D. Cohen, *Josephus in Galilee and Rome: His* Vita *and Development as a Historian* (Leiden: Brill, 1979), 80.
54. Josephus, *Life* 358. See also Josephus, *Life* 342; *Ag. Ap.* 1.56; *Ant.* 15.174, et al.
55. Cohen, *Josephus in Galilee and Rome,* 80. On other theories, see 22nn70–71.
56. See Gurd, "Cicero: Collective Revision and a Literary Republic" and "Pliny the Younger: Genetic and General Publics" in his *Work in Progress*, 49–76 and 105–26.
57. *LSJ*, s.v. I–II.
58. Steve Mason, "Of Audience and Meaning: Reading Josephus' *Bellum Iudaicum* in the Context of a Flavian Audience," in *Josephus and Jewish History in Flavian Rome and Beyond*, ed. J. Sievers and G. Lembi (Leiden/Boston: Brill, 2005) 70–100.
59. Mason, "Of Audience and Meaning," 88–90.
60. Mason, "Of Audience and Meaning," 88.
61. Mason, "Of Audience and Meaning," 89; emphasis in original.
62. Huitink and van Henten have critiqued Mason's view of publication as too focused on oral recitation and therefore close-minded. Their critiques on publication and oral recitation do not relate to the purposes of my argument here. See L. Huitink and J. W. van Henten, "The Publication of Flavius Josephus' Works and Their Audiences," *Zutot* 6 (2009) 49–60.
63. Josephus, *Ant.* 20.259.
64. Josephus, *Ant.* 20.267.
65. Richard Laqueur, *Der jüdische Historiker Flavius Josephus: Ein biographischer Versuch auf neuer quellenkritischer Grundlage* (1920 repr.; Rome: "L'Erma" di Bretschneider, 1970) esp. 4–5.
66. See David Barish, "The 'Autobiography' of Flavius Josephus and the Hypothesis of a Second Edition of his 'Antiquities,'" *HTR* 71 (1978): 62.
67. Josephus, *Ant.* 20.267.
68. Josephus, *Life* 363.
69. Eva Mroczek also points to the work of Malachi Beit-Arié and Israel Ta-Shma, whose identify certain medieval Hebrew manuscripts as "open books." Mroczek, *Literary Imagination*, 106–107. Ta-Shma writes, "quite often books were not meant by their authors to serve as final statements, but rather as presentations of an interim state of knowledge or opinion, somewhat like our computerized databases, which are constantly updated and which give the user a summary of the data known at the time of last updating. In a similar way, the medieval book was sometimes conceived

of as no more than a solid basis for possible future alterations by the author himself." I. M. Ta-Shma, "The 'Open' Book in Medieval Hebrew Literature: The Problem of Authorized Editions," *BJRL* 75 (1993): 17.
70. Mroczek, *Literary Imagination*, 106–107. Malachi Beit-Arié, *Hebrew Manuscripts of East and West: Towards a Comparative Codicology* (Panizzi Lectures; London: British Museum, 1993); Beit-Arié, "Perek Shirah: Introduction and Critical Edition." 2 vols., PhD thesis, Hebrew University of Jerusalem, 1966; Israel M. Ta-Shma, "The 'Open' Book in Medieval Hebrew Literature: The Problem of Authorized Editions," *BJRL* 75 (1993): 17–24.
71. Ta-Shma, "The 'Open' Book in Medieval Hebrew Literature," 17. Cited in Mroczek, *Literary Imagination*, 107.
72. Mroczek, *Literary Imagination*, 107.
73. Gurd, "Revision in Greek Literary Papyri," 162.

CHAPTER 4

1. There is no clear, natural, and eternal line, of course, that separates the category of revised version of a text from a new creation of that same text. Such ideas are socially constructed. In fact, in a pre–printing press context, every copied text can be regarded as a new version of that text, since the act of copying changed the physical appearance and almost certainly altered the wording.
2. Bryant, *The Fluid Text*, 88–90. Bryant uses the idea of the original author in the modern sense of the term.
3. On material philology (also called new philology), see Liv Ingeborg Lied and Hugo Lunghaug, "Studying Snapshots: Manuscript Culture, Textual Fluidity, and New Philology," in *Snapshots of Evolving Tradition: Jewish and Christian Manuscript Culture, Textual Fluidity, and New Philology,* ed. Liv Ingeborg Lied and Hugo Lunghaug (Texte und Untersuchungen zur Geschichte der altchristlichen Literatur 175; Berlin: Walter de Gruyter, 2017), 1–19.
4. For a detailed account of the discoveries, see Weston Fields, *The Dead Sea Scrolls: A Full History,* vol. 1 (Leiden: Brill, 2009). For an introduction to the Dead Sea Scrolls, see James C. VanderKam, *The Dead Sea Scrolls and the Bible* (Grand Rapids, MI: Eerdmans, 2012). For a critical assessment of the discovery stories at Qumran (as well as discovery stories of other ancient texts), see Eva Mroczek, "True Stories and the Poetics of Biblical Discovery," *BSR* 45 (2016): 21–31.
5. See, for example, James C. VanderKam, *An Introduction to Early Judaism* (Grand Rapids, MI: Eerdmans, 2002), 150.
6. Yonder Moynihan Gillihan, *Civic Ideology, Organization, and Law in the Rule Scrolls: A Comparative Study of the Covenanters' Sect and Contemporary Voluntary Associations in Political Context* (Leiden/Boston: Brill, 2012), 505.
7. See Mroczek, *Literary Imagination*, 19–45, in which Mroczek attends to the various manuscripts of Psalms found at Qumran and to their pluriformity. She argues

persuasively that there were many Psalms in the ancient Jewish imagination (sometimes as many as 4,050 psalms of David), but there was not yet a "Book of the Psalms."

8. On the language of unilinear development, see Hindy Najman, "Traditionary Processes and Textual Unity in *4 Ezra*," 107.

9. On a traditional source critical approach, see Philip S. Alexander, "The Redaction-History of *Serekh ha-Yahad*: A Proposal," *RevQ* 17 (1996): 437–56; Sarianna Metso, "The Textual Traditions of the Qumran Community Rule," in *Legal Texts and Legal Issues: Proceedings of the Second Meeting of the International Organization for Qumran Studies, Cambridge 1995*, ed. M. Bernstein et al. (STDJ 23; Leiden: Brill, 1997), 141–47; Geza Vermes, "The Leadership of the Qumran Community: Sons of Zadok–Priests–Congregation," in *Geschichte-Tradition-Reflexion: Festschrift für Martin Hengel zum 70. Geburtstag*, 3 vols., ed. H. Cancik et al. (Tübingen: Mohr Siebeck, 1996), 1:375–85. On a more complicated approach, see Charlotte Hempel, "Shifting Paradigms Concerning the Literary Development of the Serekh," in *The Qumran Rule Texts in Context: Collected Studies*, ed. Charlotte Hempel (Tübingen: Mohr Siebeck, 2013), 109–19; "Rewritten Rule Texts," in *The Qumran Rule Texts in Context: Collected Studies*, ed. Charlotte Hempel (Tübingen: Mohr Siebeck, 2013), 137–50; Alison Schofield, "Rereading S: A New Model of Textual Development in Light of the Cave 4 *Serekh* Copies," *DSD* 15 (2008): 96–120.

10. Sarianna Metso, *The Textual Development of the Qumran Community Rule* (Leiden: Brill, 1997), 154.

11. See Foucault, "What Is an Author?," 101–20, esp. 107–108.

12. On the question of authority and interpretation at Qumran, see Steven Fraade, "Interpretive Authority in the Studying Community at Qumran," *JJS* 44.1 (1993): 46–69, esp. 47.

13. On the issue of author figures, authorship, authority, and authorizing figures in Second Temple Jewish texts, see Najman, *Seconding Sinai*, 497–518; Hindy Najman, "Text and Figure in Ancient Jewish *Paideia*," in *Past Renewals: Interpretive Authority, Renewed Revelation, and the Quest for Perfection in Jewish Antiquity*, ed. Hindy Najman (Boston: Leiden, 2010), 243–57.

14. The question of use and authorization of the community rules is not unrelated to but must be kept separate from the question of authoritative interpretation of scripture at Qumran. 1QS 6.6–8 and 8.12–16 paint a picture of scriptural interpretation as a regular part of community life, and one that was done collectively. See Fraade, "Interpretative Authority at Qumran," 51–58. While the picture of interpretation in these passages is a collective one, we must be careful to remember the highly stratified leadership of the sectarian movement. The passages still leave room for the interpretations of a handful of members being more authoritative than others. Moreover, 8.11–12 refers to a community leader who plays a leadership role in the act of collective interpretation (Fraade, "Interpretative Authority at Qumran," 62).

15. See 1QS 3.13; 9.12, 21; 1 QSb 1.1; 3.22; 5.20; 4Q258 1.1; 8.5; 4Q259 3.7. See Metso, *Textual Development*, 111–12; Carol A. Newson, *The Self as Symbolic Space: Constructing Identify and Community at Qumran* (Leiden: Brill, 2004), 108. Philip Alexander noted nearly two decades ago that the *Rule of the Community* "is best taken as a manual of instruction to guide the Instructor in his duties towards the community" (Alexander, "Redaction-History," 439).
16. Josephus does mention the baths and washing rituals of the Essenes in *J.W.* 2.128–53, although it is not clear whether or not he refers to Qumran when he writes about the Essenes.
17. Alexander, "Redaction-History," 439.
18. Alexander, "Redaction-History," 439.
19. Peter Kivy, *The Performance of Reading: An Essay in the Philosophy of Literature* (Malden, MA: Wiley-Blackwell, 2009). On legal study as performative at Qumran, see also Fraade, "Interpretive Authority at Qumran," 63.
20. Neh. 8 also contains information about the interaction between the reader and those listening, which need not necessarily be assumed in the teaching of the Two Spirits by the instructor, although 1QS 7.15 refers to proper physical gestures while speaking (i.e., not with the left hand), which may indicate an expectation of how to listen and interact. On listening as embodied experience in antiquity, see Matthew Larsen, "Listening with the Body, Seeing through the Ears: Contextualizing Philo's Lecture Event in *On the Contemplative Life*," *JSJ* 47 (2016): 447–74.
21. Steven Fraade similarly argues for seeing the Damascus Document (CD) as a performative script rather than simply a composite document drawn from a variety of sources. See Fraade, "Ancient Jewish Law and Narrative in Comparative Perspective: The Damascus Document and the Mishnah," *Diné Israel* 24 (2007): 87. See also Fraade, "Interpretive Authority at Qumran," 63.
22. Alexander, "Redaction-History," 439: "*1 QS* is not a rule-book or code of practice for new members, but an aide-mémoire for someone well-versed in the Community's ways." See also Jonathan Draper, "Vice Catalogues as Oral Mnemonic Cues: A Comparative Study of the Two Ways Traditions in the *Didache* and Parallels from the Perspective of Oral Tradition," in *Jesus, the Voice, and the Text*, ed. Tom Thatcher (Waco, TX: Baylor Press, 2008), 112. Draper refers to the Two Ways traditions as a skeleton for the teacher to use. On scribal and reading cultures at Qumran, see David Andrew Teeter, *Scribal Laws: Exegetical Variation in the Textual Transmission of Biblical Law in the Late Second Temple Period* (FAT 92; Tübingen: Mohr Siebeck, 2014).
23. Philo, *Contempl.* 75b–76 (Colson, LCL).
24. See Larsen, "Listening with the Body," 447–74.
25. On this emendation and its significance, see James Nati, "The *Community Rule* or *Rules for the Communities*?: Contextualizing the Qumran *Serakhim*," in *Sibyls, Scriptures, and Scrolls: John Collins at 70*, ed. Joel Baden et al. (*JSJ*Sup 175;

Leiden: Brill, 2016), 2:916–39, esp. 925–26. I am thankful to Nati for his article and his helpful engagement in this section of my chapter over personal conversations.

26. On brackets in the Dead Sea scrolls, see Emanuel Tov, *Scribal Practices and Approaches Reflected in the Texts Found in the Judean Desert* (Atlanta, GA: SBL Press, 2009).

27. Sarianna Metso, *The Serekh texts* (London/New York: T&T Clark, 2007), 70.

28. 1QS 6.16, 22, 25; 7.3, 16, 19, 20, 25; 8.17, 24. On the different approaches to the pure food in 1QS and 4QS, see Nati, "The *Community Rule* or *Rules for the Communities*," 931–93.

29. John J. Collins, "The Yahad and the 'Qumran Community,'" in *Biblical Traditions in Transmission: Essays in Honour of Michael A. Knibb*, ed. C. Hempel and J. M. Lieu (Leiden: Brill, 2006), 81–96. See also John J. Collins, *Beyond the Qumran Community: The Sectarian Movement of the Dead Sea Scrolls* (Grand Rapids, MI: Eerdmans, 2009).

30. See the comparison of the *Yaḥad* and modern religious movements in Eyal Regev, *Sectarianism in Qumran: A Cross-Cultural Perspective* (Berlin: Walter de Gruyter, 2007).

31. Hempel, "Shifting Paradigms," 110.

32. Hempel, "Shifting Paradigms," 110. Translation by Hempel.

33. Another way of reading this passage is to speak of the "Zadokite takeover." See Vermes, "The Leadership of the Qumran Community: Sons of Zadok—Priests—Congregation," 1:375–84.

34. On the difficulty of speaking about the leadership structures of the sectarians, see Sarianna Metso, "Problems in Reconstructing the Organizational Chart of the Essenes," *DSD* 16 (2009): 388–415.

35. See James Nati, "The *Community Rule* or *Rules for the Communities*?," 913–39, especially 937.

36. See Deleuze and Guatarri, *A Thousand Plateaus*, 3–25, especially 15.

37. See Jan Vansina, *Oral Tradition as History* (Madison: University of Wisconsin Press, 1985), 54 (cited in Draper, "Vice Catalogues as Oral Mnemonic Cues," 113). On work as energy, see John Bryant, *The Fluid Text*, 44–63. See also Jennifer Knust, "In Pursuit of a Singular Text: New Testament Textual Criticism and the Desire for the True Original," *RC* 2 (2008): 1–15.

38. On different editions of other texts in antiquity, Mroczek writes that "[d]ifferent editions of Ben Sira may have existed already during his or his students' time." Mroczek, *Literary Imagination*, 105.

39. See *LSJ*, s.v. II.4.

40. Josephus, *Ant.* 7.110, 293; 10.5, 55; 11.94, 96, 104, 208, 248; 15.174; *Life* 342, 358; *Ag. Ap.* 1.56.

41. See also the textual pluriformity of the versions of the Damascus Document found in the Cairo genizah. On the history of the transmission of the Damascus Document, see Lara Guglielmo, "Manuscripts, Editions, and Translations of the

Damascus Document from 1896 to 2007: Towards a (re-)Edition of 4Q266," *Materia Giudaica* 13 (2008): 251–78.
42. Tertullian, *Praescr.* 7.
43. Greg Woolf, "Approaching the Ancient Library," in *Ancient Libraries*, ed. Jason König et al. (New York: Cambridge University Press, 2013), 11. Woolf does not clarify what language is shared. Greek fragments have been found at Qumran.
44. *PHerc.* 155 and *PHerc.* 339 both contain Philodemus's *On the Stoics*. Paleographically, *PHerc.* 339 appears older than *PHerc.* 155. *PHerc.* 339 has the subscription ΦΙΛΟΔΗΜΟΥ | ΠΕΡΙ ΤΩΝ ΣΤΩΙΚΩΝ. P155 is more fragmentary and contains no subscription. See Tiziano Dorandi, "Filodemo, Gli Stoici," *Cronache Ercolanesi* 12 (1982): 91–92.
45. Marcello Gigante, *Filodemo in Italia* (Firenze: Felice Le Monnier, 1990), 27.
46. Tiziano Dorandi, ed., *Filodemo. Storia dei filosofi. Platone e L'Academia (PHerc. 1021 e 164)* (Napoli: Bibliopolis, 1991). Dorandi then tries to use this information about Philodemus's writing technique in this one instance and extrapolate it out to a process of writing for the Greco-Roman world. Dorandi, *Le stylet et la tablette*, 11–13. As Sean Gurd has shown, ancient writing and revision practices were not so one-size-fits-all. See Gurd, *Work in Progress*. I am thankful to David Sider for the suggestion through a personal conversation that the excerpts in *PHerc.* 164 were possibly taken by a scribe.
47. Marcello Gigante, *Philodemus in Italy,* English trans. Dirk Obbink (Ann Arbor: University of Michigan Press, 1995), 17.
48. Here I follow the content, style, and presentation of the catalogue of titles given in Gianluca Del Mastro, *Titoli e annotazioni bibliologiche nei papiri greci di Ercolano* (Napoli: Centro Internazionale per lo Studio dei Papiri Ercolanensi "Marcello Gigante," 2014), 417.
49. All five are taken from Gianluca Del Mastro, *Titoli e annotazioni bibliologiche nei papiri greci di Ercolano*, 420–21.
50. Dorandi, *Le stylet et la tablette*, 11–13; Gigante, *Filodemo in Italia*, 17. David Blank disagrees with this interpretation of the word ὑπομνημάτικον. He argues that it indicates that these books were recorded lecture notes and therefore intended for limited circulation. David Blank, "Versionen oder Zwillinge? Zu den Handschriften der ersten Bücher von Philodems Rhetorik," in *Editing Texts—Texte edieren*, ed. Glenn W. Most (Göttingen: Vandenhoeck und Ruprecht, 1999), 123–40. See also Daniel Delattre, *La Villa de Papyrus et les rouleaux d'Herculanum: la bibliothéque de Philodème* (Liège: CEDOPAL et Les Editions de l'Université de Liège, 2006), 84–85.
51. Blank, "Versionen oder Zwillige?," 123–40.
52. Bryant, *The Fluid Text*, 30–63.
53. See discussion of Poseidonactos of Biton above, who is mentioned as the scribe or corrector in *PHerc.* 1426.

54. Thanks to Greg Given for helping me with the language of unattributed to attributed, rather than unauthored to authored, which opens up a modern discourse with much baggage.

CHAPTER 5

1. It is clear that what constitutes publication and the concept of a book are also technologically determined, and such technological factors influence social constructions, perceptions, and negotiations.
2. For an overview, see Richard Burridge, *What Are the Gospels?: A Comparison with Graeco-Roman Biography* (New York: Cambridge University Press, 2004), 3–24. See also R. H. Gundry, "Recent Investigations into the Literary Genre 'Gospel,'" in *New Dimensions in New Testament Study*, ed. R. N. Longenecker and M. C. Tenney (Grand Rapids, MI: Zondervan, 1974), 97–114.
3. See Eve-Marie Becker, "The Reception of 'Mark' in the 1st and 2nd Centuries c.e. and Its Significance for Genre Studies," in *Mark and Matthew II: Comparative Readings: Reception History, Cultural Hermeneutics, and Theology*, ed. Eve-Marie Becker and Anders Runesson (Tübingen: Mohr Siebeck, 2013), 15–36, esp. 24, 25. While she seems to fit best in the category of viewing the Gospel according to Mark as a "historical monograph," Becker also uses language that views "Mark" as the "inventor of written gospel-concept" and as a "person-centered pre-historiographical account," which would amount to a new genre.
4. See, for example, Martin Dibelius, *Die Formsgeschichte des Evangeliums*, 2nd ed. (Tübingen: J. C. B. Mohr, 1933); Rudolf Bultmann, *Die Geschichte der synoptischen Tradition* (Göttingen: Vandenhoeck und Ruprecht, 1961); Philipp Vielhauer, *Geschichte der Urchristlichen Literatur: Einleitung in das Neue Testament, die Apokryphen und die Apostolischen Väter* (New York: De Gruyter, 1975); Robert Guelich, "The Gospel Genre," in *Das Evangelium und die Evangelien*, ed. Peter Stuhlmacher (Tübingen: Mohr Siebeck, 1983), 183–219.
5. On biography, see Ernest Renan, *Life of Jesus* (London: Kegan Paul, 1893); Clyde Votaw, "The Gospels and Contemporary Biographies," *AmJT* 19 (1915): 45–73, 217–49; Charles Talbert, *What Is a Gospel? The Genre of the Canonical Gospels* (Philadelphia: Fortress, 1977); Burridge, *What Are the Gospels?*; Richard Burridge, "About People, By People, For People: Gospel Genre and Audiences," in *The Gospels for All Christians: Rethinking the Gospel Audiences*, ed. Richard Bauckham (Grand Rapids, MI: Eerdmans, 1997), 113–46; Hubert Cancik, "Die Gattung Evangelium: Das Evangelium des Markus im Rahmen der antiken Historigraphie," in *Markus Philologie: historische, literargeschichtliche und stilistische Untersuchungen zum zweiten Evangelium*, ed. Hubert Cancik (Tübingen: J. C. B. Mohr, 1984), 85–113; Hubert Cancik, "Bios und Logos: Formengeschichtliche Untersuchungen zu Lukians 'Demonax,'" in *Markus Philologie: historische, literargeschichtliche und stilistische Untersuchungen zum zweiten Evangelium*, ed. Hubert Cancik

(Tübingen: J. C. B. Mohr, 1984), 115–30. On aretalogy, see Moses Hadas and Morton Smith, *Heroes and Gods: Spiritual Biographies in Antiquity* (London: Routledge and Kegan Paul, 1965); Jonathan Z. Smith, "Good News Is No News: Aretology and Gospel," in his *Map Is Not Territory* (Chicago: University of Chicago Press, 1978), 190–207.

6. See Collins, *Mark*; Eva-Marie Becker, *Das Markus-Evangelium im Rahmen antiker Historiographie* (Tübingen: Mohr Siebeck, 2006). How a history about a single person is different from a biography in the ancient world remains unclear to me.

7. See Wittgenstein, *Philosophische Untersuchungen-Philosophical Investigations*, 36–41 (§67–77).

8. Detlev Dormeyer, *Evangelium als literarische und theologische Gattung* (Darmstadt: Wissenschaftliche Buchgesellschaft, 1989).

9. Dormeyer, *Evangelium als literarische und theologische Gattung*, 7–25. He provides a quick sketch of how the gospels are discussed in Papias, Justin, Irenaeus, and Origen, along with a discussion of the literary and theological "solutions" and the generic names for the gospel in the second century. Then Dormeyer moves immediately to Hermann Samuel Reimarus and G. E. Lessing, who were active in the eighteenth century.

10. See, for example, Collins, *Mark*, 2–6.

11. On Irenaeus's use of the term "gospel," see Annette Yoshiko Reed, "ΕΥΑΓΓΕΛΙΟΝ: Orality, Textuality, and the Christian Truth in Irenaeus' *Adversus haereses*," *VC* 56 (2002): 11–46.

12. Furthermore, when I say the Gospels according to Matthew, Mark, and Luke, I mean such gospels *as we have them* in the manuscript tradition, and not necessarily as they existed in a definitive form in the first century CE. Of course, this is not far enough, as the idea of the Gospel according to Mark as distinguished from, say, the Gospel according to Matthew is itself a later development, but for chapters 5 and 6, it will have to suffice. A completely new framework for thinking about the gospel tradition and gospel writing lies beyond the scope of the present book. I will compare the text of the Gospel according to Mark with the Gospels according to Matthew and Luke as we have them in the Nestle-Aland critical edition of the Greek New Testament, not because I think they were perceived as separate books in the first and most of the second centuries, but in order to show that the textual traditions as we now have them are best understood in the first centuries as the same open, growing textual tradition of gospel rather than different books with different authors. Additionally, I will argue there was no such thing as the idea of the Gospel according to Mark before the end of the second century, and thus no conception of the Gospel according to Mark in distinction from the Gospel according to Matthew. There was simply the gospel, and it existed in an unfinished, pluriform, and open textual constellation. Thus, when I write "the Gospel according to [Name]," I am more precisely referring to the textual tradition behind the text we now call "the Gospel according to [Name]." Since such a formula is

tedious to the reader, I will usually write "the Gospel according to [Name]" and trust my reader will understand I, in fact, mean the textual tradition behind the text we now call "the Gospel according to [Name]."

13. Eusebius, *Hist. eccl.* 3.24.5.
14. Origen, *Cels.* 2.13.
15. Tertullian, *Jejun.* 10.3. Here Tertullian is speaking specifically of Acts of the Apostles.
16. On the preface as a later addition, see Joseph B. Tyson, *Marcion and Luke-Acts: A Defining Struggle* (Columbia: University of South Carolina, 2006), 109–16.
17. Loveday Alexander, *The Preface to Luke's Gospel: Literary Convention and Social Context in Luke 1.1–4 and Acts 1.1* (SNTSMS 78; Cambridge: Cambridge University Press, 1993); Loveday Alexander, "Luke's Preface in the Context of Ancient Preface Writing," *NovT* 28 (1986): 48–74.
18. Galen, *On Anat. Proc.* 1.1, 2.1.
19. Galen, *On Anat. Proc.* 1.1, 2.1.
20. Galen, *On Anat. Proc.* 2.1. Translation from Singer, *Galen, On Anatomical Procedures* 32.
21. Luke 1:1–4.
22. The translation is my own, but I consult Michel Patillon and Giancarlo Bolognesi, *Aelius Théon Progymnasmata: Texte établi et traduit* (Paris: Les Belles Lettres, 1997), 39; George Kennedy, *Progymnasmata: Greek Textbooks of Prose Composition and Rhetoric* (Leiden/Boston: Brill, 2002), 28.
23. Nicolaus of Damascus, *Vit. Caes.* 2.
24. Theon, *Progymnasmata* 78.25, 79.7, et al.
25. Q is short for the German *Quelle*, which means "source." It is a hypothetical document based on the agreements of Matthew and Luke, assuming that Luke did not use Matthew as a source, or vice versa. Q-hypothesis has enjoyed wide acceptance among scholars for a long time, though it has had a recent surge of critics. See Francis Watson, *Gospel Writing: A Canonical Perspective* (Grand Rapids, MI: Eerdmans, 2013), 117–285; Mark Goodacre, *The Case Against Q: Studies in Markan Priority and the Synoptic Problem* (Harrisburg, PA: Trinity International Press, 2002).
26. Francis Watson calls "Luke's" compositional procedures a "radical rewriting of his source material." Watson, *Gospel Writing*, 200. Based on what I have argued here, I would not call Luke's reworking of the unpolished sources "radical."
27. Compare Demosthenes, *Fals. leg.* 19.257, which presents Demosthenes as knowing and tracing accurately all of Philip's actions, using language similar to the preface to the Gospel according to Luke. Demosthenes claims a unique ability to make an accusation, because he knows everything well (ἀκριβέστατ' εἰδὼς) and has followed everything closely (παρηκολουθηκὼς ἅπασι).
28. I categorize the producer of the preface as a reader and the producer of the Gospel according to Matthew as a user, since the Gospel according to Matthew does

not comment explicitly on the text we now call the Gospel according to Mark. I recognize that readers are users of texts and users of texts are also in some sense readers. Yet for the purpose of this book, I find the distinction useful, as explicitly commenting on a text and reworking a text have different functions.

29. Eusebius, *Hist. eccl.* 3.24.14–15 (Lake, LCL).
30. See Josephus, *Ant.* 15.37, 52.
31. Lucian, *How to Write History* 48.
32. See Eusebius, *Hist. eccl.* 3.24.5, a passage in which Eusebius calls the Gospels according to Matthew and John ὑπομνήματα.
33. See Johannes Quasten, *Patrology, Vol. 1: The Beginnings of Patristic Literature* (Notre Dame, IN: Christian Classics, 1983), 82–85.
34. On the fragments of Papias, see Josef Kürzinger, *Papias von Hierapolis und die Evangelien des Neuen Testaments* (Regensburg: F. Pustet, 1983); Daniel Armin Baum, "Der Presbyter des Papias über einen 'Hermeneuten' des Petrus. Zu Eusebius, Hist. eccl. 3,39,15," *TZ* 56 (2000): 21–35; Enrico Norelli, *Papia di Hierapolis, Esposizione degli Oracoli del Signore. I frammenti. Introduzione, testo, traduzione e note* (Milan: Paoline, 2005); Dennis R. MacDonald, *Two Shipwrecked Gospels: The Logoi of Jesus and Papias's Exposition of Logia about the Lord* (Atlanta: Society of Biblical Literature Press, 2012).
35. Eusebius, *Hist. eccl.* 3.39.
36. Eusebius, *Hist. eccl.* 3.39.1.
37. François Bovon, *Luke 1: A Commentary on the Gospel of Luke 1:1–9:50* (Minneapolis: Fortress, 2002), 9. Strangely, Bovon does not provide a citation supporting his claim.
38. Eusebius, *Hist. eccl.* 3.39.3.
39. Eusebius, *Hist. eccl.* 3.39.3–4 (Ehrman, LCL).
40. *LSJ*, s.v. I–II
41. Eusebius, *Hist. eccl.* 3.39.2: κατὰ τὸ προοίμιον.
42. Eusebius, *Hist. eccl.* 3.39.4–7.
43. Eusebius, *Hist. eccl.* 3.39.3–7.
44. Eusebius, *Hist. eccl.* 3.39.14 (LCL, Lake).
45. See George Kennedy, "Classical and Christian Source Criticism," in *The Relationships between the Gospels: An Interdisciplinary Dialogue*, ed. William O. Walker (San Antonio, TX: Trinity International Press, 1978), 125–55; David Aune, *The New Testament in its Literary Environment* (Philadelphia: Westminster Press, 1987), 66–67; Yoon-Man Park, *Mark's Memory Resources and the Controversy Stories (Mark 2:1–3:6): An Application of the Frame Theory of Cognitive Science to the Markan Oral-Aural Narrative* (Leiden: Brill, 2010), 53. See also Wally V. Cirafesi and Gregory P. Fewster, "Justin's ἀπομνημονεύματα and Ancient Greco-Roman Memoir," *Early Christianity* 7 (2016): 186–212.
46. Philostratus, *Vit. Apoll.* 1.3; Porphyry, *Vit. Plot.* 3.37–39. I thank Greg Given both for guiding me to this passage and for helping me understand it more correctly.

47. Galen, *On the Order of My Own Books*, 1.1–2. (19a.49–56K).
48. Eusebius, *Hist. eccl.* 3.39.16.
49. See Porphyry, *Vit. Plot.* 3.37–39, where ordering one's work was an activity that sought to control the reading of one's work. I disagree with Francis Watson, *Gospel Writing*, 130, who takes the order to refer to a difference of sequence of stories.
50. It should be noted that it is not entirely certain that "Mark's" notes and "Matthew's" rearrangement can be identified in a one-to-one relationship with the texts we now call the Gospels according to Mark and Matthew.
51. Lucian, *How to Write History* 47–48.
52. Justin Martyr primarily thought of gospel tradition as a fluid constellation of textual objects with a collective authorship of the apostles. These texts were the residue of the apostles' oral teaching, and they were preserved as an *aide-mémoire* for later generations. In one instance, however, Justin hones in on a specific section of the textual tradition of the Gospel according to Mark and makes a claim about its textual genetics. See Justin Martyr, *Dial.* 106.3. The passage is about the changing of the names of the sons of Zebedee to Boanerges, which means "sons of thunder," is unique to the Gospel according to Mark (Mark 3:17). Miroslav Marcovich and Johann Karl Theodor von Otto, in their respective critical editions of *Dialogue with Trypho*, make conjectural emendations of the Greek phrase ἐν τοῖς Ἀπομνημονεύμασιν αὐτοῦ (Miroslav Marcovich, *Iustini Martyris Dialogus cum Tryphone* [New York: De Gruyter, 1997]; Johann Karl Theodor von Otto, *Justini Philosophi et Martyris cum Tryphone Judaeo* [Jena: Prostat in Libraria, Hermann Dufft, 1876]). Marcovich changes the text to ἐν τοῖς Ἀπομνημονεύμασιν <τῶν ἀποστόλων> αὐτοῦ and Otto to ἐν τοῖς Ἀπομνημονεύμασιν αὐτῶν (i.e., ἀποστόλων). The manuscript tradition, however, reads ἐν τοῖς ἀπομνημονεύμασιν αὐτοῦ and this reading also seems to be the *lectio difficilior*, since it goes against the way Justin usually refers to gospel tradition. Justin refers to the textual tradition we now call the Gospel according to Mark, like Papias, as ἀπομνημονεύματα. He does not, though, call the text "the Gospel according to Mark" nor even use the name "Mark."
53. Analogously, Eva Mroczek has written about the literary imagination in Jewish antiquity, textual production is often about "projects," "not products." Mroczek, *Literary Imagination*, 106.
54. See Reed, "ΕΥΑΓΓΕΛΙΟΝ," 11–56.
55. Greek and Latin texts are taken from Adelin Rousseau and Louis Doutreleau, *Irénée de Lyon, Contre Les Hérésies. Livre III* (Sources Chrétiennes 211; Paris: Les Éditions du Cerf, 1974), 22–25.
56. *LSJ*, s.v. 7. It is difficult for me to determine a substantive difference in meaning between the words *exdidōmi* and *ekpherō* in the context of *Haer.* 3.1.1. Both have to do with bringing a piece of writing out into a public sphere. The Latin translation renders both words with the same word: *edo*.
57. *OLD*, s.v 9.
58. *LSJ*, s.v. 6.

59. Irenaeus, *Haer.* 1.*praef.*2: ἐντυχὼν τοῖς ὑπομνήμασι τῶν ὡς αὐτοὶ λέγουσιν Οὐαλεντίνου μαθητῶν. These ὑπομνήματα are usually translated as commentaries, but, as I have shown, such a gloss may need to be reconsidered.
60. On Clement and gospel tradition, see Stephen Carlson, "Clement of Alexandria on the 'Order' of the Gospels," *NTS* 47 (2001): 118–25; Annewies van den Hoek, "Divergent Gospel Traditions in Clement of Alexandria and Other Authors of the Second Century," *Apocrypha* 7 (1996): 43–62; James A. Brooks, "Clement of Alexandria as a Witness to the Development of the New Testament Canon," *JECS* 9.1 (1992): 41–55; Carl P. Cosaert, *The Text of the Gospels in Clement of Alexandria* (Atlanta: SBL Press, 2008).
61. Bart D. Ehrman, *The Apostolic Fathers II* (LCL 25; Cambridge, MA: Harvard University Press, 2005), 96–97; Michael W. Holmes, *The Apostolic Fathers: Greek Texts and English Translation*, 3rd ed. (Grand Rapids, MI: Baker Academic, 2007), 758–59.
62. On παρατίθημι as citing or quoting, see *LSJ*, s.v. 5.
63. Eusebius, *Hist. eccl.* 2.15.
64. The manuscript R from the Library of the Holy Synod of Moscow contains the plural ὑπομνήματα, not the singular ὑπόμνημα.
65. See discussion this volume, chapter 3, pages 43–45.
66. Kennedy, "Classical and Christian Source Criticism," 125–55.

CHAPTER 6

1. See Gamble, *Books and Readers in the Early Church*, 125.
2. Artemidorus, *Onir.* 2.70.167. Greek text is taken from Daniel E. Harris-McCoy, *Artemidorus' Oneirocritica: Text, Translation, and Commentary* (New York: Oxford University Press, 2012), 257; translation mine.
3. Artemidorus, *Onir.* 1. *praef.* 1–2; 2. *praef.*
4. Altering, reworking, or using previous pieces of high literature (as opposed to practical types of texts) seems to have had a different discourse. On the topic of plagiarism in ancient Roman context, see Scott McGill, "The Right of Authorship in Symmachus' *Epistulae* 1.31," *CP* 104 (2009): 229–32; McGill, *Plagiarism in Latin Literature*.
5. Artemidorus, 1. *praef.* 1–2; 2. *praef.*
6. Thanks to Greg Given for pointing out the need to remind the reader of this book at this point that the text we now call the Gospel according to Mark does not reflect a stable first-century text. That is, the Gospel according to Mark as we now have it in early manuscripts does not necessarily reflect a first-century text. Ὑπομνήματα were especially fluid and it is likely the textual tradition we now call the Gospel according to Mark changed in the time between the end of the first century and the time when we have good manuscript evidence (the fourth century). It is clear that there were multiple versions of unfinished note collections in the first few centuries.

7. Of course, the exceptions that may come readily to mind, such as the Greek and Hebrew versions of Esther or the Greek and Latin versions of the *Golden Ass*, prove my point. Such are different versions of the same work. From a modern scholarly discourse point of view, we tend to think of the Greek and Latin versions of *The Golden Ass* as different versions of the same work. The same holds true for the Greek and Hebrew versions of Jeremiah and Esther (and many others could be included, such as the different recensions of the *Acts of Justin* and so forth). Alternatively, while the texts we now call the Gospel according to Mark and the Gospel according to Matthew are at least as similar as these texts, modern scholars have tended to think of them as different books, and this is one of the assumptions I hope to challenge.
8. On the similarity of Mark and Matthew, see the comment from E. P. Sanders and Margaret Davies, *Studying the Synoptic Gospels* (Philadelphia: Trinity International Press, 1989), 51.
9. See Brown, *Introduction to the New Testament*, 111, who cites 80 percent.
10. I offer hearty thanks to A. Seth Reese, who made the following three illustrations. Used with permission of the creator.
11. The Eusebian canons are defined by the *The Concise Oxford Dictionary of the Christian Church* as "The system of tables ('canons') devised by Eusebius of Caesarea to enable the reader of one Gospel to turn up parallel passages ('sections') in the other Gospels or passages containing similar matter. The numbering of the sections was formerly attributed to Ammonius Saccas" (E. A. Livingston, ed., *The Concise Oxford Dictionary of the Christian Church*, rev. 2nd ed. [New York: Oxford University Press, 2006], 205).
12. In so doing, as I mentioned in chapter 1, I do not believe the Aland synopsis gives me access to the *definitive* versions of two different first-century texts called the Gospel according to Matthew and the Gospel according to Mark. I acknowledge methodological limitations to my approach, yet I believe it remains productive in pointing out problems in modern scholarly discourse, as well as beginning to construct a new understanding of how the textual traditions behind the text we now call the Gospels according to Matthew and Mark interact with each other.
13. Of course, all the strategies mentioned have the limitation of relying on a construction of the two texts based on manuscripts that come from a period when the Gospels according to Matthew and Mark are already regarded as "book" with "authors," yet it nonetheless remains a productive framework for exploring my thesis, and looking at stories as units seems less problematic than the alternatives. In this way, my work here may in the end serve an intermediary role, while a new way of talking about the relationship between gospel texts is left open to future work.
14. On the value of using large-scale statistical analysis to aid in interpretation, see Franco Moretti, *Distant Reading* (Brooklyn: Verso, 2013).
15. Venn diagram proportions were generated using the website http://jura.wi.mit.edu/bioc/tools/venn.php.

16. Martial, *Epigram* 10.1.1–2.4. Gurd, *Work in Progress*, 111.
17. Ovid, *Am.* 1.1. Gurd, *Work in Progress*, 91.
18. Emanuel Tov, *Textual Criticism of the Hebrew Bible*, 2nd ed. (Minneapolis, MN: Fortress, 2001), 320.
19. Metso, *Textual Development*, 107–108.
20. For example, Francis Watson in an interview with Eerdman's Publishing Company about his book *Gospel Writing*, stated that if there were no differences between Matthew, Mark, Luke, and John, there would not be four Gospels. There would be one Gospel and four copies, since it is the differences that make the four Gospels discrete entities. See www.youtube.com/watch?v=HuA6OBR_abA. He seems to assert this as an intuitive and incontrovertible statement, from which he can build a more complex argument about why differences matter. I imagine that rhetorically he is correct to assume that in the minds of many biblical scholars one can safely build upon such a claim. From a material philology point of view, however, his statement is hard to maintain, as we do not have four gospels but thousands of different gospel texts, as each one of those thousands differs from one another.
21. See Papias's comments in Eusebius, *Hist. eccl.* 3.39.15–16 from chapter 5.
22. In 13:24–30, 33, 36–52, the Gospel according to Matthew augments the Jesus's kingdom parables found in the Gospel according to Mark. The Gospel according to Matthew adds discourses in 18:10–35; 24:37–25:46. The Gospel according to Matthew adds the individual pericopae of 3:7–10; 12:38–45; 17:24–27; 20:1–16; 21:28–32; 22:1–14; 23:37–39; 27:3–10, 62–66.
23. The Gospel according to Matthew fully omits only eight stories: Mark 1:21–22, 23–28, 35–38; 3:20–21; 4:21–29; 8:22–26; 11:18–19; 12:41–44.
24. The Gospel according to Matthew rearranges the stories in Mark 4:35–5:43.
25. Lucian, *How to Write History*, 47–48.
26. Matt. 3:7–10; 8:5–13; 12:38–42, 43–45; 17:24–27; 23:37–39; 27:3–10.
27. See J. Andrew Doole, *What Was Mark for Matthew?: An Examination of Matthew's Relationship and Attitude to his Primary Source* (WUNT 344; Tübingen: Mohr Siebeck, 2013). Doole argues that Matthew was essentially a Markan Christian and that he followed Mark's text like a faithful but creative scribe. He even goes so far as to call Matthew a "new edition" of the Gospel according to Mark. He still speaks, however, about Matthew as an author figure who created a separate text from the one authored by Mark. For example, he writes about "the writing of his [Matthew's] own Gospel" (169) and "Matthew's use of Mark as a source in composing his Gospel" (164). For him, the Gospel according to Matthew and the Gospel according to Mark are two different works in the first century CE.
28. Luke 21:1–4 preserves the story.
29. Günther Bornkamm, "The Stilling of the Storm in Matthew," in *Tradition and Interpretation in Matthew*, ed. Günther Bornkamm et al. (Philadelphia: Westminster, 1963), 52–57. See also Norman Perrin, *What Is Redaction Criticism?* (Eugene, OR: Wipf and Stock, 2002).

30. See Matthew D. C. Larsen, "Accidental Publication, Unfinished Texts and the Traditional Goals of New Testament Textual Criticism," *JSNT* 39 (2017): 362–87.
31. Note that the text Galen interacts with is different from many modern critical editions of Hippocrates, *Epid.* 6.2.25. See 17b.13K. In the Loeb volume, the Greek reads: Ὅτι ἐν θερματέρῳ τὸ ἐν τοῖσι δεξιοῖσι, καὶ μελανθὲς διὰ τοῦτο, καὶ ἔξω αἱ φλέβες μᾶλλον. For the purposes of the present argument, either text of *Epid.* 6.2.25 supports the larger point. Translation from Gurd, "Galen on ἔκδοσις," 172.
32. 17b.13K. Greek text and translation taken from Sean Gurd, "Galen on ἔκδοσις," 172, 181.
33. For a similar situation regarding a note made by Nietzsche in one of his notebooks, compare Jacques Derrida, "'J'ai oublié mon parapluie' / 'I have forgotten my umbrella,'" in *Spurs: Nietzsche's Styles/Éperons: Les styles de Nietzsche,* trans. Barbara Harlow (Chicago, IL: University of Chicago Press, 1978), 122–45.
34. Hippocrates, *Epid.* 6.3.1; Galen, 17b.13K. Greek text and translation taken from Gurd, "Galen on ἔκδοσις," 172, 181. Note that Galen's text differs slightly from other modern critical editions. The Loeb volume of Hippocrates *Epidemics* reads καθαιρέσιος instead of καθαιρέσεως, as is found in the Kühn edition of Galen's text.
35. 17b.13K. Greek text and translation from Gurd, "Galen on ἔκδοσις," 172, 182.
36. Michel Foucault, "Self Writing," in *Ethics: Subjectivity and Truth,* ed. Paul Rabinow (New York: New Press, 1997), 211.
37. Michel Foucault, "On the Genealogy of Ethics: An Overview of Work in Progress," in *The Foucault Reader,* ed. Paul Rabinow (New York: Vintage Books, 2010), 364.
38. See Doole, *What Was Mark for Matthew?*; David C. Sim, "Matthew's Use of Mark: Did Matthew Intend to Supplement or Replace His Primary Source?," *NTS* 57 (2011): 176–92.
39. Bornkamm, "The Stilling of the Storm in Matthew," 52–57.
40. On gospel texts originally circulating without titles or ascribed human authors, see Annette Yoshiko Reed, "ΕΥΑΓΓΕΛΙΟΝ," 11–46, esp. 20; Bart Ehrman, *Forgery and Counterforgery: The Use of Literary Deceit in Early Christian Polemics* (New York: Oxford University Press, 2013), 51; Gamble, *Book and Readers,* 153–54; François Bovon, "The Synoptic Gospels and the Noncanonical Acts of the Apostles," *HTR* 81 (1988): 20–23.
41. Porphyry, *Vit. Plot.* 7.13–14.
42. See Tricia Miller, *Three Versions of Esther: Their Relationship to Anti-Semitic and Feminist Critique of the Story* (Leuven: Peeters, 2014); Lawrence M. Wills, *The Jewish Novel in the Ancient World* (Ithaca and London: Cornell University Press, 1995), 104–105.
43. Irene Peirano, "Epilogue: Towards a Rhetoric of the Roman Fake—The Helen Episode in *Aeneid 2,*" in her *The Rhetoric of the Roman Fake: Latin Pseudepigrapha in Context* (Cambridge: Cambridge University Press, 2012), 242–63.
44. I borrow the language of vitality from Hindy Najman, "The Vitality of Scripture Within and Beyond the Canon," 497–518. She points out that vitality is a sign of health.

45. Codex Sinaiticus and Codex Vaticanus, two important fourth century witnesses, end the Gospel according to Mark at 16:8. See James A. Kelhoffer, *Miracle and Mission: The Authentication of Missionaries and Their Message in the Longer Ending of Mark* (Tübingen: Mohr Siebeck, 2000); Collins, *Mark*, 120–25, 780–81, 797–800; Lynn Cox, *A History and Critique of Scholarship Concerning the Markan Endings* (Lewiston, NY: Edwin Mellen, 1993); Metzger, *Textual Commentary of the Greek New Testament*, 102–106.
46. See Kelly R. Iverson, "A Further Word on Final Γάρ (Mark 16:8)," *CBQ* 68.1 (2006): 79–94.
47. Mark 14.28; see also 8:31; 9:31; 10:34.
48. For heuristic purposes, I retain the traditional ways of identifying the endings, but as should be clear, such titles work only within the bookish framework I critique. See, for example, Jouette M. Bassler and Wayne A. Meeks, eds., *The HarperCollins Study Bible: New Revised Standard Version, With the Apocraphal/Deuterocanonical Books* (San Francisco: Harper Collins, 1993), 1951–2.
49. The ἀμήν is added in C* D$^s$ L W Θ Ψ $f^{13}$ 892. 1006. 1342. 2427, as well as in the majority text, some Coptic and Boharic manuscripts, and the Wordsworth-White-Sparks Vulgate.
50. See H. A. G. Houghton, *The Latin New Testament: A Guide to its Early History, Texts, and Manuscripts* (Oxford: Oxford University Press, 2016), 22, 210–11.
51. Houghton, *The Latin New Testament*, 10.
52. Houghton, *The Latin New Testament*, 10.
53. Bruce M. Metzger, *A Textual Commentary on the Greek New Testament*, 2nd ed. (Stuttgart: Bibelgesellschaft, 1994), 101–102.
54. The events inside the tomb are also absent from the other canonical gospels, although the Gospel according to Peter does contain a similar story about two people descending into the tomb during the moment of resurrection. *Gos. Pet.* 35–40. See Metzger, *Textual Commentary*, 102.
55. Walter Benjamin, "The Task of the Translator," in *Walter Benjamin: Selected Writings, Volume 1, 1913–1926*, ed. Marcus Bullock and Michael W. Jennings (Cambridge, MA: Harvard University Press, 1996), 253–63.
56. See Bruce M. Metzger and Bart D. Ehrman, *The Text of the New Testament: Its Transmission, Corruption, and Restoration*, 4th ed. (New York: Oxford University Press, 2005), 80–81. See also Caspar René Gregory, *Das Freer-Logion* (Leipzig: J. C. Hinrichs, 1908); Jörg Frey, "Zu Text und Sinn des Freer-Logion," *ZNW* 93 (2002): 12–34.
57. Taken from the critical apparatus of Nestle-Aland 28. Some examples of manuscripts that contain more than one ending are L (8th century), Ψ (9th/10th century), 083 (6th/7th century), 099 (7th century), the margins of 274 (10th century; the longer ending is preserved in the main body of the text of the manuscript), $l^{1602}$ (8th century). Some Syriac, Coptic, and Ethiopic manuscripts record both the shorter ending and the longer ending alongside one another.

58. See Metzger and Ehrman, *Text of the New Testament* 77, 84–85.
59. Greek: Ἔν τισι μὲν τῶν ἀντιγράφων ἕως ὧδε πληροῦται ὁ εὐαγγελιστὴς ἕως οὗ καὶ Εὐσέβιος ὁ Παμφίλου ἐκανόνισεν· ἐν πολλοῖς δὲ καὶ ταῦτα φέρεται. See Kirsopp Lake, *Codex 1 of the Gospels and Its Allies: Greek Text*. (Texts and Studies vol. 7. no. 3; Cambridge: Cambridge University Press, 1902), 92. Amy S. Anderson, *The Textual Tradition of the Gospels: Family 1 in Matthew* (Leiden/Boston: Brill, 2004), 68.
60. Anderson, *Textual Tradition of the Gospels*, 69. Greek: εἰρηναῖος ὁ τῶν | ἀποστόλων πλη | σίον. ἐν τῶι πρὸς | τὰς αἱρέσεις τρί | τωι λόγωι. τοῦτο | ἀνήνεγκεν | τὸ ῥητὸν. | ὡς μάρκω | εἰρημέ | ν | ο | ν.
61. Kelhoffer, *Miracle and Mission*, 48–150.
62. Kelhoffer, *Miracle and Mission*, 155.
63. Kelhoffer, *Miracle and Mission*, 150–54.
64. Kelhoffer does write that "The term forgery denotes a particular method of composition, and is not intended to connote a value judgment concerning Mark 16:9–20 or other early Christian forgeries" (*Miracle and Mission*, 150n84). Whether or not the term forgery can be used without attaching a value judgment, Kelhoffer's remark does not define what he means by the term.
65. Kelhoffer, *Miracle and Mission*, 150–54.
66. Kelhoffer, *Miracle and Mission*, 150–54.
67. On forgery, see Pamela O. Long, *Openness, Secrecy, and Authorship: Technical Arts and the Culture of Knowledge from Late Antiquity to the Renaissance* (Baltimore, MD: Johns Hopkins University Press, 2001), 27–28; Bart D. Ehrman, *Forgery and Counterforgery*, 1n1.

CHAPTER 7

1. See the accompanying book created for the exhibit, Kelly Baum, Andrea Bayer, and Sheena Wagstaff, eds., *Unfinished: Thoughts Left Visible* (New York: Metropolitan Museum of Art, 2016).
2. See Alice Neel's painting, *James Hunter Black Draftee*, 1965, in Baum et al., *Unfinished*, 125.
3. See Mikhail M. Bakhtin, *Problems of Dostoevsky's Poetics*, ed. and trans. Caryl Emerson (Minneapolis: University of Minnesota Press, 1984), esp. 166; Mikhail M. Bakhtin, *Speech Genres & Other Late Essays*, trans. Vern W. McGee and ed. Caryl Emerson and Michael Holquist (Austin: University of Texas Press, 1986), 170.
4. Ernest Mandel, introduction to *Capital, Volume 1*, by Karl Marx, trans. Ben Fowkes (New York: Penguin Classics, 1992), 25–38.
5. Walter Benjamin, *The Arcade Project*, trans. Howard Eiland (Cambridge, MA: Harvard University Press, 2002). "To great writers, finished works weigh lighter than those fragments on which they labor their entire lives." Quotation taken from the blurb on the Harvard University Press version of the *Arcade Project*.

6. Gurd, "Revision in Greek Literary Papyri," 160–84. Gurd shows how the author does not always set out knowing what he is aiming for. Later revisions are not necessarily preferred versions. Authors often produced multiple variants from which they would choose later.
7. See papyrus nr. 86 (*P.Oxy.* XVII 2070), in Lincoln H. Blumell and Thomas A. Wayment, eds., *Christian Oxyrhynchus: Texts, Documents, and Sources* (Waco, TX: Baylor University Press, 2015), 314–21. I thank AnneMarie Luijendijk for bringing *P.Oxy.* 2070 to my attention and showing me its relevance to my project.
8. *T.Ab.* 10.2–14 (Rec.B). Translation from C. A. Evans from Accordance Bible software.
9. For an insightful comparandum of archival practices, see *P.Lond.* 259, which presents tax rolls organized in numbered columns. I thank Ann Hanson for pointing this papyrus out to me and indicating its relevance to my project.
10. David Ferris, *The Cambridge Introduction to Walter Benjamin* (New York: Cambridge University Press, 2008), 115.
11. Foucault, "Self Writing," 209–10.
12. A. Locher and R. C. A. Rottländer, "Überlegungen zur Entstehungsgeschichte der Naturalis historia des älteren Plinius und die Schrifttäfelchen von Vindolanda," in *Lebendige Altertumswissenschaft, Festgabe zur Vollendung des 70. Lebensjahres von H. Vetters: Festgabe H. Vetters*, ed. Hermann Vetters et al. (Vienna: A. Holzhausen, 1985), 140–47. Cited in Dorandi, *Le stylet et la tablette*, 31–39.
13. Dorandi, *Filodemo. Storia dei filosofi*, Tiziano Dorandi, "Commentarii opistographi," *ZPE* 65 (1986): 71–75; Tiziano Dorandi, "Den Autoren über die Schulter geschaut. Arbeitweise und Autographie bei den antiken Schriftsteller," *ZPE* 87 (1991): 11–33; Dorandi, *Le stylet et la tablette*, 31–39, 46–50.
14. Aulus Gellius, *Noct. att. praef.* 1–2 (Rolfe, LCL).
15. See van den Hoek, "Techniques of Quotation in Clement of Alexandria," 223–43.
16. Lorenzo Perilli, "Conservazione dei testi e circolazione della conoscenza in Grecia," in *Biblioteche del mondo antico: Dalla tradizione orale alla cultura dell'Impero*, ed. Angela Maria Andrisano (Rome: Carocci editore, 2009), 36–71, esp. 64. Cited in Victor M. Martinez and Megan Finn Senseney, "The Professional and his Books: Special Libraries in the Ancient World," in *Ancient Libraries*, ed. Jason König, Katerina Oikonomopoulou, and Greg Woolf (New York: Cambridge University Press, 2013), 409.
17. See Martin Kähler, *The So-Called Historical Jesus and the Historic, Biblical Christ*, trans. and ed. Carl E. Braaten (Philadelphia: Fortress Press, 1964), 80n11. Interestingly, Kähler's comment, which is usually quoted as being about the Gospel according to Mark, is directed to all the (canonical) gospels: "To state the matter somewhat provocatively, one could call the Gospels passion narratives with extended introductions." This now famous sound bite comes from an aside in a footnote on "pragmatism" in the writing of history.

18. For a helpful and concise overview, see Collins, *Mark*, 85–93.
19. Robert H. Gundry, *Mark: A Commentary on His Apology for the Cross*, vol. 2 (9–16) (Grand Rapids, MI: Eerdmans, 2004), 1046.
20. Gundry, *Mark*, 2:1045–49.
21. Collins, *Mark*, 85–93. She divides the Gospel according to Mark into the following narrative units: 1:16–45 (Jesus's First Mighty Deeds: The Nearness of the Kingdom), 2:1–3:6 (Jesus in Conflict: The Law and the Kingdom), 3:7–35 (Jesus the Son of God: In Relation to the Demons, the Twelve, and His Family), 4:1–34 (Jesus Speaks in Parables), 4:35–6:6a (Epiphanies of Divine Power), 6:6b–8:26 (Renewed Proclamations), 8:27–10:45 (The Mystery of the Kingdom), 11:1–13:37 (Proclamation in Jerusalem), 14:1–16:8 (The Passion Narrative), 16:9–20 (Additional Endings of Mark).
22. Rudolf Bultmann already noticed an element of what I am suggesting here regarding groupings of words within the Synoptic Gospels. He noted that the redaction of the tradition material was at times done by catchwords (*Stichwort*). See Bultmann, *Die Geschichte synoptischen Tradition*, 351; ET: Rudolf Bultmann, *The History of the Synoptic Tradition*, trans. John Marsh (Peabody, MA: Hendrickson, 1994), 324–25. The difference between what Bultmann noted and what I am suggesting is that (1) Bultmann lacked a historical context of ancient writing practices in his discussion; (2) Bultmann notes rather limited clusters of examples, such as μόδιος in Mark 4:21 and 24 or prayer in Luke 11:1–4, 5–8, and 9–13 as causing passages to be collected next to each other and not providing structure to the text as a whole; and (3) Bultmann viewed the linking of passages together by words as a mnemonic device, whereas the utility for which I argue extends beyond memory. See also Joanna Dewey, "Mark as Interwoven Tapestry: Forecasts and Echoes for a Listening Audience," *CBQ* 53 (1991): 221–36.
23. Codex Alexandrinus and other early Greek manuscripts understand Mark 1:1–22 as the *prooimion* of the text. Collins, *Mark*, 86–87; Metzger and Ehrman, *Text of the New Testament*, 34. I also see the first verses as some sort of a preface, perhaps added at a later point in the process of production. I see the preface, however, stopping in 1:20, since Mark 1:21–22 deals directly with activity on the Sabbath in a synagogue.
24. On the various textual connections between Mark 4:35–41 and Ps. 107:25–30 and Jonah, see Robert H. Stein, *Mark* (Grand Rapids, MI: Baker Academic, 2008), 240–46.
25. See Elizabeth Struthers Malbon, *Mark's Jesus: Characterization as Narrative Christology* (Waco, TX: Baylor University Press, 2009), 38; Collins, *Mark*, 391; Norman Perrin, "Toward an Interpretation of the Gospel according to Mark," in *Christology and a Modern Pilgrimage*, ed. Hans Dieter Betz (Claremont, CA: New Testament Colloquium, 1971), 4–5; Werner Kelber, *The Oral and the Written Gospel* (Philadelphia: Fortress, 1983), 110.
26. Mark 8:23, 24 (twice), 25 (twice); 9:8; 10:21, 23, 27, 51, 52.

27. For σάββατον, Mark 1:21; 2:23, 24, 27 (twice), 28; 3:2, 4. For συναγωγὴ, Mark 1:21, 23, 29, 39; 3:1.
28. The keywords of *Sabbath* and *synagogue* do not appear in 2:13–17 and 2:18–22.
29. Joanna Dewey, *Markan Public Debate: Literary Technique, Concentric Structure, and Theology in Mark 2:1–3:6* (Chico, CA: Scholars Press, 1980).
30. For δώδεκα, Mark 3:14, 16; 4:10; 5:25, 42; 6:7. For ἀποστέλλω, Mark 3:14, 31; 4:29; 5:10; 6:7, 17, 27.
31. Διαστέλλω also occurs in Mark 5:43, when Jesus gives orders that no one tell about him raising the twelve-year-old girl from the dead.
32. Collins, *Mark*, 621–27, 819.
33. See Joel F. Williams, "Literary Approaches to the End of Mark's Gospel," *JETS* 42 (1999): 21–35; T. E. Boomershine, "Mark 16:8 and the Apostolic Commission," *JBL* 100 (1981): 225–39.
34. Alternatively, it may be an intricately crafted "cliff-hanger," but treating it as a subtle literary ending does not fit well with the raw and unpolished style of the rest of text.
35. I distinguish the foreshadowing of Jesus's death, which appears throughout the Gospel according to Mark (as well as generally throughout many early Christian texts), from the "Suffering Son of Man" motif, which highlights the necessity of the Son of Man to suffer, die, and rise again. The Suffering Son of Man motif appears most clearly in the 8:22–10:52 set of notes—specifically in 8:31–32, 9:31–32, and 10:33–34. It also appears in a different form in 14:17–42.
36. See, for example, Mark 1:22; 6:2, 34.
37. Since writing this chapter, I have become aware of Loren Stuckenbruck's article, "The Dead Sea Scrolls: Insight into Traditioning Processes and the Growth of Gospel Traditions," *DSD* 23 (2016): 304–28. Stuckenbruck uses the textual models at Qumran to rethink the Synoptic problem and growth of gospel traditions.
38. Bakhtin, *Problems of Dostoevsky's Poetics*, 43; emphasis mine.
39. Bakhtin, *Problems of Dostoevsky's Poetics*, 15.
40. Bakhtin, *Problems of Dostoevsky's Poetics*, 69–72.
41. Bakhtin, *Problems of Dostoevsky's Poetics*, 80–1.
42. Bakhtin, *Problems of Dostoevsky's Poetics*, 84.
43. A similar point is made in Friedrich Nietzsche, "Homer und klassische Philologie," 248–69. I am indebted to Hindy Najman's work on Nietzsche, author, textual unity, and textual growth. See especially Najman, "Traditionary Processes and Textual Unity," 99–117 and her as yet unpublished "Between Greek and Hebrew Philology," Keynote lecture at conference on Marginality, Canonicity, and Passion, Yale University, Department of Classics, March 2012.
44. See, for example, Elizabeth Struthers Malbon, *Mark's Jesus*: "The result of [her approach] is a *multilayered* Markan narrative christology" (231). "Mark's Gospel *subverts its own* narrator's manifest sense of what it means for Jesus to be the Christ,

the Son of God, by its protagonist's manifest sense of what it means for God to be God" (256).
45. Étienne Trocmé, "Is There a Markan Christology?," in *Christ and Spirit in the New Testament. In Honour of Charles Francis Digby Moule*, ed. B. Lindars and S. S. Smalley (New York: Cambridge University Press, 1973), 3–13.
46. Telford, *Theology of the Gospel According to Mark*, 30.
47. Mark 6:48.
48. Collins, *Mark*, 334. Collins points to Exod. 34:5–6 and 3 Kgdms 19:11 LXX (= 1 Kings 19:11 ET).
49. Collins, *Mark*, 334–5. See Exod. 3:6, 14.
50. Collins, *Mark*, 476–7. She also points to the contrast between 10:17–22 and 14:61–64.
51. Mark 6:5a.
52. Mark 5:30.
53. See Candida R. Moss, "The Man with the Flow of Power: Porous Bodies in Mark 5:25–34," *JBL* 129 (2010): 507–19.
54. William Wrede, *Das Messiasgeheimnis in den Evangelien* (Göttingen: Vandenhoeck & Ruprecht, 1901); English translation, *The Messianic Secret*, trans. J. C. G. Greig (Cambridge: James Clark, 1971).
55. See Collins, *Mark*, 171. See also Ulrich Luz, "Das Geheimnismotiv und die markinische Christologie," *ZNW* 56 (1965): 9–30; Jürgen Roloff, "Das Markusevangelium als Geschichtsdarstellung," *EvTh* 29 (1969): 73–93 (both cited by Collins, *Mark*, 171).
56. On the portrayal of Herod in Mark 6:14–29, see Abraham Smith, "Tyranny Exposed: The Characterization of Herod Antipas in Mark 6:14–29," *BibInt* 14 (2006): 259–93.
57. Foucault, "Self Writing," 212.
58. On Milton and anachronistic ideas of authorship, see esp. Eva Mroczek, *Literary Imagination*.
59. See, for example, Roland Barthes, *S/Z*, trans. Richard Miller (New York: Hill and Wang, 1974); Derrida, *Dissemination*; Stanley Fish, *Is There a Text in This Class?: The Authority of Interpretive Communities* (Cambridge, MA: Harvard University Press, 1982).
60. Barthes, *S/Z*, 4–5.

EPILOGUE

1. On breaking down the division between textual traditions and modern scholarship on texts, as well as bringing modern scholars into the process of tradition, see Yii-Jan Lin, *The Erotic Life of Manuscripts: New Testament Textual Criticism and the Biological Sciences* (New York: Oxford University Press, 2016), 158.

2. Kathryn Tanner, "Scripture as Popular Text," *Modern Theology* 14 (1998): 279–98. I characterize Tanner's popular texts, as opposed to classic texts, as follows: texts that (1) are meant to be read not only by an elite class of readers, (2) do not establish the terms of their own interpretation but invite the reader to participate in the meaning-making process, without creating new rules for their reading, (3) are geared toward practical utility more than literary consumption, and (4) challenge and subvert both popular readers' cultural expectations and prevailing elite cultural ideologies.
3. Walter Ong, *Orality and Literacy: Technologizing the Word* (New York: Routledge, 1982), 132.
4. On the "perpetual present" of writerly texts, see Barthes, *S/Z*, 5. See also Michael J. Thate, *Remembering Things Past?: Albert Schweitzer, the Anxiety of Influence, and the Untidy Jesus of Markan Memory* (Tübingen: Mohr Siebeck, 2013), 270: "With these approaches in mind, something startling happens for the Reader: they become the star of the Markan Script, and themselves become the missing ending/new beginning of Mark's Gospel."
5. Bakhtin, *Problems of Dostoevsky's Poetics*, 166: "Nothing conclusive has yet taken place in the world, the ultimate word of the world and about the world has not yet been spoken, the world is open and free, everything is still in the future and will always be in the future."
6. I am working on an article in which I make the case that the genre of the Gospel according to Thomas is best understood as ὑπομνήματα.
7. See page 83.
8. *Acts of Timothy* 8–10. I thank Brent Nongbri for bringing this text to my attention.
9. See Brent Nongbri, *Constructing God's Library* (New Haven, CT: Yale University Press, in press).
10. Robert Darnton, *The Great Cat Massacre and Other Episodes in French Cultural History* (New York: Basic Books, 1984), 18.
11. Darnton, *The Great Cat Massacre*, 18.
12. Darnton, *The Great Cat Massacre*, 19.
13. Darnton, *The Great Cat Massacre*, 64.
14. Darnton, *The Great Cat Massacre*, 64.
15. For my understanding of how GitHub works I am heavily indebted to D. Daniel Larsen. The initial idea to connect gospel writing in antiquity with GitHub comes from conversation with Slate Liu-Ballard. I recognize and thank both people for their help and contribution.

APPENDIX A

1. On the text of *PHerc.* 1506 and 1426, I am using Jürgen Hammerstaedt, "Der Schlussteil von Philodems drittem Buch über Rhetorik," *Cronache Ercolanesi* 8 (1992): 9–118.

2. Col. CLVIII, line 31–32. Hämmerstaedt, 23–25.
3. Col. I, line 4–5. Hämmerstaedt, 23–25.
4. Col. IL, line 25–26. Hämmerstaedt, 24.
5. Col. II, line 4–6. Hämmerstaedt, 25.
6. Col. LV, lines 28–32. Hämmerstaedt, 38.
7. Col. XI, lines 2–7. Hämmerstaedt, 39.
8. Col. LVI, lines 25–28. Hämmerstaedt, 42.
9. Col. XII, lines 26–30. Hämmerstaedt, 43.
10. Col. LVII, lines 3–4. Hämmerstaedt, 42.
11. Col. XIII, line 25. Hämmerstaedt, 43.
12. Col. LVII, lines 12–13. Hämmerstaedt, 44.
13. Col. XIV, lines 4–6. Hämmerstaedt, 45.
14. Col. LVII, line 35–Col. LVIII, line 2. Hämmerstaedt, 44–46.
15. Col. XV, lines 5–11. Hämmerstaedt, 45–47.

### APPENDIX B

1. Latin text of Codex Bobiensis taken from John Wordsworth et al., eds. *Portions of the Gospels according to St. Mark and St. Matthew from the Bobbio Ms. (k) Now Number G. VII. 15 at the National Library at Turin, together with Other Fragments of the Gospels from Six Mss. at the Libraries of St. Gall, Coire, Milan, and Berne (usually cited as n, o, p, a2, s and t)* (Oxford: Clarendon Press, 1886).

# Bibliography

Alexander, Loveday. "Luke's Preface in the Context of Ancient Preface Writing." *NovT* 28 (1986): 48–74.
Alexander, Loveday. *The Preface to Luke's Gospel: Literary Convention and Social Context in Luke 1.1–4 and Acts 1.1*. Cambridge: Cambridge University Press, 1993.
Alexander, Loveday. "Ancient Book Production and the Circulation of the Gospels." In *The Gospels for All Christians*, edited by Richard Bauckham, 71–112. Grand Rapids, MI: Eerdmans, 1998.
Alexander, Philip S. "The Redaction-History of *Serekh ha-Yahad*: A Proposal." *RevQ* 17 (1996): 437–56.
Anderson, Amy S. *The Textual Tradition of the Gospels: Family 1 in Matthew*. Leiden/Boston: Brill, 2004.
Aune, David. *The New Testament in Its Literary Environment*. Philadelphia, PA: Westminster Press, 1987.
Babbit, Frank Cole. Introduction to *Moralia, Vol. 1*, by Plutarch. Translated by Frank Cole Babbit. Cambridge, MA: Harvard University Press, 2000.
Bagnall, Roger S. *Early Christian Books in Egypt*. Princeton, NJ: Princeton University Press, 2009.
Bakhtin, Mikhail M. *Problems of Dostoevsky's Poetics*. Edited and translated by Caryl Emerson. Minneapolis: University of Minnesota Press, 1984.
Bakhtin, Mikhail M. *Speech Genres & Other Late Essays*. Translated by Vern W. McGee and edited by Caryl Emerson and Michael Holquist. Austin: University of Texas Press, 1986.
Barish, David A. "The 'Autobiography' of Flavius Josephus and the Hypothesis of a Second Edition of his 'Antiquities.'" *HTR* 71 (1978): 61–75.
Barthes, Roland. *S/Z*. Translated by Richard Miller. New York: Hill and Wang, 1974.
Bassler, Jouette M., and Wayne A. Meeks, eds. *The HarperCollins Study Bible: New Revised Standard Version, with the Apocraphal/Deuterocanonical Books*. San Francisco, CA: HarperCollins, 1993.

Baum, Daniel Armin. "Der Presbyter des Papias über einen 'Hermeneuten' des Petrus. Zu Eusebius, Hist. eccl. 3,39, 15." *TZ* 56 (2000): 21–35.

Baum, Kelly, Andrea Bayer, and Sheena Wagstaff, eds. *Unfinished: Thoughts Left Visible*. New York: Metropolitan Museum of Art, 2016.

Beard, Mary. *SPQR: A History of Ancient Rome*. New York: W. W. Norton, 2015.

Beck, Richard Gustav. *Einleitung und Disposition zu Ciceros fragmentarisch erhaltener Rede in Clodium et curionem*. Zwickau: Druck von Zückler, 1886.

Becker, Eve-Marie. *Das Markus-Evangelium im Rahmen antiker Historiographie*. Tübingen: Mohr Siebeck, 2006.

Becker, Eve-Marie. "The Reception of 'Mark' in the 1st and 2nd Centuries C.E. and Its Significance for Genre Studies." In *Mark and Matthew II: Comparative Readings: Reception History, Cultural Hermeneutics, and Theology*, edited by Eve-Marie Becker and Anders Runesson, 15–36. Tübingen: Mohr Siebeck, 2013.

Benjamin, Walter. "The Task of the Translator." In *Walter Benjamin: Selected Writings, Volume 1, 1913–1926*, edited by Marcus Bullock and Michael W. Jennings, 253–63. Cambridge, MA: Harvard University Press, 1996.

Benjamin, Walter. *The Arcade Project*. Translated by Howard Eiland. Cambridge, MA: Harvard University Press, 2002.

Behr, Holger. *Die Selbstdarstellung Sullas: ein aristokratischer Politiker zwischen persönlichem Führungsanspruch und Standessolidarität*. Frankfurt am Main: Peter Lang, 1993.

Birt, Theodore. *Das antike Buchwesen in seinem Verhältniss zur Litteratur*. Berlin: Hertz, 1882.

Blank, David. "Versionen oder Zwillinge? Zu den Handschriften der ersten Bücher von Philodems Rhetorik." In *Editing Texts—Texte edieren*, edited by Glenn W. Most, 123–40. Göttingen: Vandenhoeck und Ruprecht, 1999.

Blumell, Lincoln H., and Thomas A. Wayment, eds. *Christian Oxyrhynchus: Texts, Documents, and Sources*. Waco, TX: Baylor University Press, 2015.

Boomershine, T. E. "Mark 16:8 and the Apostolic Commission." *JBL* 100 (1981): 225–39.

Bornkamm, Günther. "The Stilling of the Storm in Matthew." In *Tradition and Interpretation in Matthew*, edited by Günther Bornkamm et al., 52–57. Philadelphia, PA: Westminster, 1963.

Bourdieu, Pierre. *Outlines of a Theory of Practice*. Translated by Richard Nice. Cambridge: Cambridge University Press, 1977.

Bovon, François. "The Synoptic Gospels and the Noncanonical Acts of the Apostles." *HTR* 81 (1988): 19–36.

Bovon, François. *Luke 1: A Commentary on the Gospel of Luke 1:1–9:50*. Minneapolis, MN: Fortress, 2002.

Bowie, E. L. "Apollonius of Tyana: Tradition and Reality." *ANRW* 16.2 (1978): 1652–99.

Breed, Brennen W. *The Nomadic Text: A Theory of Biblical Reception*. Indiana Studies in Biblical Literature. Bloomington: Indiana University Press, 2014.

Brooks, James A. "Clement of Alexandria as a Witness to the Development of the New Testament Canon." *JECS* 9.1 (1992): 41–55.

Brown, Raymond. *An Introduction to the New Testament.* New Haven, CT: Yale University Press, 1997.
Bryant, John. *The Fluid Text: A Theory of Revision and Editing for Book and Screen.* Ann Arbor: University of Michigan Press, 2002.
Bultmann, Rudolf. *Die Geschichte der synoptischen Tradition.* Göttingen: Vandenhoeck und Ruprecht, 1931. English translation: *The History of the Synoptic Tradition*, trans. John Marsh. Peabody, MA: Hendrickson, 1994.
Burridge, Richard. "About People, By People, For People: Gospel Genre and Audiences." In *The Gospels for All Christians: Rethinking the Gospel Audiences*, edited by Richard Bauckham, 113–46. Grand Rapids, MI: Eerdmans, 1997.
Burridge, Richard. *What Are the Gospels?: A Comparison with Graeco-Roman Biography*, 2nd ed. New York: Cambridge University Press, 2004.
Cancik, Hubert. "Die Gattung Evangelium: Das Evangelium des Markus im Rahmen der antiken Historigraphie." In *Markus Philologie: historische, literargeschichtliche und stilistische Untersuchungen zum zweiten Evangelium*, edited by Hubert Cancik, 85–113. Tübingen: J. C. B. Mohr, 1984.
Cancik, Hubert. "Bios und Logos: Formengeschichtliche Untersuchungen zu Lukians 'Demonax.'" In *Markus Philologie: historische, literargeschichtliche und stilistische Untersuchungen zum zweiten Evangelium*, edited by Hubert Cancik, 115–30. Tübingen: J. C. B. Mohr, 1984.
Carlson, Stephen. "Clement of Alexandria on the 'Order' of the Gospels." *NTS* 47 (2001): 118–25.
Cirafesi, Wally V., and Gregory P. Fewster. "Justin's ἀπομνημονεύματα and Ancient Greco-Roman Memoir." *Early Christianity* 7 (2016): 186–212.
Cohen, Shaye J. D. *Josephus in Galilee and Rome: His* Vita *and Development as a Historian.* Leiden: Brill, 1979.
Collins, Adela Yarbro. *Mark: A Commentary.* Minneapolis, MN: Fortress, 2009.
Collins. John J. "The Yahad and the 'Qumran Community.'" In *Biblical Traditions in Transmission: Essays in Honour of Michael A. Knibb*, edited by C. Hempel and J. M. Lieu, 81–96. Leiden: Brill, 2006.
Collins, John J. *Beyond the Qumran Community: The Sectarian Movement of the Dead Sea Scrolls.* Grand Rapids, MI: Eerdmans, 2009.
Cosaert, Carl P. *The Text of the Gospels in Clement of Alexandria.* Atlanta, GA: SBL Press, 2008.
Cox, Lynn. *A History and Critique of Scholarship Concerning the Markan Endings.* Lewiston, NY: Edwin Mellen, 1993.
Crawford, Jane W. *M. Tullius Cicero: The Lost and Unpublished Orations.* Göttingen: Vandenhoeck und Ruprecht, 1984.
Cribiore, Raffaella. *Gymnastics of the Mind: Greek Education in Hellenistic and Roman Egypt.* Princeton, NJ: Princeton University Press, 2001.
Darnton, Robert. *The Great Cat Massacre and Other Episodes in French Cultural History.* New York: Basic Books, 1984.

Del Mastro, Gianluca. *Titoli e annotazioni bibliologiche nei papiri greci di Ercolano.* Napoli: Centro Internazionale per lo Studio dei Papiri Ercolanensi 'Marcello Gigante,' 2014.

Delattre, Daniel. *La Villa de Papyrus et les rouleaux d'Herculanum: la bibliothéque de Philodème.* Liège: CEDOPAL et Les Editions de l'Université de Liège, 2006.

Deleuze, Gilles, and Félix Guatarri. *A Thousand Plateaus: Capitalism and Schizophrenia 2.* Translated by Brian Massumi. Minneapolis: University of Minnesota, 1987.

Derrida, Jacques. *Spurs: Nietzsche's Styles/Éperons: Les styles de Nietzsche.* Translated by Barbara Harlow. Chicago, IL: University of Chicago Press, 1978.

Derrida, Jacques. *Dissemination.* Translated by Barbara Johnson. Chicago, IL: University of Chicago Press, 1981.

Dewey, Joanna. *Markan Public Debate: Literary Technique, Concentric Structure, and Theology in Mark 2:1–3:6.* Chico, CA: Scholars Press, 1980.

Dewey, Joanna. "Mark as Interwoven Tapestry: Forecasts and Echoes for a Listening Audience." *CBQ* 53 (1991): 221–36.

Dibelius, Martin. *Die Formsgeschichte des Evangeliums*, 2nd ed. Tübingen: J. C. B. Mohr, 1933.

Didion, Joan. *South and West.* New York: Knopf, 2017.

Doole, J. Andrew. *What Was Mark for Matthew?: An Examination of Matthew's Relationship and Attitude to his Primary Source.* Tübingen: Mohr Siebeck, 2013.

Donahue, John R. "The Quest for the Community of Mark's Gospel." In *The Four Gospels 1992: Festschrift Frans Neirynck*, edited by F. Van Segbroeck et al., 823–28. Leuven: Leuven University Press, 1992.

Dorandi, Tiziano. "Filodemo, Gli Stoici." *Cronache Ercolanesi* 12 (1982): 91–133.

Dorandi, Tiziano. "Commentarii opistographi." *ZPE* 65 (1986): 71–75.

Dorandi, Tiziano. "Den Autoren über die Schulter geschaut. Arbeitweise und Autographie bei den antiken Schriftsteller." *ZPE* 87 (1991): 11–33.

Dorandi, Tiziano, ed. *Filodemo. Storia dei filosofi. Platone e L'Academia (PHerc. 1021 and 164).* Napoli: Bibliopolis, 1991.

Dorandi, Tiziano. *Le stylet et la tablette: dans le secret des auteurs antiques.* Paris: Les Belle Lettres, 2000.

Dormeyer, Detlev. *Evangelium als literarische und theologische Gattung.* Darmstadt: Wissenschaftliche Buchgesellschaft, 1989.

Draper, Jonathan. "Vice Catalogues as Oral Mnemonic Cues: A Comparative Study of the Two Ways Traditions in the *Didache* and Parallels from the Perspective of Oral Tradition." In *Jesus, the Voice, and the Text*, edited by Tom Thatcher, 111–34. Waco, TX: Baylor Press, 2008.

Dzielska, Maria. *Apollonius of Tyana in Legend and History.* Rome: L'Erma Bretschneide, 1986.

Edwards, James R. *The Gospel According to Mark.* Grand Rapids, MI: Eerdmans, 2002.

Ehrman, Bart D. *The Apostolic Fathers II.* Loeb Classical Library 25. Cambridge, MA: Harvard University Press, 2005.

Ehrman, Bart D. *Forgery and Counterforgery: The Use of Literary Deceit in Early Christian Polemics.* New York: Oxford University Press, 2013.
Ferris, David. *The Cambridge Introduction to Walter Benjamin.* New York: Cambridge University Press, 2008.
Fields, Weston. *The Dead Sea Scrolls: A Full History*, Vol. 1. Leiden: Brill, 2009.
Fish, Stanley. *Is There a Text in This Class?: The Authority of Interpretive Communities.* Cambridge, MA: Harvard University Press, 1982.
Foucault, Michel. "What Is an Author?" In *The Foucault Reader*, edited by Paul Rabinow, 101–20. New York: Pantheon Books, 1984.
Foucault, Michel. "Self Writing." In *Ethics: Subjectivity and Truth*, edited by Paul Rabinow, 207–21. New York: New Press, 1997.
Foucault, Michel. "On the Genealogy of Ethics: An Overview of Work in Progress." In *The Foucault Reader*, edited by Paul Rabinow, 340–73. New York: Vintage Books, 2010.
Fraade, Steven. "Interpretive Authority in the Studying Community at Qumran." *JJS 44.1* (1993): 46–69.
Fraade, Steven. "Ancient Jewish Law and Narrative in Comparative Perspective: The Damascus Document and the Mishnah." *Diné Israel* 24 (2007): 65–99.
Frey, Jörg. "Zu Text und Sinn des Freer-Logion." *ZNW* 93 (2002): 12–34.
Gamble, Harry A. *Books and Readers in the Early Church.* New Haven, CT: Yale University Press, 1997.
Geffcken, Katherine A. *Comedy in Pro Caelio: With an Appendix on the In Clodium et Curionem.* Waukunda, IL: Bolchazy and Carducci, 1995.
Gigante, Marcello. *Filodemo in Italia.* Firenze: Felice Le Monnier, 1990. English translation: *Philodemus in Italy*, translated by Dirk Obbink. Ann Arbor: University of Michigan Press, 1995.
Gillihan, Yonder Moynihan. *Civic Ideology, Organization, and Law in the Rule Scrolls: A Comparative Study of the Covenanters' Sect and Contemporary Voluntary Associations in Political Context.* Leiden/Boston: Brill, 2012.
Goodacre, Mark. *The Case Against Q: Studies in Markan Priority and the Synoptic Problem.* Harrisburg, PA: Trinity International Press, 2002.
Gregory, Caspar René. *Das Freer-Logion.* Leipzig: J. C. Hinrichs, 1908.
Guelich, Robert. "The Gospel Genre." In *Das Evangelium und die Evangelien*, edited by Peter Stuhlmacher, 183–219. Tübingen: Mohr Siebeck, 1983.
Guglielmo, Lara. "Manuscripts, Editions, and Translations of the Damascus Document from 1896 to 2007: Towards a (Re-)Edition of 4Q266." *Materia Giudaica* 13 (2008): 251–78.
Gundry, Robert H. "Recent Investigations into the Literary Genre 'Gospel.'" In *New Dimensions in New Testament Study*, edited by R. N. Longenecker and M. C. Tenney, 97–114. Grand Rapids, MI: Zondervan, 1974.
Gundry, Robert H. *Mark: A Commentary on His Apology for the Cross*, Vol. 2 (9–16). Grand Rapids, MI: Eerdmans, 2004.

Gurd, Sean. "Galen on ἔκδοσις." In *Regards sur la Seconde Sophistique et son époque—Perceptions of the Second Sophistic and its Times*, edited by Thomas Schmidt and Pascale Fleury, 169–84. Toronto: University of Toronto Press, 2011.

Gurd, Sean A. *Work in Progress: Literary Revision as Social Performance*. New York: Oxford University Press, 2012.

Gurd, Sean. "Revision in Greek Literary Papyri." In *Probabilities, Hypotheticals, and Counterfactuals in Ancient Greek Thought*, edited by Victoria Wohl, 160–84. New York: Cambridge University Press, 2014.

Hadas, Moses, and Morton Smith. *Heroes and Gods: Spiritual Biographies in Antiquity*. London: Routledge and Kegan Paul, 1965.

Hall, Lindsay J. H. "Hirtius and the *Bellum Alexandrinum*." *ClQ* 46 (1996): 411–15.

Hammerstaedt, Jürgen. "Der Schlussteil von Philodems drittem Buch über Rhetorik." *Cronache Ercolanesi* 8 (1992): 9–118.

Hanson, Ann E. "Memorandum and Speech of an Advocate." *ZPE* 8 (1971): 15–27.

Hanson, Ann E. "Galen: Author and Critic." In *Editing Texts-Texte edieren*, edited by Glenn Most. Göttingen: Vandenhoeck und Ruprecht, 1998.

Harris-McCoy, Daniel E. *Artemidorus' Oneirocritica: Text, Translation, and Commentary*. New York: Oxford University Press, 2012.

Hay, Louis. "Genetic Criticism: Origins and Perspectives." In *Genetic Criticism: Texts and Avant-textes*, edited by Jed Deppman et al., 17–27. Philadelphia: University of Pennsylvania Press, 2004.

Hedrick, Jr., Charles W. "Literature and Communication." In *The Oxford Handbook of Social Relations in the Roman World*, edited by Michael Peachin, 167–90. New York: Oxford University Press, 2011.

Hempel, Charlotte. "Rewritten Rule Texts." In *The Qumran Rule Texts in Context: Collected Studies*, edited by Charlotte Hempel, 137–50. Tübingen: Mohr Siebeck, 2013.

Hempel, Charlotte. "Shifting Paradigms Concerning the Literary Development of the Serekh." In *The Qumran Rule Texts in Context: Collected Studies*, edited by Charlotte Hempel, 109–19. Tübingen: Mohr Siebeck, 2013.

Hitchcock, Louise. *Theory for Classics: A Student's Guide*. New York: Routledge, 2008.

Holmes, Michael W. *The Apostolic Fathers: Greek Texts and English Translation*, 3rd ed. Grand Rapids, MI: Baker Academic, 2007.

Hooker, Morna D. *The Gospel According to Mark*. Peabody, MA: Hendrickson, 1991.

Houghton, H. A. G. *The Latin New Testament: A Guide to its Early History, Texts, and Manuscripts*. Oxford: Oxford University Press, 2016.

Huitink, L., and J. W. van Henten. "The Publication of Flavius Josephus' Works and Their Audiences." *Zutot* 6 (2009) 49–60.

Incigneri, Brian. *The Gospel to the Romans: The Setting and Rhetoric of Mark's Gospel*. Leiden/Boston: Brill, 2003.

Iverson, Kelly R. "A Further Word on Final Γὰρ (Mark 16:8)." *CBQ* 68.1 (2006): 79–94.

Johnson, William. *Readers and Reading Culture in the High Roman Empire: A Study of Elite Communities*. New York: Oxford University Press, 2010.

Johnson, W. A., and H. N. Parker, eds. *Ancient Literacies: The Culture of Reading in Greece and Rome*. New York: Oxford University Press, 2009.

Jones, Christopher P. *Philostratus: The Life of Apollonius of Tyana, Books I–IV*. Loeb Classical Library 16. Cambridge, MA: Harvard University Press, 2005.

Kähler, Martin. *The So-Called Historical Jesus and the Historic, Biblical Christ*. Translated and edited by Carl E. Braaten. Philadelphia: Fortress Press, 1964.

Kelber, Werner. *The Oral and the Written Gospel*. Philadelphia: Fortress, 1983.

Kelhoffer, James A. *Miracle and Mission: The Authentication of Missionaries and Their Message in the Longer Ending of Mark*. Tübingen: Mohr Siebeck, 2000.

Kennedy, George. "Classical and Christian Source Criticism." In *The Relationships Between the Gospels: An Interdisciplinary Dialogue*, edited by William O. Walker, 125–55. San Antonio, TX: Trinity International Press, 1978.

Kennedy, George. *Progymnasmata: Greek Textbooks of Prose Composition and Rhetoric*. Leiden/Boston: Brill, 2002.

King, Karen. "What Is an Author?: Ancient Author-Function in the *Apocryphon of John* and the *Apocryphon of James*." In *"A Share in All Good Things": Essays in Honour of John S. Kloppenborg*, edited by William Arnal et al. BETL. Leuven: Peeters, in press.

Kivy, Peter. *The Performance of Reading: An Essay in the Philosophy of Literature*. Malden, MA: Wiley-Blackwell, 2009.

Knust, Jennifer. "In Pursuit of a Singular Text: New Testament Textual Criticism and the Desire for the True Original." *RC* 2 (2008): 1–15.

Kraus, Christina Shuttleworth. "Hair, History, and Hegemony: Caesar's Style and its Earliest Critics." In *Aspects of the Language of Latin Prose*, edited by Tobias Reinhardt et al., 97–116. New York: Oxford University Press, 2005.

Kürzinger, Josef. *Papias von Hierapolis und die Evangelien des Neuen Testaments*. Regensburg: F. Pustet, 1983.

Lake, Kirsopp. *Codex 1 of the Gospels and Its Allies: Greek Text*. Texts and Studies vol. 7, no. 3. Cambridge: Cambridge at the University Press, 1902.

Laqueur, Richard. *Der jüdische Historiker Flavius Josephus: Ein biographischer Versuch auf neuer quellenkritischer Grundlage*. 1920 Repr. Rome: "L'Erma" di Bretschneider, 1970.

Larsen, Matthew. "Listening with the Body, Seeing through the Ears: Contextualizing Philo's Lecture Event in *On the Contemplative Life*." *JSJ* 47 (2016): 447–74.

Larsen. Matthew D. C. "Accidental Publication, Unfinished Texts and the Traditional Goals of New Testament Textual Criticism." *JSNT* 39 (2017): 362–87.

Larsen, Matthew D. C. "Correcting the Gospel: Putting the Titles of the Gospels in their Historical-Literary Context." In *Rethinking 'Authority' in Late Antiquity: Authorship, Law, and Transmission in Jewish and Christian Tradition*, edited by Mark Letteney and A. J. Berkowitz. London: Routledge, forthcoming.

Leigh, Matthew. "Epic and Historiography in Rome." In *Companion to Greek and Roman Historiography*, edited by John Marincola, 483–92. Chichester: Blackwell, 2007.

Letteney, Mark. "Authenticity and Authority: The case for Dismantling a Dubious Correlation." In *Rethinking 'Authority' in Late Antiquity: Authorship, Law, and Transmission in Jewish and Christian Tradition*, edited by Mark Letteney and A. J. Berkowitz. London: Routledge, forthcoming.

Lied, Liv Ingeborg, and Hugo Lunghaug. "Studying Snapshots: Manuscript Culture, Textual Fluidity, and New Philology." In *Snapshots of Evolving Tradition: Jewish and Christian Manuscript Culture, Textual Fluidity, and New Philology*, edited by Liv Ingeborg Lied and Hugo Lunghaug, 1–19. Texte und Untersuchungen zur Geschichte der altchristlichen Literatur 175. Berlin: Walter de Gruyter, 2017.

Lin, Yii-Jan. *The Erotic Life of Manuscripts: New Testament Textual Criticism and the Biological Sciences*. New York: Oxford University Press, 2016.

Livingston, E. A., ed. *The Concise Oxford Dictionary of the Christian Church*. Rev. 2nd ed. New York: Oxford University Press, 2006.

Locher, A., and R. C. A. Rottländer. "Überlegungen zur Entstehungsgeschichte der Naturalis historia des älteren Plinius und die Schrifttäfelchen von Vindolanda." In *Lebendige Altertumswissenschaft, Festgabe zur Vollendung des 70. Lebensjahres von H. Vetters: Festgabe H. Vetters*, edited by Hermann Vetters et al., 140–47. Vienna: A. Holzhausen, 1985.

Long, Pamela O. *Openness, Secrecy, and Authorship: Technical Arts and the Culture of Knowledge from Late Antiquity to the Renaissance*. Baltimore, MD: Johns Hopkins University Press, 2001.

Luz, Ulrich. "Das Geheimnismotiv und die markinische Christologie." *ZNW* 56 (1965): 9–30.

MacDonald, Dennis R. *Two Shipwrecked Gospels: The Logoi of Jesus and Papias's Exposition of Logia about the Lord*. Atlanta, GA: Society of Biblical Literature Press, 2012.

Malbon, Elizabeth Struthers. *Mark's Jesus: Characterization as Narrative Christology*. Waco, TX: Baylor University Press, 2009.

Mandel, Ernest. Introduction to *Capital, Volume 1*, by Karl Marx. Translated by Ben Fowkes. New York: Penguin Classics, 1992.

Mansfield, Jaap. *Prolegomena: Questions to be Settled before the Study of an Author or a Text*. Leiden: Brill, 1997.

Marcovich, Miroslav. *Iustini Martyris Dialogus cum Tryphone*. New York: De Gruyter, 1997.

Marcus, Joel. *Mark 1–8: A New Translation with Introduction and Commentary*. New York: Doubleday, 2000.

Marquis, Timothy Luckritz. *The Transient Apostle: Paul, Travel, and the Rhetoric of Empire*. New Haven, CT: Yale University Press, 2013.

Marrou, H. I. "La technique de l'édition à l'époque patristique." *VC* 3 (1949): 208–24.

Martinez, Victor M., and Megan Finn Senseney. "The Professional and His Books: Special Libraries in the Ancient World." In *Ancient Libraries*, ed. Jason König et al., 401–17. New York: Cambridge University Press, 2013.

Marxsen, Willi. *Introduction to the New Testament*. Translated by G. Buswell. Philadelphia: Fortress Press, 1968.

Mason, Steve. "Of Audience and Meaning: Reading Josephus' *Bellum Iudaicum* in the Context of a Flavian Audience." In *Josephus and Jewish History in Flavian Rome and Beyond*, edited by J. Sievers and G. Lembi, 70–100. Leiden/Boston: Brill, 2005.

McCutcheon, R. W. "Silent Reading in Antiquity and the Future History of the Book." *Book History* 18 (2015): 1–32.

McGill, Scott. "The Right of Authorship in Symmachus' *Epistulae* 1.31." *CP* 104 (2009): 229–32.

McGill, Scott. *Plagiarism in Latin Literature*. New York: Cambridge University Press, 2012.

Metso, Sarianna. *The Textual Development of the Qumran Community Rule*. Leiden: Brill, 1997.

Metso, Sarianna. "The Textual Traditions of the Qumran Community Rule." In *Legal Texts and Legal Issues: Proceedings of the Second Meeting of the International Organization for Qumran Studies, Cambridge 1995*, edited by M. Bernstein et al., 141–48. Leiden: Brill, 1997.

Metso, Sarianna. *The Serekh texts*. London/New York: T&T Clark, 2007.

Metso, Sarianna. "Problems in Reconstructing the Organizational Chart of the Essenes." *DSD* 16 (2009): 388–415.

Metzger, Bruce M. *A Textual Commentary on the Greek New Testament*, 2nd ed. Stuttgart: Bibelgesellschaft, 1994.

Metzger, Bruce M., and Bart D. Ehrman. *The Text of the New Testament: Its Transmission, Corruption, and Restoration*, 4th ed. New York: Oxford University Press, 2005.

Meyer, Edvard. "Apollonius von Tyana und die Biographie des Philostratos." *Hermes* 52 (1917): 317–424.

Meyer, Elizabeth. *Legitimacy and Law in the Roman World:* Tabulae *in Roman Belief and Practice*. New York: Cambridge University Press, 2004.

Millard, Alan. *Reading and Writing in the Time of Jesus*. Sheffield: Sheffield Academic Press, 2000.

Miller, Tricia. *Three Versions of Esther: Their Relationship to Anti-Semitic and Feminist Critique of the Story*. Leuven: Peeters, 2014.

Moretti, Franco. *Distant Reading*. Brooklyn: Verso, 2013.

Moss, Candida R. "The Man with the Flow of Power: Porous Bodies in Mark 5:25–34." *JBL* 129 (2010): 507–519.

Mroczek, Eva. *The Literary Imagination in Jewish Antiquity*. New York: Oxford University Press, 2016.

Mroczek, Eva. "True Stories and the Poetics of Biblical Discovery." *BSR* 45 (2016): 21–31.

Myers, Jacob M. *I and II Esdras: Introduction, Translation, and Commentary*. Garden City, NY: Doubleday, 1974.

Najman, Hindy. "How Should We Contextualize Pseudepigrapha? Imitation and Emulation in *4 Ezra*." In *Flores Florentino: Dead Sea Scrolls and Other Early Jewish*

*Studies in Honor of Florentino García Martínez*, edited by Anthony Hilhorst et al., 529–36. Leiden: Brill, 2007.

Najman, Hindy. *Seconding Sinai: The Development of Mosaic Discourse in Second Temple Judaism*. Leiden/Boston: Brill, 2009.

Najman, Hindy. "Text and Figure in Ancient Jewish *Paideia*." In *Past Renewals: Interpretive Authority, Renewed Revelation, and the Quest for Perfection in Jewish Antiquity*, edited by Hindy Najman, 243–57. Boston: Leiden, 2010.

Najman, Hindy. "Configuring the Text in Biblical Studies." In *A Teacher for All Generation: Essays in Honor of James C. VanderKam*, edited by Eric F. Mason et al., 3–22. Leiden/Boston: Brill, 2012.

Najman, Hindy. "The Vitality of Scripture Within and Beyond the 'Canon.'" *JSJ* 43 (2012): 497–518.

Najman, Hindy. "Between Greek and Hebrew Philology." Keynote lecture at conference on Marginality, Canonicity, Passion. Yale University, Department of Classics, March 2012. [unpublished]

Najman, Hindy. "Traditionary Processes and Textual Unity in *4 Ezra*." In *Fourth Ezra and Second Baruch: Reconstruction After the Fall*, edited by Matthias Henze and Gabriele Boccaccini, 99–118. Leiden/Boston: Brill, 2013.

Najman, Hindy, Itamar Manoff, and Eva Mroczek. "How to Make Sense of a Pseudonymous Attribution: The Cases of *4 Ezra* and *2 Baruch*." In *A Companion to Biblical Interpretation in Early Judaism*, edited by Matthias Henze, 308–36. Grand Rapids, MI: Eerdmans, 2012.

Nati, James. "The *Community Rule* or *Rules for the Communities*?: Contextualizing the Qumran *Serakhim*." In *Sibyls, Scriptures, and Scrolls: John Collins at 70*, vol. 2, edited by Joel Baden et al., 916–39. Leiden: Brill, 2016.

Newson, Carol A. *The Self as Symbolic Space: Constructing Identify and Community at Qumran*. Leiden: Brill, 2004.

Nietzsche, Friedrich. "Homer und die klassische Philologie." *KGW* 2.1 (1869): 248–69.

Nongbri, Brent. *Constructing God's Library*. New Haven, CT: Yale University Press, in press.

Norelli, Enrico. *Papia di Hierapolis, Esposizione degli Oracoli del Signore. I frammenti. Introduzione, testo, traduzione e note*. Milan: Paoline, 2005.

Nutton, Vivian. *Avoiding Distress*. In *Galen: Psychological Writings*, edited by P. N. Singer, 43–106. New York: Cambridge University Press, 2014.

Ong, Walter. *Orality and Literacy: Technologizing the Word*. New York: Routledge, 1982.

von Otto, Johann Karl Theodor. *Justini Philosophi et Martyris cum Tryphone Judaeo*. Jena: Prostat in Libraria, Hermann Dufft, 1876.

Park, Yoon-Man. *Mark's Memory Resources and the Controversy Stories (Mark 2:1–3:6): An Application of the Frame Theory of Cognitive Science to the Markan Oral-Aural Narrative*. Leiden: Brill, 2010.

Parker, David C. *The Living Text of the Gospels*. New York: Cambridge University Press, 1997.

Patillon, Michel, and Giancarlo Bolognesi, *Aelius Theón Progymnasmata: Texte établi et traduit*. Paris: Les Belles Lettres, 1997.
Peirano, Irene. *The Rhetoric of the Roman Fake: Latin Pseudapigrapha in Context*. Cambridge: Cambridge University Press, 2012.
Pelling, Christopher. "Plutarch's Method of Work in the Roman Lives." *JHS* 99 (1979): 74–96.
Perilli, Lorenzo. "Conservazione dei testi e circolazione della conoscenza in Grecia." In *Biblioteche del mondo antico: Dalla tradizione orale alla cultura dell'Impero*, edited by Angela Maria Andrisano, 36–71. Rome: Carocci editore, 2009.
Perrin, Norman. "Toward an Interpretation of the Gospel of Mark." In *Christology and a Modern Pilgrimage*, edited by Hans Dieter Betz, 1–78. Claremont, CA: New Testament Colloquium, 1971.
Perrin, Norman. *What Is Redaction Criticism?* Eugene, OR: Wipf and Stock, 2002.
Pesch, Rudolf. *Das Markusevangelium, 1. Teil: Einleitung und Kommentar zu Kap. 1,1– 8,26*. Freiburg: Herder, 1976.
Pfann, Stephen. "The Use of Cryptographic and Esoteric Scripts in Second Temple Judaism and Surrounding Cultures." In *Interpreting* 4 Ezra *and* 2 Baruch: *International Studies*, edited by Gabriele Boccaccini and Jason M. Zurawski, 173–96. New York: T&T Clark, 2015.
Puccioni, Giulio. *Frammenti delle orazioni perdute*. Milan: A. Mondadori, 1971.
Pulis, John W. "'In the Beginning': A Chapter from the Living Testament of Rastafari." In *The Social Life of Scriptures: Cross-Cultural Perspectives on Biblicism*, edited by James S. Bielo, 30–43. New Brunswick, NJ: Rutgers University Press, 2009.
Quasten, Johannes. *Patrology. Vol. 1: The Beginnings of Patristic Literature*. Notre Dame, IN: Christian Classics, 1983.
Reed, Annette Yoshiko. "ΕΥΑΓΓΕΛΙΟΝ: Orality, Textuality, and the Christian Truth in Irenaeus' *Adversus haereses*." *VC* 56 (2002): 11–46.
Regev, Eyal. *Sectarianism in Qumran: A Cross-Cultural Perspective*. Berlin: Walter de Gruyter, 2007.
Renan, Ernest. *Life of Jesus*. London: Kegan Paul, 1893.
Riggsby, Andrew. *Caesar in Gaul and Rome: War in Words*. Austin: University of Texas Press, 2006.
Riggsby, Andrew. "Memoir and Autobiography in Republican Rome." In *Companion to Greek and Roman Historiography*, edited by John Marincola, 266–74. Chichester: Blackwell, 2007.
Roloff, Jürgen. "Das Markusevangelium als Geschichtsdarstellung." *EvTh* 29 (1969): 73–93.
Rothschild, Clare K., and Trevor W. Thompson. "Galen's *On the Avoidance of Grief*: The Question of a Library at Antium." *CP* 107 (2012): 131–45.
Rousseau, Adelin, and Louis Doutreleau, *Irénée de Lyon, Contre Les Hérésies. Livre III*. Paris: Les Éditions du Cerf, 1974.
Rudd, Niall. *Horace: Satires and Epistles*. New York: Penguin, 2005.

Sanders, E. P., and Margaret Davies. *Studying the Synoptic Gospels*. Philadelphia: Trinity International Press, 1989.

Schofield, Alison. "Rereading S: A New Model of Textual Development in Light of the Cave 4 *Serekh* Copies." *DSD* 15 (2008): 96–120.

Sherwin-White, A. N. *The Letters of Pliny: A Historical and Social Commentary*. Oxford: Clarendon, 1966.

Sim, David C. "Matthew's Use of Mark: Did Matthew Intend to Supplement or Replace His Primary Source?." *NTS* 57 (2011): 176–92.

Singer, Charles. *Galen, On Anatomical Procedures: Translation of the Surviving Books with Introduction and Notes*. New York: Oxford University Press, 1956.

Smith, Abraham. "Tyranny Exposed: The Characterization of Herod Antipas in Mark 6:14–29." *BibInt* 14 (2006): 259–93.

Smith, Jonathan Z. *Map Is Not Territory*. Chicago, IL: University of Chicago Press, 1978.

Speyer, W. *Die literarische Fälschung im heidnischen und christlichen Altertum: Ein Versuch ihrer Deutung*. Munich: Beck, 1971.

Starr, Raymond. "The Circulation of Literary Texts in the Roman World." *ClQ* 37 (1987): 213–23.

Stein, Robert H. *Mark*. Grand Rapids, MI: Baker Academic, 2008.

Stone, Michael Edward. *Fourth Ezra: A Commentary on the Book of Fourth Ezra*. Minneapolis, MN: Fortress, 1990.

Stuckenbruck, Loren. "The Dead Sea Scrolls: Insight into Traditioning Processes and the Growth of Gospel Traditions." *DSD* 23 (2016): 304–28.

Ta-Shma, Israel M. "The 'Open' Book in Medieval Hebrew Literature: The Problem of Authorized Editions," *BJRL* 75 (1993): 17–24.

Talbert, Charles. *What Is a Gospel? The Genre of the Canonical Gospels*. Philadelphia: Fortress, 1977.

Tanner, Kathryn. "Scripture as Popular Text." *Modern Theology* 14 (1998): 279–98.

Teeter, David Andrew. *Scribal Laws: Exegetical Variation in the Textual Transmission of Biblical Law in the Late Second Temple Period*. FAT 92. Tübingen: Mohr Siebeck, 2014.

Telford, W. R. *The Theology of the Gospel According to Mark*. New York: Cambridge University Press, 1999.

Thate, Michael J. *Remembering Things Past?: Albert Schweitzer, the Anxiety of Influence, and the Untidy Jesus of Markan Memory*. Tübingen: Mohr Siebeck, 2013.

Tov, Emanuel. *Textual Criticism of the Hebrew Bible*, 2nd ed. Minneapolis, MN: Fortress, 2001.

Tov, Emanuel. *Scribal Practices and Approaches Reflected in the Texts Found in the Judean Desert*. Atlanta, GA: SBL Press, 2009.

Trocmé, Étienne. "Is There a Markan Christology?" In *Christ and Spirit in the New Testament. In Honour of Charles Francis Digby Moule*, edited by B. Lindars and S. S. Smalley, 3–13. New York: Cambridge University Press, 1973.

Tyson, Joseph B. *Marcion and Luke-Acts: A Defining Struggle*. Columbia: University of South Carolina, 2006.

van den Hoek, Annewies. "Divergent Gospel Traditions in Clement of Alexandria and Other Authors of the Second Century." *Apocrypha* 7 (1996): 43–62.
van den Hoek, Annewies. "Techniques of Quotation in Clement of Alexandria. A View of Ancient Literary Working Methods." *VC* 50 (1996): 223–43.
van der Stockt, Luc. "A Plutarchan Hypomnema on Self-Love." *AJP* 120 (1999): 575–99.
van der Stockt, Luc. "Plutarch in Plutarch: The Problem of the Hypomnemata." In *La Biblioteca di Plutarco, Atti del IX Convegno plutarcheo Pavia, 13–15 giugno*, edited by Italo Gallo, 331–40. Naples: D'Auria. 2004.
van Groningen, Bernard A. "ΕΚΔΟΣΙΣ." *Mnemosyne* 16 (1963): 1–17.
VanderKam, James C. *An Introduction to Early Judaism*. Grand Rapids, MI: Eerdmans, 2002.
VanderKam, James C. *The Dead Sea Scrolls and the Bible*. Grand Rapids, MI: Eerdmans, 2012.
Vansina, Jan. *Oral Tradition as History*. Madison: University of Wisconsin Press, 1985.
Vermes, Geza. "The Leadership of the Qumran Community: Sons of Zadok–Priests–Congregation." In *Geschichte-Tradition-Reflexion: Festschrift für Martin Hengel zum 70. Geburtstag*, edited by H. Cancik et al.; *Vol. 1: Judentum*, edited by Peter Shäfer, 375–84. Tübingen: Mohr Siebeck, 1996.
Vielhauer, Philipp. *Geschichte der Urchristlichen Literatur: Einleitung in das Neue Testament, die Apokryphen und die Apostolischen Väter*. New York: De Gruyter, 1975.
Votaw, Clyde. "The Gospels and Contemporary Biographies." *AmJT* 19 (1915): 45–73, 217–49.
Watson, Francis. *Gospel Writing: A Canonical Perspective*. Grand Rapids, MI: Eerdmans, 2013.
Watson, Francis. "How Did Mark Survive?" In *Matthew and Mark across Perspectives: Essays in Honor of Stephen C. Barton and William R. Telford*, edited by Kristian A. Bendoraitis and Nijay K. Gupta, 1–17. New York: T&T Clark, 2016.
Williams, Joel F. "Literary Approaches to the End of Mark's Gospel." *JETS* 42 (1999): 21–35.
Wills, Lawrence M. *The Jewish Novel in the Ancient World*. Ithaca, NY: Cornell University Press, 1995.
Wittgenstein, Ludwig. *Philosophische Untersuchungen-Philosophical Investigations*, 4th ed. Translated by G. E. M. Anscombe, P. M. S. Hacker, and Joachim Schulte. Malden, MA: Wiley-Blackwell, 2009.
Wolfson, Elliott R. "Gazing Beneath the Veil: Apocalyptic Envisioning the End." In *Reinterpreting Revelation and Tradition: Jews and Christians in Conversation*, edited by John Pawlikowski and Hayim Goren Perelmuter, 77–103. Franklin, WI: Sheed and Ward, 2000.
Woolf, Greg. "Approaching the Ancient Library." In *Ancient Libraries*, ed. Jason König et al., 1–22. New York: Cambridge University Press, 2013.
Wordsworth, John, et al., eds. *Portions of the Gospels according to St. Mark and St. Matthew from the Bobbio Ms. (k) Now Number G. VII. 15 at the National Library at*

Turin, together with Other Fragments of the Gospels from Six Mss. at the Libraries of St. Gall, Coire, Milan, and Berne (usually cited as n, o, p, a2, s and t). Oxford: Clarendon Press, 1886.

Wrede, William. *Das Messiasgeheimnis in den Evangelien*. Göttingen: Vandenhoeck und Ruprecht, 1901. English translation: *The Messianic Secret*, translated by J. C. G. Greig. Cambridge: James Clark, 1971.

X, Malcolm, and Alex Haley. *The Autobiography of Malcolm X as Told to Alex Haley*. New York: Grove Press, 1965.

Xenophontos, Sophia A. "Plutarch's Compositional Technique in the *Au seni respublica gerenda sit*." *AJP* 133 (2012): 61–91.

# *Index of Modern Authors*

Alexander, Loveday, 84, 168n.23, 178n.17
Alexander, Philip S., 60, 172n.9, 173nn.15, 17–18, 22
Anderson, Amy S., 186n.59
Aune, David, 179n.45

Babbit, Frank Cole, 165n.56
Bagnall, Roger S., 164n.33
Bakhtin, Mikhail M., 121–22, 135–36, 186n.3, 189nn.38–42, 191n.5
Barish, David A., 170n.66
Barthes, Roland, 145, 190nn.59–60, 191n.4
Bassler, Jouette M., 185n.49
Baum, David Armin, 179n.34
Baum, Kelly, 186nn.1–2
Bayer, Andrea, 186nn.1–2
Beard, Mary, 164n.53
Beck, Richard Gustav, 167n.7
Becker, Eve-Marie, 176n.3, 177n.6
Behr, Holger, 165n.63
Benjamin, Walter, 122, 125, 185n.55, 186n.5
Birt, Theodore, 162n.29
Blank, David, 175n.50
Blumell, Lincoln H., 187n.7
Bolognesi, Giancarlo, 178n.22
Boomershine, T. E., 189n.33
Bornkamm, Günther, 109, 183n.29, 184n.39

Bourdieu, Pierre, 37, 166n.1
Bovon, François, 88, 179n.37, 184n.40
Bowie, E. L., 166n.83
Breed, Brennen W., 160n.13
Brooks, James A., 181n.60
Brown, Raymond, 159n.3, 160n.4, 182n.9
Bryant, John, 7–8, 17, 59, 72, 162nn.31–33, 163n.29, 164n.41, 171n.2, 174n.37, 175n.52
Bultmann, Rudolf, 176n.4, 188n.22
Burridge, Richard, 176n.2

Cancik, Hubert, 172n.9, 176n.5
Carlson, Stephen, 181n.60
Cirafesi, Wally V., 179n.45
Cohen, Shaye J. D., 53, 170nn.53, 55
Collins, Adela Yarbro, 127, 132, 139, 159nn.1–2, 160n.4, 177nn.6, 10, 185n.45, 188nn.18, 21, 23, 25, 189n.32, 190nn.48–50, 55
Collins, John J., 66, 174n.29
Cosaert, Carl P., 181n.60
Cox, Lynn, 185n.45
Crawford, Jane W., 167n.7
Cribiore, Raffaella, 166n.84

Darnton, Robert, 152–53, 191nn.10–14
Davies, Margaret, 182n.8
Del Mastro, Gianluca, 175nn.48–49

Delattre, Daniel, 175n.50
Deleuze, Gilles, 68, 160n.8, 174n.36
Derrida, Jacques, 145, 164n.36, 184n.33, 190n.59
Dewey, Joanna, 130, 188n.22, 189n.29
Dibelius, Martin, 176n.4
Didion, Joan, 162n.30
Doole, J. Andrew, 183n.27
Donahue, John R., 160n.4
Dorandi, Tiziano, 6–7, 49, 70, 126, 162nn.26, 1, 169nn.34, 44, 47, 175nn.44, 46, 50, 187nn.12–13
Dormeyer, Detlev, 82, 177nn.8–9
Doutreleau, Louis, 180n.55
Draper, Jonathan, 173n.22, 174n.37
Dzielska, Maria, 166n.83

Edwards, James R., 159n.2
Ehrman, Bart D., 97, 181n.61, 184n.40, 186n.58, 188n.23

Ferris, David, 125, 187n.10
Fewster, Gregory P., 179n.45
Fields, Weston, 171n.4
Fish, Stanley, 190n.59
Foucault, Michel, 8–9, 125, 144, 159n.1, 162n.34, 169n.40, 172n.11, 184nn.36–37, 187n.11, 190n.57
Fraade, Steven, 172nn.12, 14, 173nn.19, 21
Frey, Jörg, 185n.56

Gamble, Harry A., 6–7, 49, 162nn.27–28, 181n.1, 184n.40
Geffcken, Katherine A., 167n.6
Gigante, Marcello, 70, 175nn.45, 47–48, 50
Gillihan, Yonder Moynihan, 60, 171n.6
Goodacre, Mark, 178n.25
Gregory, Caspar René, 185n.56
Guatarri, Félix, 68, 160n.8, 174n.36
Guelich, Robert, 176n.4

Gundry, Robert H., 127, 176n.2, 188nn.19–20
Gurd, Sean, 33, 57, 122, 163n.24, 164nn.43–44, 166nn.78–80, 167nn.14, 20, 169nn.42–43, 170n.56, 171n.73, 175n.46, 183nn.16–17, 184nn.32, 34–35, 187n.6

Hadas, Moses, 177n.5
Hall, Lindsay J. H., 163n.25
Hammerstaedt, Jürgen, 191n.1, 192nn.2–15
Hanson, Ann E., 166n.2, 167n.20, 187n.9
Harris-McCoy, Daniel E., 181n.2
Hay, Louis, 169n.8
Hedrick, Jr., Charles W., 164n.33
Hempel, Charlotte, 77, 172n.9, 174nn.31–32
Hitchcock, Louise, 166n.1
Holmes, Michael W., 107, 181n.61
Hooker, Morna D., 159n.2
Houghton, H. A. G., 185nn.50–52
Huitink, L., 170n.62

Incigneri, Brian, 159n.3
Iverson, Kelly R., 185n.46

Johnson, William, 162n.29
Jones, Christopher P., 45, 166nn.82–83, 86

Kähler, Martin, 137, 187n.17
Kelber, Werner, 188n.25
Kelhoffer, James A., 119–20, 185n.45, 186nn.61–66
Kennedy, George, 108, 178n.22, 179n.45, 181n.66
King, Karen, 169n.39
Kivy, Peter, 173n.19
Knust, Jennifer, 174n.37

Kraus, Christina Shuttleworth, 11, 162n.2, 163nn.21, 23
Kürzinger, Josef, 179n.34

Lake, Kirsopp, 186n.59
Laqueur, Richard, 65–66, 170n.65
Larsen, Matthew D. C., 158, 161n.15, 173nn.20, 24, 184n.30
Leigh, Matthew, 163n.18
Letteney, Mark, 161n.15, 169n.41
Lied, Liv Ingeborg, 171n.3
Lin, Yii-Jan, 190n.1
Livingston, E. A., 182n.11
Locher, A., 126, 187n.12
Long, Pamela O., 186n.67
Lunghaug, Hugo, 171n.3
Luz, Ulrich, 190n.55

MacDonald, Dennis R., 179n.34
Malbon, Elizabeth Struthers, 188n.25, 189n.44
Mandel, Ernest, 122, 186n.4
Mansfield, Jaap, 162n.29
Marcovich, Miroslav, 180n.52
Marcus, Joel, 159n.2
Marquis, Timothy Luckritz, 167n.16
Marrou, H. I., 162n.26
Martinez, Victor M., 187n.16
Marxsen, Willi, 159n.2
Mason, Steve, 63–64, 170nn.58–62
McCutcheon, R. W., 168n.20
McGill, Scott, 164n.32, 181n.4
Meeks, Wayne A., 185n.49
Metso, Sarianna, 60–61, 65–66, 172nn.9–10, 173n.15, 174nn.27, 34, 183n.19
Metzger, Bruce M., 127, 185n.45, 186n.58, 188n.23
Meyer, Edvard, 166n.83
Meyer, Elizabeth, 165n.55
Meyers, Jacob M., 168n.29
Millard, Alan, 166n.85

Miller, Tricia, 184n.42
Moretti, Franco, 182n.14
Moss, Candida R., 190n.53
Mroczek, Eva, 3–4, 14, 23, 56–57, 144, 160nn.10–14, 163nn.16–17, 164n.45, 168n.25, 170n.69, 171nn.70–72, 174n.38, 180n.53, 190n.58

Najman, Hindy, 159n.1, 168nn.25–26, 29, 169n.40, 172nn.8, 13, 184n.44, 189n.43
Nati, James, 64, 68, 173n.25, 174n.35
Newson, Carol A., 173n.15
Nietzsche, Friedrich, 159n.1, 184n.33, 189n.43
Nongbri, Brent, 161n.15, 191nn.8–9
Norelli, Enrico, 179n.34
Nutton, Vivian, 165n.73

Ong, Walter, 191n.3

Park, Yoon-Man, 179n.45
Parker, David C., 161n.16
Patillon, Michel, 178n.22
Peirano, Irene, 114, 168n.25, 184n.43
Pelling, Christopher, 165n.59
Perilli, Lorenzo, 126, 187n.16
Perrin, Norman, 183n.29, 188n.25
Pesch, Rudolf, 159n.2
Pfann, Stephen, 168n.29
Puccioni, Giulio, 167n.7

Quasten, Johannes, 179n.33

Reed, Annette Yoshiko, 177n.11
Regev, Eyal, 174n.30
Renan, Ernest, 176n.5
Riggsby, Andrew, 162nn.1, 3, 5, 163n.30
Roloff, Jürgen, 190n.55
Rothschild, Clare K., 165n.73
Rottländer, R. C. A., 126, 187n.12

Rousseau, Adelin, 180n.55
Rudd, Niall, 168n.24

Sanders, E. P., 182n.8
Schofield, Alison, 172n.9
Senseney, Megan Finn, 187n.16
Sherwin-White, A. N., 164n.32
Sim, David C., 184n.38
Singer, Charles, 165nn.75–76, 178n.20
Smith, Abraham, 190n.56
Smith, Jonathan Z., 177n.5
Smith, Morton, 177n.5
Speyer, W., 162n.29
Starr, Raymond, 6, 59, 161nn.23–25
Stein, Robert H., 188n.24
Stone, Michael Edward, 168n.29
Stuckenbruck, Loren, 189n.37

Ta-Shma, Israel M., 56, 170n.69, 171n.70
Talbert, Charles, 176n.5
Tanner, Kathryn, 148, 191n.2
Teeter, David Andrew, 173n.22
Telford, W. R., 137–38, 159n.2, 190n.46
Thate, Michael J., 191n.4
Thompson, Trevor W., 165n.73
Tov, Emanuel, 174n.26, 183n.18
Trocmé, Étienne, 137, 190n.45
Tyson, Joseph B., 178n.16

van den Hoek, Annewies, 126, 162n.1, 164n.32, 181n.60, 187n.15
van der Stockt, Luc, 28, 165nn.59–61
van Groningen, Bernard A., 6, 49, 161nn.21, 25
van Henten, J. W., 170n.62
VanderKam, James C., 171nn.4–5
Vansina, Jan, 174n.37
Vermes, Geza, 60, 172n.9, 174n.33
Vielhauer, Philipp, 176n.4
von Otto, Johann Karl Theodor, 180n.52
Votaw, Clyde, 176n.5

Wagstaff, Sheena, 186nn.1–2
Watson, Francis, 160n.9, 178nn.25–26, 180n.49, 183n.20
Wayment, Thomas A., 187n.7
Williams, Joel F., 189n.33
Wills, Lawrence M., 184n.42
Wittgenstein, Ludwig, 81, 166n.77, 177n.7
Wolfson, Elliott R., 168n.29
Woolf, Greg, 69–70, 175n.43, 187n.16
Wordsworth, John, 117, 192n.1
Wrede, William, 142, 190n.54

X, Malcolm, 5, 161n.19
Xenophontos, Sophia A., 165n.62

# Subject Index

accidental publication, 6–7, 37–39, 41–45, 47, 49, 51, 53, 55, 57, 59, 79
*Acts of Timothy*, 150
adding, 13, 29, 33, 41–42, 48, 63, 76, 85, 93, 99–100, 103, 107, 113–114, 118, 120, 154
advance copies, 54
*aide-mémoire*, 30, 48, 63
*akribēs*, 29, 41, 84–86
Aland synopsis, 103–104
ambiguity, 19
  between writer and author, 49
  in Hippocrates, 33–34, 109–113
  in Markan endings, 118
  purpose of, 148
  in text, 62, 68, 143, 145
Amelius, 91
Ammonian sections, 103
*Amores*, 49, 104
anachronistic concept, 2, 3, 23, 37, 79, 88, 91, 99, 148–149, 152
anonymity, 1, 3, 8, 19–21, 30, 34, 40, 42, 44, 48, 62, 82, 97, 111
aphorism
  of Hippocrates, 33–34, 62, 109–111
  of Martin Kähler, 127
Apollo, 24
Apollonius, 34, 89

*apologia*, 89, 118
apostle, 86, 88–90, 97, 119, 130, 142. *See also* disciple
Aristarchus, 9, 40
Ariston, 89–90
Aristophanes, 50–51
arrange, 89, 124, 126, 132, 144, 151
arranged, 87, 91–92, 126, 133
arrangement, 85–86, 88–89, 91–92, 107–108, 123–124, 126–128, 143
arranging, 19, 84, 127
Arrian, 47–49, 98
Artemidorus, 100
ascension, 117
Asklepius, 24
assumption, 1–2, 4–5, 33, 87, 109, 112, 120, 122, 135–137, 151
Atticus, 12–14, 39–40, 50–51
attribution, 1, 38, 50, 76–77, 81, 93–94, 119, 150
*auctor*, 43–44, 98
audience, 7, 19, 44
  of Galen, 29
  of the Gospel according to Mark, 1, 119, 128, 142
  of the Gospel according to Matthew, 112
  of *hypomnēmata*, 123

auditor, 45, 97–98, 112
Augustine of Hippo, 12
Augustus, 26, 85
Aulus Gellius, 126
Aulus Hirtius, 15–16
aural experience of text, 62–63
author, 1–9, 11–19, 21–23, 26, 28–29,
    35–38, 43–45, 47, 49–50, 55–57, 59,
    61, 68, 70, 74–75, 79–84, 87–88,
    90–93, 96, 100–102, 104, 106, 109,
    114, 119, 122–123, 130, 134–138, 140,
    143–144, 147, 149–150, 152–154
authored text, 1–2, 7–9, 11, 13, 15–17, 19,
    21–23, 25, 27, 29, 31, 33, 35, 47, 49, 59,
    77, 81, 83, 85, 91, 93–94, 96, 120, 134
authoriality, 8, 35
authoring, 13, 15, 18–19, 28, 100
authority, 8–9, 29, 45, 49, 59, 61–62,
    67–68, 70, 75, 81, 87, 90, 94, 96, 98,
    116, 130–131, 134, 137
authorization, 17, 22, 61, 49, 59, 61–62,
    136–137
authorized text, 7, 22, 42, 49, 59, 61, 63,
    65–69, 71, 73, 75, 77, 79, 97, 135
authorizer, 22, 62, 64, 67, 75, 98, 134
authorship, 2, 5, 8–9, 11, 22, 29, 38, 47,
    49, 59, 76, 83, 87–88, 90, 92, 96, 98,
    101–102, 109, 113
autobiography, 5, 9, 13–14, 55

barbarisms, 12–13
Ben Sira, 3–4, 14, 23, 57
bible, 3, 80
    Hebrew Bible, 69, 128, 139
*biblion*, 86, 94–95, 124
binary, 134
    authored and nonauthored, 8
    narrative vs note structure, 130
    private/public, 28
    readerly or writerly, 145
    unfinished and finished, 121
    unpublished/published, 28

biography
    of Cicero, 13
    genre of the Gospel according to
        Mark, 80–81, 83, 108, 122, 133, 144
    of Sulla, 29
*bios*, 80–81, 133, 144
birth, 11, 53, 81, 85, 107
Boëthus (Flavius), 30–31
book, 1–7, 9, 12–15, 17–18, 23–25, 27,
    29–31, 33, 35, 38, 42, 46–47, 49–50,
    53–54, 56–57, 61, 63, 70–71, 73–75,
    79–83, 86–101, 104, 106–110, 112,
    114, 117, 119–120, 122–126, 128,
    133–136, 140, 143–144, 148–154
bracketing, 64, 128–133, 135
bread, 66, 113, 129, 132
*buxos*, 46

Caligula, 26
canons, 80
    Eusebian, 103, 119 (*see also* Ammonian
        sections)
Celsus, 2, 150
character, 19, 85
    of Catius, 43
    of Jesus, 80
    of Josephus, 56
    of Lampo, 25
childhood, 32, 81, 85, 107, 134
*chreiai*, 91
christology of Mark, 137–138, 140,
    143–144
church, 93–94, 97–98, 113, 134, 137
Cicero, 12–17, 26, 28, 38–40, 50–52, 55
circulation, 1, 6, 9, 14, 22, 38–40, 48, 54,
    71, 74, 97
Clement of Alexandria, 96–98, 126
codes, 123
    of the Community Rule, 64
    of GitHub
    of the Torah, 143
Codex Athous Laurae, 119

Codex Bobiensis, 116–118
Codex Regius, 119
Codex Washingtonianus, 118
collaboration, 22, 53, 153
collect, 112, 123, 127, 144
collected, 28, 107, 121, 124, 130–131, 140, 147–148
collecting, 24, 125–126, 143
collection, 3, 34–35, 69–70, 100, 120, 122–123, 125–128, 130–136, 140, 147–152
*commentarii*, 11, 13–19, 26, 28, 33, 38, 53, 68–69, 114, 126, 128. See also *hypomnēmata*
commentary, 1, 9, 11, 110, 127
commentator, 120, 148
communal nature of texts, 53, 62, 66–67
community, 4, 23, 105, 108, 118, 122–123, 134–135, 153
*Rule of the*, 9, 59–70, 73–77, 101
compilation, 19, 41, 66, 83, 86, 123, 135, 153
concentric circles, 6, 96, 134
constellation, 2, 5, 11, 32, 67, 81, 83, 88, 91, 99, 102–104, 106, 114, 150–151, 153
consulship
of Cicero, 12–14, 17
contaminations
of text, 67–68
continuation, 16, 91, 93
continuator, 16, 148
continue, 15, 20, 56, 60, 90, 93, 108, 112–113
continued, 6, 17, 56, 61, 120, 133
continuing, 45, 88, 99–100, 106, 114, 120
contract, 8
conventions
literary, 95
copying, 8, 17–18, 31, 39–40, 42, 51, 54, 60–61, 70–71, 117, 119, 122
copyists, 40, 50–51
Corfidius, 51

correction, 12, 21–22, 40–42, 50–51, 64–65, 67, 76, 101, 108, 114, 117
cost
of Pliny the Elder's notes, 17–18
of producing scroll, 61
Covenanters, 60
crafting, 27, 54, 121–123, 130, 144
curation, 40, 50, 121
Curio, 39
currency, 17, 152
Cyprian, 117

Damis, 34–35, 89, 91
Daniel, 47, 112
daughter, 89, 124, 131, 138, 141–144
Dead Sea Scrolls, 9, 23, 59–61, 66, 69–70
death, 39, 85, 93, 95, 124
of Jesus, 81, 107–108, 116, 129, 132–134, 141, 143
of Karl Marx, 122
of Sulla, 28
definition, 7–8, 11, 38, 42, 49, 81, 108, 119, 137
definitive moment, 2, 6
definitive version, 7, 14, 21, 49, 52, 56–57, 71, 73–75, 152
demand, 31
demarcation, 103
Demonax, 81
Demosthenes, 95
*diēgēsis*, 85, 133–134, 144
digital humanities, 153
Diodorus Siculus, 41–43
disciple, 43, 74, 89, 91, 93–95, 118–119, 131–133, 138–140, 142, 150. *See also* apostle
distribution, 6
doctor, 11, 20–21, 24–25, 30–31, 36, 39, 134, 141
draft, 11–13, 15, 18–19, 33–36, 38, 57, 70–71, 76, 87, 93, 107, 110–111, 114, 151

eating, 15, 66, 129, 132
edition, 4, 55, 65, 70, 84, 97, 101, 104, 117, 119, 123, 151
*edo*, 94
*eisegesis*, 147
*ekdidōmi*, 46, 94
*ekpherō*, 46, 94
embarrassment, 39–40, 108
ending, 76, 145
   in Josephus, 54–56
   in the Gospel according to Mark, 99, 114–120, 133, 148–149, 151
Enlightenment, 80
Epictetus, 47–49, 98
epilogue, 81
epistle, 45, 105, 120
Esther, 101, 114
*euaggelion*, 88, 150
Eusebius, 83, 86–92, 96–98, 103, 119, 150
everyday language, 23–26, 95
excerpts, 17, 19, 70, 126

family, 32, 34–35, 81, 85, 108, 119, 137, 143–144
Farrer Hypothesis, 102
feeding, 129, 131–132
finishedness, 1–3, 6–8, 12–18, 16–17, 25, 28–29, 32–34, 36, 40–41, 46, 49, 53–55, 57, 75, 81, 83–87, 93, 96, 100, 106, 108–110, 120–123, 128, 133–136, 143, 150, 153–154
fluidity of text, 2, 4–5, 7–8, 11, 17, 20–26, 29, 35, 42, 56, 59–60, 69, 75, 77, 81, 83, 101, 106, 109, 113–114, 122, 133, 135, 148, 150–151, 154
folktales, 152–153
forgery, 114, 119–120
founding of the church (Irenaeus), 93–94
Freer Logion, 116, 118
function, 5, 8–9, 20, 22–23, 27, 29–30, 35, 53, 57, 64, 66, 68, 76–77, 82, 87, 98, 101, 124–125, 134–135, 139–141
Fyodor Dostoevsky, 135–136

Galen, 29–34, 62, 76, 84–85, 91–92, 98, 107, 109–112
gender, 110, 137
genre, 5, 14, 35, 70, 95, 114, 135
   of the Gospel according to Mark, 80–82
   speech, 49, 80, 82, 94, 148
geographically dispersed community, 66–67
ghostwriting, 13
GitHub, 153
gospel, 1–5, 7, 9, 36, 52, 79–120, 122–123, 125, 127–145, 147–154
Gospel according to John, 2, 83, 96, 151, 153–154
Gospel according to Luke, 2, 5, 79–80, 83–96, 103, 134, 144, 148–151, 154
Gospel according to Mark, 1–4, 36, 79–120, 122–123, 125, 127–145, 147–154
Gospel according to Matthew, 1–2, 4–5, 79–80, 82–83, 88–90, 92–94, 96, 99–101, 103–114, 120, 134, 144, 148–149, 151–152, 154
Gospel according to Thomas, 1, 150, 153–154
grief, 30, 39, 125

*habitus*, 23, 37, 46, 56, 74, 80, 106, 121, 149
handbook, 32, 85
hearing, 27, 45, 48, 64, 88, 97, 129, 131, 138, 148
Herculaneum, 69–70, 72, 74–75
hermeneutical Procrustean bed, 136
Hippocrates, 32–34, 62, 109–112
historian, 1–2, 15–16, 23–24, 37, 52–53, 88, 90, 134, 145
historical-critical method, 2, 79, 93
historicity, 34
historiography, 81–82

## Subject Index

history, 3, 11–15, 17, 24–25, 41–42, 52, 55, 70, 80–81, 83, 87–88, 90–91, 93, 97, 107, 121, 132–133, 148, 153
Homer, 9, 40
Horace, 43–45, 50, 98
*hypomnēmata*, 11–14, 16–17, 19–32, 34–36, 48–49, 53, 56, 68–70, 74, 83–87, 90–91, 93, 95–98, 100, 107, 112, 118, 120, 122–125, 127–129, 131, 133–136, 143–144, 150
Hypothesis, 101–103
  Farrer, 102
  Neo-Griesbach, 102
  Two-/Four-Source, 101

identity
  of "the desecration that makes desolate," 67
  of Jesus, 112, 142–144
imagery, 3
intention, 2, 17, 38, 49–50, 52, 112, 122
interpolation, 25, 124, 131, 142
interpreter, 91, 93, 95, 100, 123, 127, 135–136, 140, 147
Irenaeus of Lyon, 2, 82, 93–96, 119, 150
Isidore, 69
iteration, 67–69, 103, 105, 151

Jason of Cyrene, 83
Jeremiah, 101, 105
Jerusalem, 69, 128–129, 132–133, 139
Jesus, 81, 83–89, 91, 107–108, 113, 115–120, 128–135, 137–144, 147, 149–151
Josephus, 23, 52–56, 68–69, 88
journal, 24, 26
Jubilees, 23
Julia Domna, 34–35
Julius Caesar, 14, 26
Justin Martyr, 2, 180
Justus, 55
juxtaposition, 69, 125

*katatithēmi*, 95
*kathexēs*, 85
keyword, 125–129, 131–134

Lampo, 25–26
law, 19–20, 67, 127
lawbook, 66
leadership, 61, 67–68
lecture, 11, 31, 43–44, 47–48, 63–64, 71, 74–76, 98
*lemaskil*, 61, 74
lengthening, 99
letter, 8–9, 11–13, 17, 25, 27, 45, 51, 71, 103
library, 30, 41–42, 69–72, 74–75, 153
list, 11, 56, 63–66
listening, 48, 51, 62, 64, 133
literary raw material, 13–14, 18–19, 21–23, 27–28, 93
literature, 5, 11–14, 17, 19–21, 23, 26–27, 29–30, 35–36, 38, 40–41, 44, 48–49, 53, 63, 68–69, 77, 80–83, 95, 97–98, 124, 126, 135, 148
Little Red Riding Hood, 152
Livy, 76
location, 1, 66–67, 69, 76, 130
*logia*, 87–93
Lucian, 12, 24–26, 81, 87, 107

Majority Text, 119
manuscript, 3–4, 6–7, 18, 23, 50–52, 55–56, 59–60, 62, 64, 74, 103, 106, 114–119, 143, 151
Marcion, 94
Marinus, 31–32, 84
Martial, 18–19, 49, 104
Marx, Karl, 122
masculinity, 15
material, 11–19, 22–24, 27–28, 34–35, 42–43, 52–53, 57, 59–60, 68, 85, 88–89, 93, 98–100, 105, 112, 116, 125–127
  textual raw, 7, 11, 17–18, 34–35, 85, 96, 98

Matthias, 89
medieval Hebrew manuscripts, 56
memoir, 12, 14, 34–35
memoranda, 11, 28, 31–32, 84
memory aid, 19, 27, 29–30, 32, 35, 38, 48, 53, 59, 69, 71, 74–75, 90, 97–98, 112, 126
messianic secret, 128, 137, 142–143
metaphor, 3–4, 23, 39, 79, 123, 149
Metropolitan Museum of Art, 121
mighty deed, 113, 129–131, 137, 140–142. *See also* miracle
Miltonian author, 23, 144
miracle, 113, 128, 134, 142–143. *See also* mighty deed
mission, 108, 142
modern scholarship, 1–2, 5, 37–38, 40, 62, 66, 75, 79, 101, 114, 145, 148–149, 152–153
modification, 21, 67, 110
monological unity, 123, 127, 135–136, 140
multiple versions, 7, 59–61, 63, 65–67, 69, 71–75, 77, 79, 81, 87, 100–101, 119, 135, 137, 140, 144, 151
mutability, 20, 23, 26

naming, 1, 3, 5, 13, 18, 28, 35–36, 40, 42–45, 51, 71, 74–75, 82–84, 90, 116, 139, 151–152
narrative, 3, 5, 21, 85–89, 91–92, 100, 106–108, 115, 120, 122–123, 125–128, 130, 132–137, 143–144, 147–148, 152
Nestle-Aland, 28th edition, 4, 117
Nicolaus of Damascus, 85, 108
notes, 6, 8, 11–12, 14–17, 20–22, 25–32, 34–35, 38, 43–44, 48–49, 53–56, 63, 70–72, 74, 76, 84–85, 90–92, 97–100, 107, 109, 114, 116, 119–120, 122–136, 139–140, 144, 147–151, 153
notebook, 13–14, 28, 34–35, 89
novel, 9, 18, 45, 135–136, 145
numbering, 75

omitted, 25, 30, 108
open text, 4, 7–8, 14, 21, 27, 29, 41–42, 56–57, 73, 76, 81, 83, 99, 118–122, 128, 135, 143–145, 148–150, 152–153
openness, 3, 23, 26, 36, 114
orality, 5, 28–30, 32, 39, 44, 47–48, 63, 66, 89–90, 95, 97–98, 148
order, 4–5, 7, 11–13, 16, 20, 25, 38, 41, 44, 48, 51, 64, 82–85, 87, 89, 91–93, 106–108, 116, 119, 121–124, 126–127, 133. *See also taxis*
organization, 25, 60, 66, 68, 87, 92, 107, 123–127, 130–131, 134–135
Origen, 83, 96, 150
origin, 1–3, 16, 29, 41, 48, 54–55, 68–69, 74–75, 93
originality, 3–4, 7, 45, 50, 59, 67–68, 74, 76, 98, 100, 114–116, 121, 133, 151
Ovid, 49, 104

*palam facere*, 46
panegyric, 12, 14
Papias, 86–93, 97–98
papyri, 122, 150
parable, 108, 128, 131
*parakolouthein*, 85
paratextual features, 21, 25, 42, 44, 68, 89, 116
passion, 127–128, 132
Paul, 45, 86–87, 93–95
peasant tales, 152
Peter, 87, 89–95, 97–98, 113, 115, 153–154
Philo, 23–26, 63–64, 69, 88, 124
Philodemus, 69–71, 74–75, 126
philology, 23, 59, 116
philosopher, 23, 44, 48, 98, 113, 134, 144
Philostratus, 34–35, 89, 91
physicians, 20
Plato, 19, 21–23, 30, 43, 45, 101
Platonic tradition of writing, 23, 27, 30, 32, 48, 68, 97
Pliny the Elder, 17–19, 126–127

Pliny the Younger, 17–19, 26, 76
Plutarch, 26–29, 85, 125–126
poem, 12, 18, 114
poet, 18, 26, 114
policy, 64
polish in texts, 7, 13–14, 16, 18–19, 24–25, 31–32, 35, 40–41, 48–49, 53, 70, 75–76, 87, 92–93, 95, 98, 107, 110, 114, 120, 123, 126, 133, 135
polyphonic, 135
Porphyry, 91, 114
Poseidonactos of Biton, 71
postpositive conjunction, 115
practical purposes of texts, 11, 20–21, 27, 59, 64, 68, 74–76, 123, 129, 135
practice, 5, 26, 29, 32, 37, 43, 46, 54, 60, 80, 83, 101, 107, 118, 122, 126, 128
    ancient reading, 63, 82, 147
    ancient writing, 5, 23, 38, 47, 52, 92, 100, 105, 113, 135, 149
praise, 12–17, 32
preaching, 80, 93, 95, 98, 118, 128, 130–131, 134, 144
preface, 15–16, 24–25, 41–44, 47–49, 68, 83–90, 100
prepublication, 54
preservation, 87, 92, 125
president, 63–64
printing, 5, 7, 37, 40, 148
private text, 8–9, 11, 24, 28, 30, 38, 45, 76
prohibition, 64
prologue, 53–54, 120
proper arrangement, 107
*propetesteron*, 86–87
proportional Venn diagram, 104–105, 153
protection of literature, 40
provenance, 1, 93
Psalms, 3, 23, 128, 139
pseudepigraphon, 40
public audience, 6–7, 11, 14, 18–19, 22, 24–25, 28–31, 34–41, 43–49, 56, 76, 94, 110–112, 143

publication, 1–7, 29, 31, 33, 36–47, 49–53, 55–57, 59, 75, 79–80, 94, 96, 98, 110, 114, 142, 149–150, 152
published text, 2, 6–7, 16, 28, 36–37, 39–42, 44, 46–47, 49–52, 55–56, 59, 76, 81, 83, 87, 93–96, 101, 104, 134, 150
publishing, 12, 19, 42, 46, 52, 74, 85, 94, 110, 136, 143
Pythagoreans, 44

Qumran, 59–62, 66–69, 72, 134–135
quotation, 50, 83, 90, 96–98, 125
quote, 1, 8, 37, 90, 96–97, 107, 125, 137

reader, 2, 4, 19–21, 23–25, 29–30, 32–38, 40–42, 44–45, 47–49, 61–62, 64, 66, 70, 74–76, 79–83, 85–93, 95, 97–100, 103–104, 106–107, 109–116, 118–123, 125, 127, 133–136, 138–139, 143, 145, 147–152, 154
readership, 19–20, 29–30, 34, 37, 45, 47, 49, 56, 76, 81, 111
reading, 1, 3, 5–7, 9, 14–17, 19, 21–24, 26–27, 30, 32–33, 37, 42, 45–46, 50–51, 53–54, 59, 61–64, 74, 76, 79–84, 86–87, 90, 92, 95–96, 98, 100, 106, 109, 112–113, 117–123, 125–137, 139–141, 143–145, 147–149
rearrangement, 106
reception, 3, 38, 121, 148
recitation, 18, 62–63, 123
record, 11, 25, 31, 43–44, 68, 90, 95, 123–125, 127, 140
recording, 32, 35, 66, 83
redaction, 4, 101–102, 109, 149
relationship, 4, 20, 22, 50, 52, 60, 65, 79, 85, 99–102, 104, 109, 122
reliability, 2, 34, 52, 88
reminder, 19, 64
removing, 21, 51, 75, 100, 103, 108, 112–113
repetition, 28, 63, 108, 128

reproduction, 4, 8, 30, 40, 62, 150
republishing, 55, 104
resurrection, 108, 117–120, 133, 142
rethinking, 4, 52, 71
revising, 7–8, 12, 20, 29, 40–42, 49–50, 55, 71, 76, 104, 106, 114, 120
revision, 5–7, 22, 35, 37, 39, 41–43, 45–49, 51–57, 59, 73, 76, 79, 81, 99–101, 103, 107, 114–115, 122
rewording, 71
reworking, 6, 12, 29, 34, 36, 43, 53, 57, 69, 85, 97, 99, 100, 109, 112–113, 118, 120, 125, 128, 132, 137, 144–145, 148, 151, 153
rewriting, 28, 33–34, 41, 45–46, 52–53, 55–56, 71, 83, 97, 99, 109, 123–125, 147, 153
rhetoric, 15, 45, 51, 70–71, 73–75, 85
rhizomatic growth, 2, 60, 68, 154
ritual, 61–62, 66, 130
Rome, 1, 14, 27, 30–31, 39, 44, 53–54, 87, 93–94
roughness, 11–13, 15, 18–19, 27, 29, 32, 36, 40, 76, 87, 93, 98–99, 105, 107, 109, 111, 120, 122, 153
rule, 9, 20, 37, 43, 52, 59–64, 66–70, 73–75, 77, 81, 101, 105, 134–135
rulebook, 74

Sabbath, 129–130
satire, 43–44
SBL Handbook of Style, 5
scholar, 1–2, 5–6, 28, 34, 37–38, 50, 53, 60, 62, 66, 79–80, 82, 88, 93, 101, 103, 114, 128, 133, 145, 148, 152–154
scholarship, 5–6, 37, 75, 101, 127
school, 35, 44, 71, 74, 85, 144
Scrapbook, 34
scribe, 3, 18, 47, 70–71, 74–75, 108, 139
scripture, 23, 63–64, 148
sectarianism, 69
security, 42

seeing, 128–129, 133
Septimus Severus, 35
Septuagint, 68–69, 139
serializing, 94
Sermon on the Mount, 108
Servius, 114
sesterces, 17–18
silence, 18, 63, 142
Socrates, 19–22, 45, 98
Socratic dialogues, 21
soteriology, 140, 143–144
source, 4, 8–9, 11, 29, 31–32, 34, 38, 41, 43–44, 49, 60, 83, 85–90, 94, 96–98, 101–102, 105, 117, 123, 130, 149, 153
  criticism, 28
speech, 15, 26, 34, 38–40, 49, 51–52, 54, 80, 82, 85, 92, 94–95, 107–108, 138, 148
stolen texts, 41
story, 13, 15, 17, 27–28, 34–36, 38, 81, 83–87, 89, 96–97, 103–104, 107–109, 111, 113–114, 119–120, 122–124, 127–135, 138–143, 152–153
stripped speeches, 15
student, 29–31, 33, 35–36, 38, 43–44, 49, 75
style, 13, 15, 22–26, 29, 31, 33–34, 40, 43, 48, 50, 89, 95, 107, 126, 128, 140, 143
subscription, 70–71, 74–75
suffering, 128–129, 132
*suggramma*, 33, 86
*sugkatataxai*, 88
*sui generis*, 80–81
Sulla, 28–29
*suntaxis*, 87, 123
synagogue, 26, 108, 129–130
Synoptic Problem, 4, 82, 104
syntax, 15

tabulating, 42
*taxis*, 13, 91–93, 106–107, 123–124

teacher, 21, 34–36, 44–46, 48, 134–135, 137–140, 144
teaching, 30, 32–33, 35, 38, 43–45, 47–49, 63–64, 71, 84, 90–91, 97–98, 108, 110, 118, 123, 130–132, 134, 143–144
technical texts, 20, 36, 46, 74, 76, 84–85, 95, 100
*telos*, 69, 75
temple, 3, 108, 112, 129, 132–133
tension, 101, 135–137, 141, 143, 148
Tertullian, 69, 83
textual criticism, 4, 52, 149
textuality, 2, 5, 28, 34, 38, 60, 68, 76, 79, 81–83, 87–88, 93, 95–96, 98–99, 102, 109, 153
textualization, 2, 4–5, 22, 36, 38, 40, 44, 48, 52, 67, 69, 75, 79, 82–84, 87–88, 90, 92–95, 97–98, 128, 135, 148–153
textualizer, 89–90
theft, 43
Theon, 85, 108
Theophilus, 84
Theophilus of Antioch, 2
theory, 39, 76, 79–80, 154
  of Deleuze and Guatarri, 68
  of Galen, 30
  of Hippocrates, 33
  of John Bryant, 7, 17, 59
  of Plato, 19
  of Richard Laqueur, 55–56
  of Robert Darnton, 152
Therapeutae, 63–64
Titus, 52, 55–56
Torah, 47, 62, 138, 143
tradition, 2–4, 14, 23, 30, 32, 45, 47, 50, 52–53, 55–56, 66–70, 74–75, 79–83, 86–88, 90–92, 95–106, 108–115, 118–120, 123, 125, 128, 132, 135–137, 139–140, 143–144, 147–154
translation, 12, 46, 53, 67, 69, 94, 117, 153
transmission, 6

transmitter, 3
tweaking, 71
twelve, 129–131, 134, 141–142

unattributed texts, 38, 76–77
unauthored texts, 5, 8, 16, 18, 76
unfinalizability, 121
unfinishedness, 4–5, 7, 11, 13–19, 21–23, 25, 27, 29–36, 38, 42, 54, 59, 76, 79, 83, 87, 91, 93, 98–100, 106–111, 114–115, 118–123, 125, 127, 129–131, 133–137, 139–141, 143–145, 147–149, 151, 154
unit, 68, 102–103, 105, 128, 130, 134
unpolished texts, 11, 97–98, 107, 111, 114, 147
unpublication, 40
unpublished texts, 18, 28, 41, 46–47, 76, 110, 122
unpublishing, 40
user of text, 56, 61–64, 66, 82, 99–101, 103, 105, 107, 109, 111, 113, 115, 117, 119, 122–123, 125, 127, 132, 134–135, 145, 147–150, 153

Valentinus, 94–95
value, 18–19, 30, 82, 143
versification, 103
version, 2, 4, 6–8, 12, 21–22, 30–32, 49–50, 52–54, 56–57, 59–61, 63, 65, 67–75, 77, 79, 84, 87, 100–101, 104–106, 114, 117–118, 152, 154
Vespasian, 52
Vindolanda tablets, 126
Virgil, 114
Vitruvius, 76
volume, 17–18, 24–25, 41–42, 71, 89, 122

walking, 65, 113, 115, 138–139
wisdom, 14
Wittgensteinian approach, 81

writer, 3, 5, 8, 11–14, 16–17, 20, 22–24, 30, 33, 36, 40–41, 43, 46–49, 52–54, 59, 69–70, 74, 76, 83, 86, 89, 93, 105, 107, 109, 126, 128, 130, 136, 148

writerly texts, 145

writing, 3, 5, 7–8, 11–19, 22–24, 26–30, 32–33, 35, 38, 40–44, 46–56, 60–61, 64, 69–70, 74–76, 79–80, 83, 87–92, 94–97, 100–101, 105, 107, 109–114, 120, 126, 128, 135–136, 144, 148–149, 152–153

written texts, 2, 5, 12–14, 17, 19–22, 25, 27–28, 30–35, 38–40, 42, 44–50, 52, 54, 59–60, 63, 74, 81, 84, 88–89, 92–94, 97–98, 110, 119, 122, 135, 150

Xenophon, 101

*Yaḥad*, 60, 62–64, 66–67, 75

Zoticus, 114

# Index of Ancient Sources

**Hebrew Bible:**
2 Samuel
   8:16: 68
*Exodus*
   3:6: 139
   3:14: 139
   34:5–6: 139
*Ezra*
   6:2: 68
Nehemiah
   8: 62
*Psalms*
   107:25–30: 128, 188, 139

**Dead Sea Scrolls:**
1QS
   1.16–3.12: 62
   1.21–22: 62
   1.22: 62
   3.13: 61
   3.13–4.26: 62–63
   5: 67
   5.13: 61–62
   6.1–8: 66
   6.2: 66
   6.3: 66
   6.4: 66
   6.6–8: 61
   6.7–8: 63
   6.16: 66
   6.22: 66
   6.25: 66
   7: 66
   7.1–9: 64–65
   7.3: 66
   7.8: 64
   7.15: 62
   7.16: 66
   7.19: 66
   7.20: 66
   7.25: 66
   8.12–16: 61
   8.17: 66
   8.24: 66
   9.12: 61
   9.12–26: 63
   9.21: 61
1QSb
   1.1: 61
   3.2: 61
   5.20: 61
4Q256
   9: 67
4Q258
   1: 67
   1.1: 61
   8.5: 61

4Q259
   3.7: 61

**Additional Jewish Sources:**
2 Maccabees
   2:19–32: 83
   2:23–32: 83
*4 Ezra*
   14:23–26: 46
   14:44–46: 46
Ben Sira:
   24:28: 14
Josephus
  *Against Apion*
    1.46: 52
    1.48: 52
    1.50: 52–53
    1.56: 53, 68
  *Jewish Antiquities*
    7.110: 68
    7.293: 68
    10.5: 68
    10.55: 68
    11.94: 68
    11.96: 68
    11.104: 68
    11.208: 68
    11.248: 68
    15.37: 87
    15.52: 87
    15.174: 53, 68
    20.259: 54–55
    20.259–66: 55
    20.267: 54–55
  *Jewish War*
    1.1–3: 53–54
    1.13–16: 54
    2.128–53: 62
  *Life*
    342: 53, 68
    358: 14, 53, 68
    363: 55–56
    430: 56

Philo
  *Against Flaccus*
    125–34: 25
    131: 25, 124
  *Allegorical Interpretation*
    1.150: 23
    2.146: 23
    2.160: 23
    4.164: 24
  *Embassey to Gaius*
    161–62: 26
  *On Abraham*
    5: 23
  *On Dreams*
    2.268: 24
  *On Flight and Finding*
    4: 23
  *On the Contemplative Life*
    75b–76: 63–64
  *On the Virtues*:
    20: 23
  *Who is the Heir*:
    176: 23
*Testament of Abraham* (Rec.B)
   10.2–14: 123–24
*Testament of Abraham* (Rec.A)
   12.7: 124

**New Testament:**
*Gospel according to Matthew*
   1–2: 107
   3:1–4:22: 106
   3:7–10: 106, 108, 183
   4:24–27:29: 108
   8:5–13: 108, 183
   10:1–39: 108
   11:1–30: 108
   12:22–22:8: 106
   12:38–42: 108, 183
   12:43–45: 108, 183
   13:24–52: 108
   13:58: 113
   17:24–27: 108, 183

18:10–35: 106, 183
19:17: 113
20:1–16: 106, 108, 183
21:28–32: 106, 108, 183
22:1–14: 106, 108, 183
23:37–39: 106, 108, 183
24:15: 112
24:15–22: 112
24:37–25:46: 106, 108, 183
27:3–10: 108, 183
27:62–66: 106, 183
28:9–20: 108

*Gospel according to Mark*
1:1–22: 188
1:2–20: 106
1:16–45: 127
1:20: 188
1:21: 129–30
1:21–22: 106, 108, 130, 137, 183, 188
1:21–28: 130
1:21–45: 130
1:21–23:6: 129
1:22: 134
1:23: 129–30
1:23–28: 106, 108, 130, 183
1:24: 137
1:25: 142
1:29: 129–30
1:29–38: 130
1:32–34: 137
1:33: 130
1:35: 130
1:35–38: 106, 183
1:38–45: 130
1:39: 129–30
1:40: 106
1:40–45: 143
1:44–45: 142
1:45: 130
2:1–3:6: 127, 130
2:1–12: 130, 139
2:2: 130
2:7: 139

2:20: 134
2:23: 129–30
2:23–29: 130
2:24: 129–30
2:27: 129–30
2:28: 129–30
3:1: 129–30
3:1–6: 130
3:2: 129–30
3:4: 129–30
3:6: 134
3:7–19: 130
3:7–35: 127
3:7–6:31: 129, 130
3:9: 131
3:11–12: 142
3:14: 131
3:14–15: 130
3:16: 131
3:17: 180
3:19: 106
3:20–21: 106, 108, 144, 183
3:20–16:8: 106
3:23: 131
3:30–35: 144
3:31: 131
4:1–34: 127
4:2: 131
4:10: 131
4:21–29: 106, 183
4:26–29: 108
4:35–41: 188, 139
4:35–45:43: 106, 183
4:35–46:6a: 127
4:38: 137
4:39: 140
5:1–20: 131
5:10: 131
5:18: 131
5:19–20: 142, 143
5:21–26:6a: 141
5:21–24: 141
5:23–26:28: 131

*Gospel according to Mark (Cont.)*
    5:25: 131
    5:25–34: 141
    5:28: 141
    5:30: 141
    5:35–43: 141, 142
    5:42: 131
    5:43: 131, 142, 143
    6:1–6a: 141
    6:2: 134
    6:5: 113
    6:5a: 141
    6:5b: 141
    6:6b–30: 130
    6:6–6:31: 131, 142
    6:6b–8:26: 127
    6:7: 131
    6:14–29: 142
    6:17: 131
    6:27: 131
    6:31–45: 131–32
    6:32–44: 139
    6:32–38:21: 129, 131–32
    6:34: 134
    6:45–52: 138–39, 140
    6:46–52: 113
    7:1–23: 138, 143
    7:24–30: 138, 144
    7:28: 137
    7:31–36: 138
    7:31–37: 132
    7:34: 138
    7:36: 142
    8:1–21: 132
    8:22–26: 106, 108, 183
    8:22–10:52: 128, 129
    8:23: 128–29
    8:24: 128–29
    8:27–28: 137
    8:27–10:45: 127
    8:29: 137
    8:31: 115

8:31–32: 134
9:5: 137
9:8: 128–29
9:9: 142
9:14–29: 144
9:31: 115
9:31–32: 134
10:17–22: 139, 140, 143
10:18: 113
10:19: 144
10:21: 128–29
10:23: 128–29
10:27: 128–29
10:28–31: 144
10:33–34: 134
10:34: 115
10:45: 137, 143
10:47: 137
10:51: 128–29
10:52: 128–29
11:1–13:37: 127
11:1–16:8: 129, 132
11:18–19: 106, 183
11:27–12:44: 132
12:18–27: 144
12:41–44: 106, 108, 183
13:1–37: 132
13:14: 112
13:14–17: 111
13:15–17: 112
13:24–30: 106, 183
13:30: 106, 183
13:36–52: 106, 183
14:1–16:8: 127
14:17–42: 134
14:24: 143
14:28: 115
15:39: 137
16:4 + Bobiensis addition: 116–17
16:8: 115, 119, 133
Shorter ending: 115, 118
16:9–20: 115–16

16:9–20 + Freer Logion: 116, 118–19
*Gospel according to Luke*
1:1–4: 84, 85
1:5–80: 85
2:41–52: 85
3:23: 85
11:1–4: 188
11:5–8: 188
11:9–13: 188
21:1–4: 108, 183
24:13–53: 85
Col. 4:16: 45
2 Tim. 4:13: 45

**Additional Early Christian Sources:**
2 Clement
   8.5: 2
*Acts of Timothy*
   8–10: 150–51
Augustine
   *Confessions*
   3.4: 12
*Didache*
   8.2: 2
Eusebius
   *Ecclesiastical History*
   2.15: 96–98
   3.24.5: 83, 87
   3.24.14–15: 86
   3.39: 88
   3.39.1: 88
   3.39.3: 88
   3.39.3–4: 89
   3.39.3–7: 90
   3.39.4–7: 89
   3.39.14: 90
   3.39.15: 90–91
   3.39.15–16: 106, 183.
   3.39.16: 92
   6.14.6–7: 1

Irenaeus:
   *Against Heresies*
   1.praef.1: 95–96, 181
   3.1.1: 1, 2, 82, 93–96, 150
Justin Martyr
   *Dialogue with Trypho*
   101.3: 2
   106.3: 180
Origen
   *Against Celsus*
   2.13: 83
   2.27: 2, 150
Tertullian
   *Prescription against Heretics*
   7: 69
   *On Fasting, against the Psychics*
   10.3
Theophilus of Antioch
   *To Autolycus*
   3.13–14: 2

**Greek and Latin Sources:**
Aristophanes
   *Acharnians*
   530–31: 50
Arrian
   *Epicteti dissertations*
   praef.1–8: 47–48
Artemidorus
   *Onirocritica*
   1.praef.1–2: 100
   2.praef.: 100
   2.70.167: 100
Aulus Gellius
   *Attic Nights*
   praef.1–2: 126
Julius Caesar
   *Gallic War*:
   8.praef: 16
Cicero:
   *Brutus*:
   262: 15

Cicero (Cont.)
  *De oratore*
    1.21.94: 39
  *Letters to Atticus*
    1.10: 40
    1.19: 12
    1.20: 14
    2.1: 13, 14
    3.12: 39
    3.15: 39
    12.6: 40
    12.6.3: 50
    13.44: 40, 51
    14.3: 40
  *Letters to friends*
    5.2: 14
    5.12: 12
    5:12.8–9: 12
  *Pro Ligario*
    33: 51
Demosthenes
  *Erotic Essay*
    61.1–2: 95
  *False Embassy*
    19.257: 86
Diodorus Siculus
  *Library of History*
    1.4.1: 41
    1.5.2: 42
    40.8: 41
Epictetus
  *Diatribai (Dissertationes)*
    praef.1–8: 47–48
Galen
  *Anatomical Procedures*
    1.1: 30–31, 84
    2.1: 31–32, 84
  *Avoiding Distress*
    29: 30
  *Hipp. 6 Epid.*
    17b.13K: 33, 109, 110
    17a.1001K: 33–34

  *On My Own Books*
    prologue: 29–30
  *On the Order of My Own Books*
    1.1–2: 91–92
Hippocrates
  *Epidemics*
    6.2.25: 33, 34, 109
    6.3.1: 33, 109
Horace
  *Ars poetica*
    390: 50
  *Satires*
    2.4: 43
Lucian
  *How to Write History*
    16: 24, 25
    47–48: 93, 107
    48: 12–13, 87
Martial
  *Epigrams*:
    1.66: 18–19
    10.1.1–2.4: 49, 105
Nicolaus of Damascus
  *Vita Caesaris*
    2: 85
Ovid
  *Amores*
    1.1: 49–50, 104
Philodemus
  *On Rhetoric*
    2–3: 71–75, 155–56
Philostratus
  *Vita Apollonii*
    1.3: 34–35, 91
    1.19: 35
    7.38: 35
Plato:
  *Phaedrus*
    275: 19
    276: 19
    278: 19

*Statesman*
  295: 19, 20, 21, 22
*Theaetetus*
  142d–143a: 21, 22
Pliny the younger
  *Epistles*
    3.5.17: 17
Plutarch
  *De tranquillitate animi*
    464e–f: 27, 28
  *Sulla*
    6.5: 28
    6.6: 28
    14.2: 28
    14.6: 28
    17.1: 28
    23.2: 28
    37.1: 28
Porphyry
  *Vita Plotini*
    3.37–39: 91, 92
    7.13–14: 114
Ps-Plato
  *Epistles*
    2.310a: 45
    2.314: 45
Quintilian
  *Institutio oratoria*
    4.1.69: 38
    10.7.30–31: 38
    10.3.31–33: 46

Seneca
  *Contraversiae*
    4.5: 167
Suetonius
  *Divus Julius*
    56: 14, 16
Terence
  *Hauton timorumenos*
    75: 50
Theon
  *Progymnasmata*
    78.25: 85
    79.7: 85

**Papyri:**
*P.Herc.* 89: 70
*P.Herc.* 155: 70
*P.Herc.* 164: 70
*P.Herc.* 168: 70
*P.Herc.* 182: 70
*P.Herc.* 339: 70
*P.Herc.* 1021: 126
*P.Herc.* 1426: 71, 73, 75, 155
*P.Herc.* 1427: 71
*P.Herc.* 1506: 71, 72, 75, 155
*P.Herc.* 1672: 71, 75
*P.Herc.* 1674: 71, 75
*P.Lond* 259: 124
*P.Oxy.* XVII 2070: 123

www.ingramcontent.com/pod-product-compliance
Ingram Content Group UK Ltd.
Pitfield, Milton Keynes, MK11 3LW, UK
UKHW022153230426
12049UKWH00003BA/75